Essential Guide to Marketing Planning

Brief contents

Full contents

Preface

What is a marketing plan and why is it essential to marketing success? How do you go about researching, preparing, presenting, controlling and evaluating a marketing plan?

Essential Guide to Marketing Planning answers these questions by guiding you step-by-step through the entire marketing planning process. You'll learn the language and basic concepts of planning, gain insights from the experiences of real companies and non-profit organizations and put your knowledge to work as you create a marketing plan of your own.

Your step-by-step guide

Each chapter is packed with special features to assist you in understanding and completing all the steps in formulating a marketing plan:

- *No-nonsense directions*. The 'how to' format explains the decisions and issues to be addressed in researching and writing a workable marketing plan. Seventeen checklist activities guide you through such details as analysing the mission statement; analysing consumer and business markets; evaluating market segments; planning for products; planning for logistics; planning for media; and planning metrics.

- *Distinct stages in planning*. A diagram at the start of each chapter shows your progress through each of the seven stages of the marketing planning process.

- *Examples and case studies*. Every chapter contains at least three 'marketing in practice' boxed examples plus a case study to show how real organizations (from Unilever and Ikea to ANZ and the BBC) really use marketing.

- *Practical exercises*. 'Apply your knowledge' exercises challenge you to put principles into practice by analysing a specific organization's marketing activities; 'Build your own marketing plan' exercises lead you through the main steps in preparing your own marketing plan.

- *Sample marketing plan*. Consult the Appendix to see a sample plan for a fictional start-up company, Lost Legends Luxury Chocolatier.

- *Definitions*. Key terms defined in each chapter and in the glossary reinforce your knowledge of marketing expressions, including newer phrases such as *sustainable marketing*, *ethnographic research*, *personas*, *buzz marketing* and *marketing dashboard*.

Real-world view of marketing planning

Seeing how different organizations approach marketing can provoke new thinking and lead to more creative marketing plans. How does Tesco plan to compete with UK and US retailers (Chapter 1)? Why would McDonald's put more marketing emphasis on increasing sales at existing restaurants than on opening new restaurants (Chapter 5)? Can Tata profit in India by marketing a small car priced at less than £1,600 (Chapter 7)? These and other up-to-date cases reveal the realities of marketing planning all around the world.

Guide to the book

Essential Guide to Marketing Planning is divided into 12 chapters, each covering a key aspect of the planning process. Chapters 1–3 introduce marketing planning, explain how to analyse the current marketing situation and discuss how to research markets and customers. Chapter 4 examines the use of segmentation, targeting and positioning. Chapter 5 looks at planning direction, objectives and strategy. Chapters 6–9 focus on the marketing mix: product, price, place (channels and logistics) and promotion (integrated marketing communication). Chapter 10 shows how customer service and internal marketing support the marketing mix. Chapters 11 and 12 present techniques for forecasting, budgeting, measuring marketing performance and controlling plan implementation.

Visit the Companion Website, www.pearsoned.co.uk/wood-mp, for supplements such as links to marketing-related websites. With a password, lecturers can access the Instructor's Manual with answers to case study questions plus additional resources.

Acknowledgements

I sincerely appreciate the valuable insights and suggestions of the academic reviewers who commented on my ideas for this book or offered helpful advice during the development of my *Marketing Planning: principles into practice* text. Thank you to Declan Bannon (University of Paisley Business School); Jill Brown (University of Portsmouth Business School); Niki Hynes (Strathclyde University); Peter Lancaster (Sheffield Hallam University); Tony Lobo (Swinburne University of Technology); Paul Oakley (University of Brighton Business School); John Rudd (Aston Business School); Beejal Shah (University of Hertfordshire); Mike Simpson (University of Sheffield); and Heather Skinner (Glamorgan Business School).

In writing this book, I benefited immensely from the expertise, commitment and support of many talented professionals at Pearson Education. Special thanks to my project champion, David Cox (Acquisitions Editor), whose indispensable knowledge and boundless enthusiasm propelled this book forward. For all they've done to transform my manuscript into a finished product to be proud of, I'm very grateful to Emma Easy (Desk

About the author

Marian Burk Wood has held vice-presidential level positions in corporate and non-profit marketing with Citibank, Chase Manhattan Bank and the National Retail Federation. She has extensive practical experience in marketing planning, having developed and implemented dozens of marketing plans over the years for a wide range of goods and services. Her US book, *The Marketing Plan Handbook*, now in its third edition, has introduced marketing planning to thousands of students worldwide.

Wood holds an MBA in marketing from Long Island University in New York and a BA from the City University of New York. She has worked with prominent academic experts to co-author undergraduate textbooks on principles of marketing, principles of advertising and principles of management. Her special interests in marketing include ethics and social responsibility, segmentation, channels and metrics.

Publisher's acknowledgements

We are grateful to the following for permission to reproduce copyright material:

Fig. 3.5 adapted from and Fig. 6.3 from *Principles of Marketing*, 4th edn, Pearson Education (Kotler P., Wang V., Saunders J. and Armstrong G. 2005). Copyright © 2005. Reprinted/Adapted by permission of Pearson Education, Harlow, Essex; Fig. 5.1 after *On Target: The Book on Marketing Plans,* 2nd edn, Palo Alto Software (Berry T. and Wilson, D. 2001). Copyright © 1993 Timothy J. Berry.

In some instances we have been unable to trace the owners of copyright material, and we would appreciate any information that would enable us to do so.

1 Introduction to marketing planning

Comprehension outcomes

After studying this chapter, you will be able to:

- Explain the benefits of marketing planning
- List the seven stages of the marketing planning process
- Describe the contents of a marketing plan
- Discuss how the mission statement guides marketing planning

Application outcomes

After studying this chapter, you will be able to:

- Begin the first stage of marketing planning
- Analyse and prepare or improve a mission statement
- Start documenting a marketing plan

PREVIEW OF THIS BOOK

The road to marketing success in today's highly dynamic business environment begins with a creative, realistic marketing plan. This book will be your essential guide to marketing planning. Through clear explanations, real-world examples and practical exercises, it will help you to:

- understand what marketing planning is, how it works and why it's important
- complete the seven stages of the marketing planning process
- formulate your own marketing plan.

Although this book touches on many marketing concepts and definitions, the emphasis is on applying your knowledge for marketing planning. By the time you reach the last chapter, you will know how to prepare a marketing plan similar to the sample plan in the Appendix. Whether you go to work for a major corporation, start your own business, or join a non-governmental organization, your knowledge of marketing planning will be a valuable asset.

Connecting marketing planning to the world of business, every chapter opens with a brief preview of how a real company is using marketing to provide value for customers, achieve its goals or address issues such as competition. The beginning of each chapter also includes a diagram showing which stage of the marketing planning process you're currently studying, to help you envision your movement through the overall process.

Later in this chapter you'll see the first *Essential Marketing Plan Checklist* activity, featuring a series of questions to guide you through specific aspects of the marketing process. (Some chapters include more than one checklist to help you work on your marketing plan.) You'll also have the opportunity to experience marketing planning first-hand through two end-of-chapter exercises, *Apply Your Knowledge* and *Build Your Own Marketing Plan*. These activities will help you develop your planning skills and formulate a stronger, more relevant marketing plan.

Please read on as this chapter's preview describes Unilever's plans for growth – plans that, paradoxically, include divesting major products. The following chapter preview sets the stage for your introduction to the practical side of marketing planning.

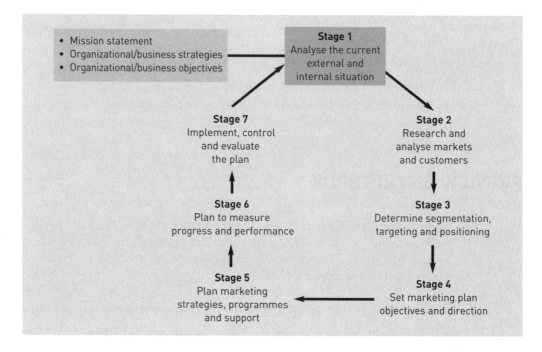

CHAPTER PREVIEW

Why would Unilever sell off two frozen-food brands that together generate more than €1.4 billion in annual turnover? Famous for its personal care, home care and food products, Unilever has been trimming its brand portfolio to free up resources for an intensive marketing initiative to increase turnover and profits. 'We can't foresee a way to get UK frozen food into growth without a huge amount of financial and management resource going into it', a spokesperson explains. 'That is money better spent elsewhere.'[1]

Even as Unilever sells slow-growth businesses like bakery supplies and dry soups, it's spending more to market 400 high-potential brands and reducing prices to battle rivals such as Procter & Gamble. Although higher marketing costs have hurt profit margins, sales are rising and the company sees higher profits ahead as it continues expansion around the world.[2] Without marketing planning, Unilever would have no clear course of action for growing sales and profits by satisfying the needs of its customers in a competitively superior way. Yet the planning decisions that lead to growth for Unilever will not necessarily work for Procter & Gamble or other rivals. Every marketing plan is therefore as unique as it is vital for the company's future.

In this chapter, you'll first be introduced to the role of marketing planning and its benefits. Next is an overview of each of the individual stages in the marketing planning process and a look at how to document a marketing plan. After you learn about the interaction among the three levels of planning with the organization, you'll see how a solid mission statement serves to guide marketing planning.

THE ROLE OF MARKETING PLANNING

Marketing planning is the structured process that leads to a coordinated set of marketing decisions and actions, for a specific organization and over a specific period, based on:

- an analysis of the current internal and external situation, including markets and customers
- clear marketing direction, objectives, strategies and programmes for targeted customer segments
- support through customer service and internal marketing programmes
- management of marketing activities through implementation, evaluation and control.

The course of action that results from marketing planning is recorded in a **marketing plan**. This internal document outlines the marketplace situation and describes the marketing strategies and programmes that will support the achievement of business and organizational goals over a specified period, usually one year.

The benefits of marketing planning

Why does an organization need marketing planning? Such planning enables marketers to examine any number of suitable opportunities for satisfying customers and achieving marketing goals, as well as current and potential threats to overall performance. The process provides a framework for systematically identifying and evaluating different possibilities and outcomes.

In particular, marketing planning keeps you focused on your customers; helps you determine what your organization can do (and what it can't do) for customers; helps you examine offerings in the context of competition and the marketing environment; and sets up the rationale for allocating resources to achieve efficiency and effectiveness in your marketing activities.[3] Marketing planning, in effect, deals with the *who, what, when, where, how* and *how much* of an organization's marketing during a certain period (usually a year).

However, the marketing plan is not simply an account of what you as a marketer hope to accomplish in the coming year. Your plan must allow for measuring progress toward objectives and making adjustments if actual results vary from projections. For example, new competitors may enter the marketplace, regulations may evolve, economic situations can improve or worsen and customer needs may change, among other shifts that can affect marketing performance.

The dynamic marketing plan

A good marketing plan must be dynamic, anticipating likely changes and providing guidelines for how to react with customer relationships in mind. The marketing environment has become so volatile that the most successful companies continually update and revise their marketing plans to maintain their competitive edge. No marketing plan lasts forever; even the most effective plan must be adjusted as the marketing situation evolves. You may, in fact, want to have several alternative plans in mind that might be implemented if significant changes occur.

Consider the experience of Australia's Coles Group.

MARKETING IN PRACTICE: COLES GROUP

Coles Group aims 'to be Australia's number one retailer in all our brands by delighting our customers, growing our shareholder value and being the best team'. Despite its strong base of 2,200 food, liquor, fuel, and general merchandise stores, Coles faces several difficult issues. One is ongoing competition from Woolworths, the market leader. Another is the challenge of dealing with local and national differences in regulatory requirements, which are subject to change at any time. Constant shifts in buying behaviour represent a third marketing challenge. For example, consumers who used to buy liquor from small local stores are seeking out the lower prices and wider selection at large discount stores – which is why Coles has changed its marketing plan to expand its chain of liquor stores. It is also adding supercentres to offer the one-stop convenience of buying food and general merchandise, at discount prices, under one roof.[4]

Marketing planning is especially important for start-up businesses and young Web-based firms like eShopAfrica, because their margin for error is so small. Based in Ghana, eShopAfrica sells high-quality sculptures and other fair-trade African goods to a global customer base. Despite significant expenses for Web hosting, product sourcing and shipment, founder Cordelia Salter-Nour has a marketing plan to reach interested buyers. 'I want to tap the snobbery market – the people who want to trade stories at dinner parties about the originality of their artefacts', she says. Salter-Nour's current marketing plan includes a yearly goal of enabling five African craftspeople to build a viable business by selling their goods online.[5]

THE MARKETING PLANNING PROCESS

The marketing plan documents decisions and actions undertaken as a result of the seven-stage marketing planning process shown in Figure 1.1. Most organizations begin this process many months before a marketing plan is scheduled to take effect. Experts warn, however, that marketing planning should not be a once-a-year exercise. Because the marketing environment can change at any time, managers should spread analysis and planning activities throughout the year and make strategic decisions after examining pressing issues at length.[6] The sections that follow provide a brief overview of all seven stages.

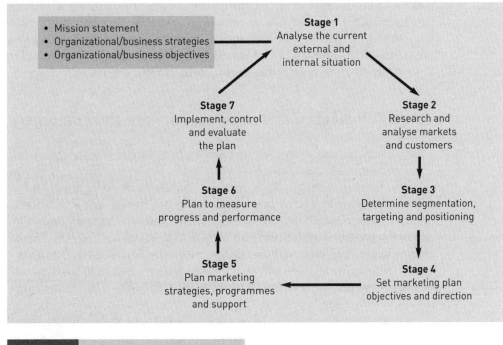

| FIGURE 1.1 | The marketing planning process |

Stage 1: Analyse the current situation

You'll use an *internal audit* to examine the current situation within the organization, including mission statement, resources, offerings, capabilities, important business relationships and – an important way of learning from the past – the results of earlier plans. As discussed later in this chapter, the mission statement is an overall guide to what the organization wants to accomplish and where, in general terms, your marketing plan should take the organization.

Using an *external audit*, you start to study trends and changes in the broad political–legal, economic, social–cultural and technological environment (abbreviated as *PEST* or, if ordered differently, as *STEP*). Research any competitive, ecological and demographic changes that might affect marketing and performance. This includes issues, threats and opportunities that might influence your ability to implement the marketing plan and achieve your objectives.

Owing to external changes such as public pressure and internal changes such as forward-looking corporate leadership, a growing number of companies are adopting **sustainable marketing**, 'the establishment, maintenance and enhancement of customer relationships so that the objectives of the parties involved are met without compromising the ability of future generations to achieve their own objectives'.[7] This entails making commitments to a broader base of **publics** (also known as *stakeholders*), groups such as stockholders, reporters, citizen action groups and neighbourhood residents that have an interest in or an influence on the organization's performance. Royal Dutch/Shell, for instance, has committed to sustainability in the many countries where it operates. 'Whatever you do, economic, social or environmental, you have to be thinking sustainably', stresses Clive Mather, the petrol company's global head of learning.[8]

See Chapter 2 for more about assessing the current situation.

Stage 2: Research and analyse markets and customers

Next you should research your markets and customers (consumers, businesses, clients or constituents). Investigate trends in market share, product useage, customer needs and perceptions, demographics, product demand, buying patterns and customer satisfaction. You want to answer questions such as: Who is buying or would buy the product being marketed, and why? How are buying patterns changing, and why? What is in demand, when is it in demand, where is it in demand and how is demand expected to change over time? What experiences, services and benefits do customers need, want or expect before, during and after each purchase? In certain industries, such as fashion, demand is so changeable that marketers need to exercise judgement when evaluating the results of customer research.[9]

During this research and analysis stage, think about what your customers might need tomorrow as well as what they need today. This will help you formulate a plan for **relationship marketing**, building ongoing connections with customers and other key stakeholders.[10] Relationship marketing starts from the premise that when organizations look beyond the immediate transaction to build trust and meet customers' long-term needs, customers are more likely to remain loyal. Successful firms clearly demonstrate a strong customer orientation through their marketing activities, recognizing that satisfying customers will ultimately lead to satisfying shareholders and other stakeholders.[11] Increasingly, top management is holding marketers accountable for reinforcing customer loyalty and long-term relationships, purchase by purchase.[12]

Gathering data about customer needs, interests and buying behaviour is faster and easier with technology. For example, Google and Yahoo! (among other online search sites) list trends based on rankings of Web searches conducted on their sites.[13] Yet certain marketing-related technologies are raising ethical questions. To illustrate, Tesco, Wal-Mart and many other companies now use radio frequency identification (RFID) tags to track items from production to cash desk. Although RFID allows companies to know the exact location of every product at every time, critics fear that this technology might be used to monitor in-home product usage, an invasion of customer privacy.[14] *See* Chapter 3 for more about analysing markets and customers.

Stage 3: Determine segmentation, targeting and positioning

No organization has the resources (people, money or time) to serve every customer in every market. You will therefore use your research and customer knowledge to identify specific subgroups that can be effectively targeted through marketing. To do this, group customers into **segments** based on characteristics, behaviours, needs or wants that affect their demand for, or usage of, the product being marketed. A segment may be as small as one consumer or business customer or as large as millions of customers in multiple nations.

Next you will decide on your **targeting** approach. Will you focus on a single segment, on two or more segments or on one entire market? How will these segments be covered through marketing? Li-Ning Sports Goods, founded by a Chinese Olympic gymnastics champion, began by targeting men aged 14 to 30 in smaller Chinese cities. Now it is expanding by targeting the same segment in other countries, where it competes with major brands such as Adidas and Nike. 'If we want to be number one in China, we have to be international as well', says the founder.[15]

You also need to formulate a suitable **positioning**, which means using marketing to create a competitively distinctive place (position) for the product or brand in the mind of targeted customers. The purpose is to set your product apart from competing products in a way that is meaningful to customers. For example, in consumer markets, Prêt À Manger differentiates its sandwiches and other ready-to-eat foods using the positioning of 'made fresh daily'. Chapter 4 discusses segmentation, targeting and positioning in further detail.

Stage 4: Set marketing plan direction and objectives

The direction of a marketing plan is based on your organization's mission statement and higher-level goals. Most use marketing plans to support a direction of growth in one of six ways: penetrating existing markets, expanding within existing markets, adding new markets, offering existing products, modifying existing products and offering entirely new products (*see* Figure 1.2).[16] A marketing plan for growth will define

	Offerings	
Market existing products in existing markets	Modify existing products for existing markets	Market new products in existing markets
Market existing products in geographical expansions of existing markets	Modify existing products for dispersed markets	Offer geographically innovative products
Market existing products in new markets	Modify existing products for new markets	Offer new products in new markets

FIGURE 1.2   Growth grid

Source: After Alan R. Andreasen and Philip Kotler, *Strategic Marketing for Non-profit Organisations*, 6th edn (Upper Saddle River, NJ: Prentice Hall, 2003), p. 81.

objectives in financial terms (such as higher turnover) and marketing terms (such as higher market share). High-performing firms may strive to retain or attain the role of **market leader**, holding the largest market share and leading other firms in new product introductions and other activities.[17]

MARKETING IN PRACTICE: NOKIA

Nokia, based in Finland, is a market leader, with one of the best-known brands in the mobile-phone business. It sells more than 200 million GSM-compatible handsets every year and frequently introduces new products with innovative features, advanced technology and special fashion accents. However, as the mobile market becomes more competitive and more technologically complex, Nokia is ready to modify its marketing plans for growth at any time. For instance, it recently joined with Sanyo to manufacture and market CDMA-compatible handsets, a move designed to boost its market share in the lucrative Japanese and US markets. In addition, Nokia took the bold but risky step of opening showcase stores in Moscow, London, Paris and Los Angeles to enhance the stylish image of its handsets, including the upmarket Vertu product line. More marketing investments are ahead as the company fine-tunes marketing plans for increasing market share and profits around the world.[18]

Instead of driving for growth, companies trying to protect their current profit situation or their market share may use their marketing plans to sustain the current turnover level. Those under severe financial strain may develop plans to survive or to retrench. For example, Edesur, the electrical utility serving southern Buenos Aires, chose not to pursue growth until a government-imposed price freeze was lifted, inflation slowed, the currency stabilized and equipment thefts were controlled – a situation that continued for several years.[19]

Note that goals and objectives are not the same, although the words are often used interchangeably. **Goals** are longer-term targets that help a business unit (or the entire organization) achieve overall performance and fulfil its mission; **objectives** are shorter-term performance targets that lead to the achievement of goals. British academic Tim Ambler notes that key corporate goals must be connected throughout the organization, all the way down to the marketing plan and individual marketing programmes, if the company is to succeed.[20] In addition to financial and marketing objectives, marketers may define societal objectives (such as for social responsibility and ecological protection). *See* Chapter 5 for more about direction and objectives.

Stage 5: Plan marketing strategies, programmes and support

In this stage, you will plan marketing strategies and tactics to achieve the objectives you set earlier. You will look not only at how to deliver value that meets customers' needs but also at the coordination of the basic marketing tools of product, price, place and promotion within individual marketing programmes. In addition, you should determine how to support the marketing effort with customer service and internal marketing. For practical reasons, you probably will not finalize all the details of your marketing activities until your plan has been approved and funded and is ready for implementation.

Product and branding

The product offering may be a tangible good such as a television or an intangible service such as expert tax-preparation assistance. Often, however, an offering combines the tangible and the intangible, as when a mobile-phone company markets phones (tangible) along with phone service (intangible) or a manufacturer markets robotic assembly equipment (tangible) and provides repair services (intangible). Tangible elements of the product include: features, design, packaging, labelling and performance.

The brand is another intangible but extremely important aspect of the product offering. Every product must live up to the **brand promise**, which marketing experts Philip Kotler and Kevin Keller define as 'the marketer's vision of what the brand must be and do for consumers'.[21] Other intangibles to consider in planning product strategy are: benefits, quality perceptions and related services. Process elements important to product planning are: the product mix/lines, new product development, the product life cycle, ecological concerns and similar issues. *See* Chapter 6 for more on planning product and brand strategy.

Hyundai, the Korean automaker, has a marketing plan for selling 800,000 vehicles in Europe by 2010 – part of its overall goal of becoming one of the world's top-five best-selling automakers. The company 'will focus on quality, reliability and durability of our models', says the brand manager. 'We need to take the global brand identity and Europeanize it.' Thus, Hyundai will be working on tangible elements such as quality and performance as well as intangible elements such as brand image.[22]

Price

What should you charge for your product offering? In planning price strategy, marketers must answer a number of key questions. Some are about external elements, such as: How do customers perceive the value of the good or service? What is the competition? How might market demand, channel requirements and legal or regulatory issues affect pricing? Internal elements raise questions such as: How can price be used to reflect the positioning of the product, brand or organization? How do costs affect revenues and profitability? How does the price fit with other marketing decisions and planning for other products? And how can pricing capture value for the organization and bring it closer to its objectives and goals?

Pricing is a vital ingredient in the marketing plan for Nestlé. This Swiss company, which specializes in food products, looks carefully at income levels and purchasing power to determine appropriate product prices (and potential profits) in its markets. For example, income in Russia has been rising and a large percentage of that income is disposable, which means consumers can afford foreign coffees and other extras. Nestlé's researchers learned that Russian consumers drink, on average, 250 cups of instant coffee each year – more than consumers anywhere else. It's easy to see why Nestlé has invested more than €500 million to market coffee and other foods to Russian consumers.[23] *See* Chapter 7 for more about price and value.

Channel and logistics

Channel and logistics strategy – place strategy – is concerned with how customers gain access to the product offering, regardless of whether it's a tangible good or an intangible service. Will you market directly to your customers or make your products available through intermediaries such as wholesalers and retailers? If you market to businesses, will you go through wholesalers, distributors or agents that serve business buyers – or deal directly with some or all of your business customers?

Other channel decisions involve customer preferences, number of channel members, market coverage and ecological impact. Also consider logistics such as shipping, storage, inventory management, order fulfilment and related functions. Current channel and logistical arrangements should be evaluated as part of the internal audit. The needs, expectations and preferences of customers should be deciding factors in planning your channels and logistics.

Consider how the owner of Jenny Lou's in Beijing deals with daily channel and logistics decisions:

MARKETING IN PRACTICE: JENNY LOU'S STORES

Jenny Wang, founder of the six Jenny Lou's grocery stores in Beijing, sells imported foods and household products to expatriate Westerners. In the early years, she focused on understanding what customers liked and finding reliable suppliers. Wang had to react quickly when Beijing officials, saying they had to eliminate overcrowded retailing conditions, demolished her small store – more than once. Each time, the entrepreneur identified a new location convenient for her customers, installed fixtures and reopened for business. Today Wang operates six stores with a combined turnover approaching £2 million and competes with international chains like Carrefour. Although Wang can't match the big chains' low prices, she competes by offering speedy, personalized services such as home delivery, which keep her customers loyal and her stores profitable.[24]

These topics are covered more thoroughly in Chapter 8.

Integrated marketing communication

Integrated marketing communication strategy – also called promotion strategy – covers all the tools you use in reaching out to your targeted segments. Media and online advertising are among the most visible and sometimes the most flamboyant; other tools include: public relations, sales promotion, special events and experiences, personal selling and direct marketing. Given the needs, interests, perceptions, expectations and buying patterns of customers in targeted segments, most organizations allow for a variety of messages and media in their marketing plans. However, you should be sure that the content and impact of the entire promotion strategy is consistent, unified and supportive of your positioning and objectives.

External elements to consider include: customer needs and perceptions; legal, regulatory, social and ethical issues; channel decisions; and clutter. Internal elements to consider include: marketing plan objectives; resources; and coordination with content and delivery. Your message and media decisions will cover message content; creative aspects; reach and frequency; media costs and characteristics; and how to evaluate audience reaction. *See* Chapter 9 for more on this topic.

Marketing support

You can plan to support your product, place, price and promotion strategies in two main ways. First, you should decide on an appropriate customer service level, in line with the chosen positioning, resource availability and customers' needs or expectations. Business customers often require service before, during and after a purchase, from tailoring product specifications to arranging installation to maintaining and repairing the product years later. For example, Siemens, based in Munich, offers training and technical support for employees of hospitals and clinics that buy its sophisticated medical equipment.

Second, you will need the commitment and cooperation of others to implement and control your plan. This requires *internal marketing*, activities designed to build relationships with colleagues and staff members backed up by personnel policies that reinforce internal commitment to the marketing effort.[25] Read more about customer service and internal marketing in Chapter 10.

Stage 6: Plan to measure progress and performance

Before implementing the marketing plan, you must decide on measures to track marketing progress and performance toward achieving your objectives. This involves developing and documenting budgets, forecasts, schedules and responsibilities for all marketing programmes. You will also forecast the effect of the marketing programmes on future turnover, profitability, market share and other measures that signal progress toward objectives. The purpose is to see whether results are better than expected, lagging expectations or just meeting projections and objectives. For perspective, it is important to put recent marketing results into context through comparisons with competitors, the overall market and the organization's previous results.

Often marketers establish quantifiable standards (*metrics*) to measure specific marketing outcomes and activities. In many cases, these metrics look at interim performance of specific brands, individual products or product lines, geographic results, financial results, customer relationship results and so on. Siemens, for instance, uses metrics to track financial results such as growth in turnover and profit margins by strategic business unit (SBU), by product and by division in each geographic region where it does business.[26]

Deciding exactly what to measure – and how – is critical to effective implementation and control of a marketing plan. The online auction firm eBay uses metrics such as the number of new users and ongoing registered users, gross value of auction sales hosted, revenue per transaction and country-by-country market share. It also looks at its competitors' results. Yet the CEO warns: 'You have to be careful because you could measure too much.'[27] Check Chapter 11 for more about planning to measure marketing progress and performance.

Stage 7: Implement, control and evaluate the plan

The real test of any marketing plan's effectiveness comes at implementation. For effective control, you will start with the objectives you have set, establish specific standards for measuring progress toward those targets, measure actual marketing performance, analyse the results and take corrective action if results are not as expected. Businesses generally apply several types of marketing control at different levels and intervals. The outcome of this stage feeds back to the beginning of the marketing planning process, paving the way for changes as needed.

Depending on your organization and your plan, you may compare results with standards daily, weekly, monthly and quarterly; you may even compare results with standards on an hourly basis if you need to maintain extremely tight control over marketing. In addition, you and your managers should evaluate performance after all programmes are complete. *See* Chapter 12 for more about effective implementation and control of your marketing plan.

Documenting a marketing plan

As you move through each stage in the marketing planning process, take time to document your decisions and actions in a written marketing plan. Every marketing plan is unique, designed specifically for the individual organization and its current marketing situation. Although some plans may be recorded in only a few pages, larger companies generally have a formal format for presenting detailed marketing plans by unit, brand and product.

Most marketing plans consist of the main sections shown in Figure 1.3 (*see* the sample plan in the Appendix as another example). In practice, marketers cannot write the executive summary until all other sections have been completed, because its purpose is to offer a quick overview of the plan's highlights. With that exception, each section of the marketing plan is developed in order, building to the details documented in the financial plans and the implementation controls at the end of the plan. And when marketers change one section of the marketing plan in response to competitive shifts or other environmental trends, they need to re-examine and change other sections as well.

Now you're ready to begin your own marketing plan. The final section of this chapter puts you into the first stage of the marketing planning process, analysing the current marketing situation. More details about internal and external audits are explained in Chapter 2.

INTERNAL AUDIT: THE STARTING POINT FOR PLANNING

Plans and decisions made at the top levels of the organization provide guidance for planning in each business unit and in the marketing function. For a thorough internal analysis, part of Stage 1 of the marketing planning process, you need to understand the interaction among the plans at all three levels.

Three levels of planning for strategy

At the top level, planning for **organizational** (or **corporate**) **strategy** governs your organization's overall purpose and its long-range direction and goals; establishes the range of businesses in which it will compete; and shapes how it will create value for customers and other stakeholders (including shareholders). Corporate strategy includes extended plans for the long term, as far as five to ten years in the future. In turn, organizational strategy

Section	Purpose
Executive summary	To describe, briefly, the plan's objectives and main points.
Current marketing situation	In the context of the mission statement, to provide background about the marketing environment; markets and customers; current marketing activities; previous results; competition.
SWOT analysis	To discuss internal strengths and weaknesses, external opportunities and threats.
Objectives and issues	To show what the marketing plan is designed to achieve in terms of financial, marketing and societal objectives; to explain key issues that might affect the plan's implementation and success.
Target market	To identify who will be targeted and how the product, brand or organization will be positioned for the selected customer segment(s).
Marketing strategy	To present the broad strategic approach that the plan will apply in providing value to achieve the objectives that have been set.
Marketing programmes	To describe the set of coordinated actions that will be implemented to create, communicate and deliver value through product, pricing, place, promotion, customer service and internal marketing.
Financial plans (budgets)	To back up the programmes with specifics about projected costs, revenue and sales forecasts, expected profit.
Implementation controls	To show the organization, responsibilities and schedule for implementation; how progess toward objectives will be monitored and measured; contingency plans for dealing with unexpected results.

FIGURE 1.3   Contents of a typical marketing plan

and goals provide a framework for the set of decisions made by business managers who must move their units forward toward the goals, given the organization's resources and capabilities (*see* Figure 1.4).

Planning for **business strategy** covers the scope of each unit and how it will compete; what market(s) it will serve; and how unit resources will be allocated and coordinated to create customer value. In establishing business strategy, senior managers must determine what portfolio of units is needed to support the organization's overall goals and

FIGURE 1.4	Planning on three organizational levels

what functions should be emphasized or possibly outsourced. The business plan for one unit may span as long as three to five years. Unilever's business strategy, for instance, called for divesting frozen foods in favour of investments in higher-growth businesses during several years.

Once the portfolio of business units is in place, planning for **marketing strategy** determines how each unit will use the *marketing-mix* tools of product, price, place and promotion – supported by customer service and internal marketing strategies – to compete effectively and meet business unit objectives. Typically, the marketing plan reflects the organization's chosen marketing strategy for the coming year (but it may cover multiple years).

Because marketing is the organizational function closest to customers and markets, it is in the pivotal role of implementing higher-level strategies while informing the market and customer definitions of these strategies. In a customer-oriented organization, marketing is a priority and concern of everyone at every level. Thus, marketing integrates floor-up, customer-facing knowledge of the market and the current environment with top-down development, direction and fine-tuning of organizational and business strategies. Figure 1.5 illustrates decisions at the three levels of strategy and shows how Unilever might apply them.[28]

Be aware that the marketing plan (prepared on the level of the marketing function) is not the same as the business plan, although the two necessarily overlap to some extent. Sir George Bull, former chairman of J. Sainsbury, observed that the marketing plan, which results from the marketing planning process, is distinguished from the business plan by its focus. 'The business plan takes as both its starting point and its objective the business itself', he said. In contrast, 'the marketing plan starts with the customer and works its way round to the business'.[29]

Marketing and the mission statement

Plans at all levels are made with the **mission statement** in mind. This statement explains the organization's purpose, points the way toward a future vision of what the organization aspires to become and drives planning at all levels. As you conduct an

Strategy level	Decisions covered	Examples of application at Unilever
Corporate	• Purpose	• To achieve sustainable, profitable growth and create long-term value for consumers, shareholders, employees
	• Direction	• Growth
	• Long-range goals	• 5–6% annual growth
	• Business definition	• Consumer goods
	• Value creation for customers	• Brand-name, quality products that meet and anticipate everyday customer needs
Business (implementing corporate strategy)	• Unit scope	• Foods, home and personal care divisions
	• Competitive approach	• Leverage brands for market leadership in high-demand product categories
	• Markets served	• Build relationships with consumers in Europe, Asia, the Americas, other markets
	• Allocation of resources for value	• Emphasize research and development to meet emerging consumer needs
Marketing (implementing business strategy, supporting corporate strategy)	• Product strategy	• Reinforce brand names in chosen categories (such as Magnum ice cream, Knorr soup)
	• Pricing strategy	• Offer quality and value
	• Channel/logistics (distribution) strategy	• Reach consumers through food wholesalers, retailers, restaurants, hotels
	• Integrated marketing communication (promotion) strategy	• Build brands through media advertising, online presence and various other techniques
	• Service	• Fill channel orders completely, on time
	• Internal marketing	• Build commitment and cooperation for marketing through ongoing communication and meetings

FIGURE 1.5   Levels of strategy

internal analysis of the current situation, take time to review your organization's mission statement because it will be an important foundation for decisions about marketing activities and resources.

A mission statement should be more than mere words on a page; it should clarify management's priorities and set the tone for all organization members – including marketing staff – by touching on five areas:[30]

- *Customer focus*. Who does the organization exist to serve? Businesses generally serve consumers, other businesses or government customers; non-profit organizations serve clients (such as patients, in the case of hospitals); government agencies serve constituents. For instance, Belgium's Médecins Sans Frontières (MSF) is a non-profit organization with the mission of 'providing medical aid wherever needed, regardless of race, religion, politics or sex and raising awareness of the plight of the people we help'.[31]

- *Value provided*. What value will the organization provide for its customers and other stakeholders, and how will it do so in a competitively superior way? Companies profit only when offerings add value that customers need or want. Krug, for example, creates value for consumers willing to spend more than £500 per bottle for vintage champagne 'of perfect craftsmanship'. Krug also creates value for employees (in the form of jobs) and shareholders of its parent company, LVMH (based on profits earned).[32]

- *Market scope*. Where and what will the organization market? Defining the market scope helps management properly align structure, strategy and resources. The CEO of Scottish & Newcastle has made the brewer's focus more international 'because frankly, we were acting basically as a UK brewing business', he says. Now the firm has forged profitable joint ventures in Russia, China and India and weeded out weaker brands to fund more marketing in stronger brands.[33]

- *Guiding values*. What values will guide managers and employees in making decisions and dealing with stakeholders? What does the organization want to stand for? Consider the values inherent in the mission of Tetra Pak, which makes shelf-stable packaging for foods. The company's mission statement is: 'We work for and with our customers to provide preferred processing and packaging solutions for food. We apply our commitment to innovation, our understanding of consumer needs and our relationships with suppliers to deliver these solutions, wherever and whenever food is consumed. We believe in responsible industry leadership, creating profitable growth in harmony with environmental sustainability and good corporate citizenship.'[34]

- *Core competencies*. What employee, process and technological capabilities give your organization its competitive edge? These are its **core competencies** (sometimes known as *distinctive competencies*) – capabilities that are not easily duplicated and that differentiate the organization from its competitors.[35] The clothing retailer Zara, headquartered in Spain, has expanded rapidly due to two core competencies: a short design-to-production-to-store cycle, based on customer buying patterns, and a constant stream of new products to freshen store inventories.[36] Competencies are 'core' when they are based on specific organization capabilities *and* contribute to competitive differentiation.

Clearly, the challenge of a good mission statement is to convey all this information in as concise a manner as possible. Now continue with your marketing plan by completing the checklist below, then read Chapter 2 for more about analysing the current marketing situation.

ESSENTIAL MARKETING PLAN CHECKLIST NO. 1:
THE MISSION STATEMENT

Before you can develop a marketing plan, you need to know who the organization exists to serve, what it expects to achieve in the long run and – in general terms – how it will compete, now and in the future. Obtain a copy of the organization's mission statement and answer each of the questions below to evaluate both the content and the likely effect. Put a tick mark next to each question after you've written your answers in the space provided. If your organization has no mission statement or if you're developing a marketing plan for a start-up or hypothetical company, use this checklist as you devise a suitable mission statement.

☐ Who will the organization focus on as customers, clients or constituents?

_____

☐ How will it provide value for customers and other stakeholders?

_____

☐ What main markets (geographic, product) will the organization serve?

_____

☐ What guiding values will the organization adopt?

_____

☐ What core competencies will the organization apply for competitive advantage?

_____

☐ How can the mission statement be improved as a guide for marketing planning?

_____

☐ Does the mission statement provide appropriate direction for organizational decisions, actions and resource allocation, including marketing planning?

_____

☐ Is the mission statement capable of rallying employees and inspiring stakeholders?

_____

☐ Is the mission statement forward-looking and enduring to guide the organization into the future?

_____

CHAPTER SUMMARY

Marketing planning is the structured process that leads to a coordinated set of marketing decisions and actions, for a specific organization and period. This process consists of seven stages: (1) analyse the external and internal situation; (2) research and analyse markets and customers; (3) determine segmentation, targeting and positioning; (4) set marketing objectives and direction; (5) plan marketing strategies, programmes and support; (6) plan to measure progress; (7) implement, control and evaluate the plan. Marketing planning is used to examine opportunities and potential threats, identify and evaluate a variety of outcomes, focus on customers, assess offerings in a competitive and environmental context, and allocate resources for marketing.

The marketing plan outlines the marketplace situation and describes the marketing strategies and programmes that will support the achievement of business and organizational goals. Organizational (corporate) strategy sets the organization's overall purpose, long-term direction, goals, businesses and approach to providing value. Business strategy sets the scope of individual units, how each will compete, the markets each will serve and how resources will be used. Marketing strategy shows how units will use the marketing mix plus service and internal marketing to achieve objectives. The mission statement outlines the organization's fundamental purpose, the future vision of what it can become and its priorities, guiding the overall development of the marketing plan.

CASE STUDY: TESCO'S MARKETING PLAN FOR GLOBAL GROWTH

Can Tesco spread its stores from Southampton to Southern California and beyond? The UK-based grocery retailer is seeking growth by expanding into new types of stores, new types of products and new markets. In addition to its retail businesses, Tesco has a profitable financial services division in alliance with Royal Bank of Scotland, offering credit, savings and insurance to more than 5 million consumers. Concerned with sustainability, the retailer is also choosing eco-friendly products and equipment such as 'green trolleys' made using energy-efficient methods.

Every year, Tesco researches consumer needs by meeting with 12,000 shoppers, reading customer comments, analysing the shopping patterns of its 13 million Clubcard customers and visiting customers at home. Its research shows that consumers vary their buying behaviour in different areas and at different times of the day. Therefore, Tesco operates 1,800 stores in four formats: small convenience stores for quick shopping trips; medium-sized high-street grocery stores with packaged foods and ready-made meals; superstores with food and non-food items; and giant Extra stores bursting with food and household items, clothing and small electronics. And it constantly expands the range of its own branded products, including organic and natural foods.

Competing with major UK merchants is a key marketing challenge, as is the difficulty of finding suitable locations for new stores. However, thanks to its strong brand, value emphasis and loyal customer base, the company has built Tesco.com into the world's largest online grocery store. Over the next five years, it is opening 'neighbourhood markets' in the competitive US market, a venture that could cost up to £2 billion. Rents are expensive, transporting food is expensive, and Tesco will be battling established supermarket chains (and discounters such as Wal-Mart). Where will Tesco's quest for growth take it next?[37]

Case questions

1. What external threats and opportunities does Tesco appear to be addressing with its multinational marketing plan?

2. To provide value to its targeted customers through such a wide product range, what core competencies must Tesco have (or have access to)?

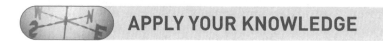

APPLY YOUR KNOWLEDGE

Choose a particular industry (such as banking or soft drinks) and research the mission statement and recent marketing activities of two competing businesses. Prepare a brief oral or written report summarizing your comments.

- What do the mission statements say about the customer focus, value creation, market scope, guiding values and core competencies of these companies?

- For each company, how do specific marketing actions appear to relate to the stated mission? As an example, does the advertising reflect the customer focus in the mission statement?

- Now look very carefully at the mission statement of one of these companies, keeping in mind the questions in this chapter's checklist. What changes would you suggest to make the statement more effective as a guide for the marketing planning process or as an inspiration for managers and employees?

BUILD YOUR OWN MARKETING PLAN

By the end of this course, you will know how to work through all the stages in the marketing planning process and how to document a marketing plan. Depending on your lecturer's instructions, you will base your marketing plan on an actual organization (as if you were one of its marketing managers), a hypothetical company or a non-profit organization. As you complete each of these cumulative exercises, record your findings and decisions in a marketing plan, following the order of topics shown in Figure 1.3.

Define the mission statement of your hypothetical organization or locate and analyse the mission statement of the organization you have chosen. If necessary, amend an existing organization's mission statement or create a new one according to this chapter's checklist. What does this mission statement suggest about the organization's purpose? Include information about the mission statement when writing about the current marketing situation in your marketing plan.

In preparation for later stages of the marketing planning process, list your ideas about the markets and customers to be researched and analysed; the product offering(s) your plan will cover; the organization's competitive stance; and its guiding values. Also look at the general direction you expect the marketing plan to take: is it likely to drive a growth strategy, sustain current turnover or support retrenching? Finally, write a few lines about what a one-year marketing plan needs to accomplish in order to lead the organization closer to its long-term goals. Save your notes for use in completing later assignments.

(STOP) ENDNOTES

1. Quoted in David Benady, 'Unilever: Going Overboard?' *Marketing Week*, 16 February 2006, p. 22.

2. Based on information from: Antonio Regalado, 'Marketers Pursue the Shallow-Pocketed; Low-Income Pool Is Seen As Untapped Resource', *Wall Street Journal*, 26 January 2007, p. B3; 'The Execution Challenge: Unilever', *Advertising Age*, 11 December 2006, p. 24; Adam Durchslag, 'Unilever Scrubs Up But Has Much To Do', *Sunday Business (London)*, 12 February 2006, n.p.; Benady, 'Unilever: Going Overboard?'; 'Unilever Posts Drop of 48% in Earnings', *Wall Street Journal*, 3 November 2006, www.wsj.com.

3. See Roger J. Best, *Market-Based Management*, 4th edn (Upper Saddle River, NJ: Pearson Prentice Hall, 2005), pp. 407–8.

4. David Pinto, 'Coles: Where It Is Exactly', *MMR*, 8 January 2007, p. 50; 'Coles Myer Takes New Direction', *MMR*, 21 August 2006, p. 15; Coles Group website (www.colesgroup.com.au/home/).

5. Sue Karlin, 'Coffins to Die For', *Fortune Small Business*, 1 February 2005, www.fortune.com; Briony Hale, 'African Crafts Go Online', *BBC Business News*, 3 February 2003, http://news.bbc.co.uk/2/hi/business/2688323.stm.

6. Paul B. Brown, 'Don't Plan Too Much. Decide', *New York Times*, 28 January 2006, p. C5.

7. Frances Brassington and Stephen Pettitt, *Principles of Marketing*, 3rd edn (Harlow, Essex: Financial Times Prentice Hall, 2003), p. 19.

8. Alison Maitland, 'Shell Takes Its Vexed Dilemmas to Business School', *Financial Times*, 7 May 2003, www.ft.com.

9. Louise Lee, 'Too Many Surveys, Too Little Passion?' *BusinessWeek*, 1 August 2005, p. 38.

10. See Philip Kotler and Kevin Lane Keller, *A Framework for Marketing Management*, 3rd edn (Upper Saddle River, NJ: Prentice Hall, 2007), Chapter 1.

11. Tim Ambler, *Marketing and the Bottom Line* (London: Financial Times Prentice Hall, 2000), pp. 19–20.

12. See Roland T. Rust, Tim Ambler, Gregory S. Carpenter, V. Kumar and Rajendra K. Srivastava, 'Measuring Marketing Productivity: Current Knowledge and Future Directions', *Journal of Marketing*, October 2004, pp. 76–89.

13. Lee Gomes, 'Web Allows People Just Like You and Me to Spot Trends. Uh-Oh', *Wall Street Journal*, 28 July 2003, p. B1.

14. Rachel Barnes, 'Privacy Issues Hit RFID', *Grocer*, 4 February 2006, p. 14; Heather Green, 'Bugging the World', *Business Week*, 25 August 2003, pp. 100–1; James Covert and Christina C. Berk, 'Consumer Groups Rip Tracking Chips', *Wall Street Journal*, 30 July 2003, p. B3D.

15. 'Chinese Niche Market Focuses on Practical', *Marketing News*, 1 October 2005, pp. 18–19; Gabriel Kahn, 'Still Going for Gold', *Wall Street Journal*, 28 January 2003, p. B1.

16. H. Igor Ansoff, 'Strategies for Diversification', *Harvard Business Review*, September–October 1957, pp. 113–24; Ade S. Olusoga, 'Market Concentration versus Market Diversification and Internationalization: Implications for MNE Performance', *International Marketing Review*, vol. 10, no. 2 (1993), pp. 40–59; Alan R. Andreasen and Philip Kotler, *Strategic Marketing for Non-profit Organizations*, 6th edn (Upper Saddle River, NJ: Prentice Hall, 2003), pp. 80–1.

17. See Philip Kotler, Veronica Wong, John Saunders and Gary Armstrong, *Principles of Marketing* (Harlow, Essex, England: Pearson Education, 2005), p. 33.

18. 'Mobile Elite Rush to Answer India's Call', *Business Week Online*, 31 January 2007, www.businessweek.com; Cassell Bryan-Low, 'Nokia Taps Curtis to Oversee Design of Its Cellphones', 3 March 2006, p. B7; Cassell Bryan-Low and Li Yuan, 'Selling Cellphone Buzz', *Wall Street Journal*, 23 February 2006, p. B1; 'Nokia Realigns for the Future', *BusinessWeek Online*, 16 February 2006, www.businessweek.com.

19. 'Edesur Losses Pile Up', *Latin American Power Watch*, 15 February 2006, p. 7; Michael Casey, 'Rain Brings Hope', *Wall Street Journal*, 13 August 2003, p. B5B.

20. Tim Ambler, 'Set Clear Goals and See Marketing Hit Its Target', *Financial Times*, 29 August 2002, p. 8.

21. Philip Kotler and Kevin Lane Keller, *Marketing Management*, 12th edn (Upper Saddle River, NJ: Prentice Hall, 2006), p. 278.

22. Jason Stein and Paul McVeigh, 'Hyundai Europe Wants to Fine-Tune Its Identity', *Automotive News Europe*, 20 February 2006, p. 8; 'Hyundai and Kia Follow Toyota's Recipe for Success', *Automotive News Europe*, 20 February 2006, p. S48.

23. Jason Bush, 'Shoppers Gone Wild', *BusinessWeek*, 20 February 2006, pp. 46–7.

24. Andrew Browne, 'In the Land of Bok Choy, Spam Hits the Spot', *Wall Street Journal*, 8 February 2005, p. B7.

25. See Ambler, *Marketing and the Bottom Line*, Chapter 6.

26. Mike Esterl, 'Siemens Chief Is Setting a Higher Bar', *Wall Street Journal*, 24 January 2006, p. C3.

27. Quote reported in Adam Lashinksy, 'Meg and the Machine', *Fortune*, 1 September 2003, pp. 68–78; also: Shailendra Bhatnagar and Doug Young, 'EBay Wins Market Share from Alibaba', *Reuters*, 2 March 2006, www.reuters.com/ business/.

28. Based on information in 'The Execution Challenge: Unilever', *Advertising Age*, 11 December 2006, p. 24; Deborah Ball, 'It Makes Dove, But Attracts Bears', *Wall Street Journal*, 31

July 2003, pp. C1, C3; Stephanie Thompson, '"Master" Plan: Bestfoods Strategy Results in Shakeup', *Advertising Age*, 7 July 2003, p. 3.

29. Quoted in Sir George Bull, 'What Does the Term Marketing Really Stand for?', *Marketing*, 30 November 2000, p. 30.

30. Adapted from Stephen J. Porth, *Strategic Management* (Upper Saddle River, NJ: Prentice Hall, 2003), pp. 53–4; Forest R. David and Fred B. David, 'It's Time to Redraft Your Mission Statement', *Journal of Business Strategy*, January–February 2003, pp. 11ff.

31. Médecins Sans Frontières website, www.msf.org.

32. Anne-Sylvaine Chassany, 'LVMH Sets Targets for Strong Growth', *Wall Street Journal*, 3 March 2006, http://online.wsj.com/article/SB11412829425698 7404. html; Tim Metcalfe, 'Spreading the Word about the King of Champagnes', *South China Morning Post*, 24 December 2005, n.p.

33. Will Oremus, 'Aussie Shakes Up U.K. Brewer', *Wall Street Journal*, 5 December 2005, p. B3.

34. Quoted on Tetra Pak website, www.tetrapak.com.

35. Stephen J. Porth, *Strategic Management* (Upper Saddle River, NJ: Prentice Hall, 2003), pp. 85–6.

36. Thomas J. Ryan, 'Uncovering Zara', *Apparel*, January 2006, p. 27; John Tagliabue, 'A Rival to Gap That Operates Like Dell', *New York Times*, 30 May 2003, pp. W1–W7.

37. Based on information from 'Ethical Shopping: Feeding Your Conscience', *Marketing Week*, 25 January, 2007, p. 42; 'Now Even Trolleys Are Getting Greener', *Grocer*, 25 November 2006, p. 14; Laura Cohn, 'A Look at Finance Efforts by Europe's "Wal-Mart"', *American Banker*, 4 December 2006, p. 1; Jerry Hirsch, 'Tesco Looking at 300 Sites for Grocery Stores', *Los Angeles Times*, 5 December 2006, p. C2; www.tesco.com.

2 Analysing the current situation

Comprehension outcomes

After studying this chapter, you will be able to:

- Explain the purpose of internal and external audits
- Discuss how the internal and external environments affect marketing planning
- Describe the use of SWOT analysis for marketing planning

Application outcomes

After studying this chapter, you will be able to:

- Conduct internal and external audits
- Prepare a SWOT analysis for your marketing plan

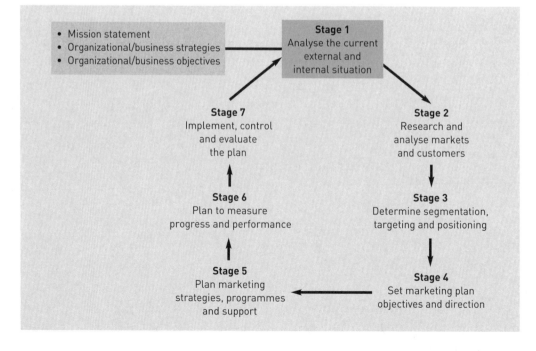

CHAPTER PREVIEW

'Our business is improving our customers' business', says CEO Henning Kagermann of SAP, based in Walldorf, Germany. As head of Europe's largest software company, Kagermann recognizes that customers want SAP to 'help them run their businesses smarter, cheaper and better'.[1] To satisfy customers while achieving corporate goals for growth and profitability, SAP's marketers track developments inside and outside the company, anticipate technological shifts and other environmental changes, then adjust internal capabilities and create a marketing plan to address the opportunities and threats they've identified.

Competition with Oracle, Microsoft and other rivals is one of the biggest external challenges for SAP. Another is the effect of changing customer preferences, which has prompted SAP to introduce new products such as 'on demand' online software. In addition, SAP wants to encourage positive media coverage by maintaining good relations with reporters and bloggers. Finally, to meet its goal of tripling the customer base by 2010, SAP would like to change the misperception that its software is for big corporations only. To do this, its marketing plan called for a multimedia campaign targeting the owners and technology managers of mid-sized companies.[2]

Like their counterparts at SAP, all marketing managers need a thorough understanding of the organization's current situation before they can create appropriate plans and programmes. This chapter continues with Stage 1 of the marketing planning process, in which you collect and interpret data about the internal and external environment. The first section is an overview of environmental scanning and analysis for the marketing plan. The following section discusses particular environmental factors that can make a difference to marketing and performance. The final section looks at how to use the data collected to evaluate your organization's strengths, weaknesses, opportunities and threats for marketing planning purposes. You can use the two checklists in this chapter as a guide to planning your internal and external audits.

ENVIRONMENTAL SCANNING AND ANALYSIS

Early in the marketing planning process, you have to look at the organization's current situation, especially within the context of the mission, higher-level plans and higher-level goals. This is accomplished through **environmental scanning and analysis**, the systematic (and ongoing) collection and interpretation of data about both internal and external factors that may affect marketing and performance. When learning about the situation inside the organization, marketers use an **internal audit**; when learning about the situation outside the organization, they use an **external audit**.

All the relevant information is accumulated, evaluated and distilled into a critique reflecting the organization's primary strengths, weaknesses, opportunities and threats, known as the **SWOT analysis**. In addition, many marketers conduct a SWOT analysis of current or potential rivals to clarify the competitive situation. This understanding helps you develop a marketing plan to leverage your internal strengths, bolster your internal weaknesses, take advantage of competitors' main weaknesses and defend against competitors' strengths, as shown in Figure 2.1.

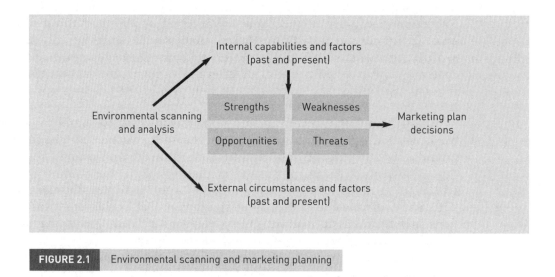

| FIGURE 2.1 | Environmental scanning and marketing planning |

Details count in any environmental scan, but professional judgement plays a vital role as well. Use your best judgement (supported by other managers' insights, expert models and so on) to develop the most reasonable marketing plan under the circumstances. Over time, work on developing your ability to discern the combined influence of various environmental factors and trends on your firm and its marketing.[3]

Internal audit: identifying strengths and weaknesses

The internal audit covers the mission statement (as discussed in Chapter 1) plus your organization's resources and capabilities, current offerings, previous performance, business relationships and key issues. These internal factors, individually and in combination, are instrumental in the way a company fulfils its mission, serves its customers and competes in the marketplace. And – just as important – they contribute to the organization's strengths and weaknesses in using marketing to deal with opportunities and threats.

A **strength** is an internal capability or factor that can help the organization achieve its objectives, making the most of opportunities or deflecting threats. For example, one of Nintendo's great strengths is its technical innovation, exhibited in products such as the Wii game console. Another is its sizeable cash position, which supports innovative new product development and other internal activities.

A **weakness** is an internal capability or factor that may prevent the organization from achieving its objectives or effectively handling opportunities and threats, especially within the competitive context. For instance, Sony had to postpone launching its

PlayStation 3 game console until its engineers finalized the standards and technology for its Blu-ray DVD format. This delay was a weakness that opened opportunities for Nintendo's Wii and Microsoft's Xbox consoles. Also it was a setback to Sony's plan for polishing its image after recalling millions of laptop computer batteries.[4]

When auditing your internal strengths and weaknesses, search company records and databases for information such as current offerings, finances, personnel and skills, technological expertise, supplier relations, distributor connections, partnerships, previous marketing plans and results. Use the checklist later in this chapter to plan your internal audit.

External audit: identifying opportunities and threats

The external audit covers political–legal factors, economic factors, social–cultural factors and technological factors (known as *PEST* or *STEP* if the order is rearranged) plus ecological and competitive factors that may present opportunities or pose threats. An **opportunity** is an external circumstance or factor that the organization can attempt to exploit for higher performance. For example, Cadbury Schweppes found that health-conscious consumers are interested in snacks with little fat and few calories. It also found that consumers now have very positive attitudes toward chewing gum. Therefore, by focusing on gum products like Trident, the firm is enjoying higher turnover and profit margins.[5]

A **threat** is an external circumstance or factor that could inhibit organizational performance, if not addressed. Cadbury Schweppes markets Dr Pepper, Mott's and other soft drinks, so competition from Coca-Cola and PepsiCo is a major threat. A threat for the company's chocolate and sweets business is the shift toward low-fat, low-calorie treats. Another threat is parents' concern about helping children choose healthier foods. This is why Cadbury Schweppes states: 'We do not vend our confectionery or carbonated beverages in primary schools and will only vend these products in secondary schools by invitation and in line with nutritional guidelines set by the school.'[6]

Sources for an external audit include internal information about customers, suppliers, partners, market share, technical standards; customer feedback through surveys, suggestions, complaints; government, academic or syndicated studies of the market, the industry, competition; industry groups; employees, suppliers, and other partners; media and online reports; special interest groups. Later in this chapter you'll read more about the external audit.

ANALYSING THE INTERNAL ENVIRONMENT

During an internal audit, you will scan and analyse five main factors: the organization's resources and capabilities; current offerings; previous performance; business relationships; and key issues. You're looking for information that can help you understand your organization's current situation and the strengths you can rely on when implementing a marketing plan.

Organizational resources and capabilities

As noted in Chapter 1, core competencies are internal capabilities that contribute to competitive superiority yet are not easily duplicated. Such capabilities are traced to the organization's human, financial, informational and supply resources (*see* Figure 2.2). One reason Wal-Mart de México has boosted its turnover and profit margin is its core competency in logistics management.

MARKETING IN PRACTICE: WAL-MART DE MÉXICO

Wal-Mart de México, a subsidiary of the world's largest retailer, has surpassed its local competitors and achieved enviable profitability through its expertise in planning inventory, warehousing goods and getting the right merchandise to the right stores. The retailer operates nearly 800 supermarkets, stores and supercentres. Its marketing plan calls for tailoring the specific mix of goods and services in each store to the tastes and buying power of the surrounding area. Just as important, the company ensures that shelves are never empty and, in fact, the most popular products are available in abundance – at low, affordable prices.[7]

Human resources: Does your company have the people, skills, commitment, rewards to successfully implement your marketing plan?

Specifically examine:
- Workforce knowledge, skills, morale, turnover
- Top management support
- Individual commitment, initiative, entrepreneurial spirit
- Recruitment, training, rewards

Informational resources: Does your company have the data, tools and access to information to successfully implement your marketing plan?

Specifically examine:
- Data capture, storage, reporting systems
- Analysis tools
- Access to timely, accurate, complete information

Financial resources: Does your company have the money to successfully implement your marketing plan?

Specifically examine:
- Funding for marketing activities
- Funding for research
- Funding for internal support
- Anticipated funding for multi-year programmes

Supply resources: Does your company have the supplies, supply systems and relationships to implement your marketing plan?

Specifically examine:
- Ample availability of materials, parts, components and services
- Supply chain relationships
- Inventory management

FIGURE 2.2 Areas of focus in organizational resources

When planning for marketing, you and your managers must balance the investment and allocation of resources. The organization's values, ethical standards and social responsibility position also affect this balancing act. From a practical standpoint, the internal audit helps managers determine the resources they have, the resources they can obtain and where their resources are currently committed. This is the starting point for identifying any resource gaps and determining how best to allocate resources in support of the marketing plan.

Outsourcing, strategic alliances and supply chain realignment are three ways that organizations can gain or supplement resource arrangements to bridge any gaps for added strength. As an example, rather than devote internal resources to maintaining manufacturing facilities in every region, BMW, Skoda and other automakers serve South Asian markets by outsourcing some manufacturing to India. Fine-tuning the supply chain can help a firm boost on-time delivery and cut the lead time for obtaining supplies.[8]

Current offerings

In this part of the internal audit, you review and analyse the goods and services you currently offer so you know where you stand before making plans to move ahead. Also understand how your organization's offerings relate to the mission and to your resources. Companies generally examine the following, looking at historic and current trends:

- composition, sales and market share of product mix and lines
- customer needs satisfied by features and benefits
- product pricing and profitability, contribution to overall performance
- product age and position in product life cycle
- links to other products.

Previous performance

Although past performance is never a guarantee of future performance, looking at previous results can reveal insights about internal strengths and weaknesses. The purpose is to build on past marketing experience in planning new marketing activities. At a minimum, you will analyse these performance indicators:

- prior year sales (in units and monetary terms)
- prior year profits and other financial results
- historic trends in sales and profits by product, geographic region, customer segment, etc.
- results of previous marketing plans
- customer acquisition, retention and loyalty trends and costs.

Some companies use **data mining**, sophisticated analyses of database information to uncover customer behaviour patterns, to understand previous sales trends, customer loyalty, even the deals that got away. Samsung Electronics America scrutinized data from 10,000 distributors to see how many and what kind of orders it had lost to rivals. It learned that one rival had won 40 per cent of the health-care industry orders that Samsung did not get. As a result, Samsung resolved to strengthen ties with hardware firms serving the health-care field.[9] Similarly, Tesco used data mining of its sales records to identify customers who had not made recent purchases, then sent each a letter with a money-off coupon. Within three months, Tesco had won back 4,800 customers.[10]

Business relationships

As the Samsung example suggests, good business relationships can act as strengths, helping organizations make the most of opportunities or defend against threats and profitably satisfy customers. Among the areas of business relationships to be examined during an internal audit are:

- value added by suppliers, distributors and strategic alliance partners
- internal relationships with other units or divisions
- capacity, quality, service, commitment and costs of suppliers and channel members
- changes in business relationships over time
- level of dependence on suppliers and channel members.

The existence of a business relationship is not in and of itself a strength. Moreover, not having strong connections with vital suppliers or channel members can be a definite weakness when an organization is seeking aggressive growth or simply struggling to survive. On the other hand, close connections with internal divisions or channel members and suppliers can be an important competitive advantage.

Key issues

What specific issues could interfere with the organization's ability to move toward its mission and goals, and what are the warning signs of potential problems? What specific issues are pivotal for organizational success? Some organizations look at key issues more closely, according to customer segment, market or product.

You may need marketing research to get a more complete picture of certain issues. Consider what Unilever's researchers learned from a multinational study of women's attitudes toward beauty and self-image. Respondents said that media and advertising messages depict standards of beauty that most women – including themselves – cannot attain. Understanding this issue helped Unilever identify an opportunity that it pursued through a marketing plan to promote its Dove products with ads featuring women who don't look like supermodels. Younger women, in particular, are responding to Dove's message – which has reshaped Dove's brand image and boosted sales.[11]

ESSENTIAL MARKETING PLAN CHECKLIST NO. 2:
THE INTERNAL ENVIRONMENT

To formulate a realistic marketing plan, you must be knowledgeable about what your organization has, where it has been and what it can leverage. Continue your marketing planning effort by adding a tick mark next to each question after writing answers in the spaces provided. If you are planning for a start-up or a hypothetical company, use this checklist to note ideas about potential weaknesses you should counter and internal strengths you'll need to support your marketing plan.

☐ Does the organization have the human, informational, financial and supply resources appropriate for marketing?

_____

☐ What do trends in marketing results and organizational performance suggest about the effectiveness of previous plans and the content of future plans?

_____

☐ What goods and services are currently offered and how do they contribute to turnover and profits?

_____

☐ How do the organization's offerings provide value to customers – and is this value competitively superior?

_____

☐ Are the offerings suitable for the organization's mission, goals and resources?

_____

☐ What are the trends in customer needs, acquisition, retention and loyalty?

_____

☐ How do business relationships affect capacity, quality, costs and availability?

_____

☐ What marketing research does the organization need to support marketing planning?

_____

☐ What lessons can be applied to the marketing plan, based on the internal audit?

_____

ANALYSING THE EXTERNAL ENVIRONMENT

In contrast to the factors in the internal environment, which offer clues to strengths and weaknesses, the factors in the external environment offer clues to opportunities and threats (*see* Figure 2.3). These factors also suggest additional lines of inquiry for researching and analysing markets and customers, as discussed in Chapter 3. The following sections look at external environmental factors in more detail.

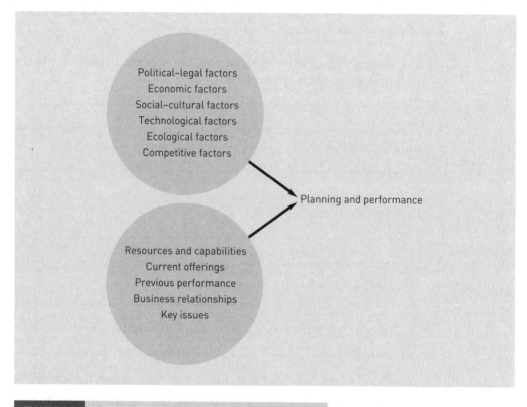

Political–legal factors
Economic factors
Social–cultural factors
Technological factors
Ecological factors
Competitive factors

Resources and capabilities
Current offerings
Previous performance
Business relationships
Key issues

Planning and performance

FIGURE 2.3   Factors in the external and internal environment

Remember, your external audit is intended to help you identify trends or situations that you can capitalize on through marketing planning – and issues or circumstances that you should defend against through marketing planning. When you write your marketing plan, you'll summarize the most important point or points about each of these factors as you explain your organization's current marketing situation. *See* the checklist at the end of this section for specific questions to ask when analysing the external environment.

Political–legal factors

Depending on where your organization is based and where it does business, political–legal factors can lead to profitable opportunities or potential threats (or both). Political instability, as one example, can pose a threat to ongoing operations; laws, regulations and governmental actions can affect product purity and labelling, promotion, pricing, distribution, competitive behaviour and consumer choices. Your analysis should look at how the various political–legal factors might affect the current marketing plan (such as in your choice of markets) and your future plans (to continue in a particular market, for instance).

Economic factors

In the interconnected global economy, recession or recovery in one region can have a cascading effect on the purchasing patterns of consumers and businesses near and far. Economic factors influence customer buying power because of the effect on consumer and business income, debt and credit usage. Economic slowdowns often discourage businesses from spending heavily on upgrading their plants, for instance, or government agencies from proceeding with infrastructure improvements. Even if the home country economy is growing slowly, however, a company may create a marketing plan around opportunities in countries where the economic outlook seems more favourable.

To illustrate, the German retailer Metro has created a marketing plan to open eight Cash and Carry superstores in Vietnam because that nation's economy has been growing at nearly 7 per cent annually and the average per capita income has also been rising. The government encourages retail expansion, knowing that new stores help Vietnamese suppliers gain market share domestically and reach new markets abroad – which, in turn, strengthens the local economy.[12] Be alert for these kinds of opportunities based on economic factors. Also be aware of economic factors when you set your marketing plan objectives (*see* Chapter 5).

Social–cultural factors

Social–cultural factors are among the most dynamic in the external environment, affecting the size and composition of markets and segments as well as customers' requirements, characteristics, attitudes and perceptions. Population shifts due to higher or lower birth rates, longer life spans and immigration can create, expand or shrink markets. Along with these shifts come changes in demand and usage of different goods and services – key changes that must be considered in marketing planning. David Wilson Homes is conducting in-depth research to better understand the social–cultural factors that affect home buyers.

MARKETING IN PRACTICE: DAVID WILSON HOMES

What do families want in a new home? David Wilson Homes, a division of William Bowden, needs to know because it annually builds more than 5,000 new homes in Britain. To add a human dimension to its research, the company constructed a 'concept home' with new features and invited a family of four to live there for six months. At times, the family wore devices to signal when someone entered and left each room. University researchers analysed this information to determine, for example, how often the dining room was used. Then they combined their findings with other marketing research and with demographic data to help project the consumer needs and expectations for which David Wilson Homes should prepare.[13]

During your planning, examine demographic details such as gender, education, occupation, ethnic and religious composition, household size, household composition and household income, any or all of which can affect purchasing and usage. Specific products may demand a closer look at characteristics such as how a certain customer segment uses technology. Companies that market to businesses look closely at trends such as the size and growth of targeted industries as measured by number of firms, number of locations or outlets, workforce size, turnover and profitability.

Customers are real people, not numbers; they have distinct feelings and attitudes toward companies, brands, products and buying situations, which in turn influence how they act. For example, marketers for the Cascais shopping centre near Lisbon, Portugal, learned that upper-income families go shopping only when they want a specific purchase. 'As a result, we decided to introduce valet parking to speed up the process for them', says the head of market research.[14] Insights such as these are important for realistic and creative marketing planning.

Paid promotions play a role in establishing a positive reputation, but consumers may give more credence to word-of-mouth communication about quality, service and other aspects of the offering. 'Word of mouth is still important because it reaches people who may not be e-commerce shoppers yet', explains a spokesperson for the online retailer Amazon.com. 'Word of mouse is important because on the Web you can reach so many more people beyond your circle of friends.'[15] This is why many marketing plans explicitly address word-of-mouth communications.

Technological factors

Fast-changing technology has an effect on customers, suppliers, competitors, channel members, marketing techniques and organizational processes. Moreover, competing technology standards (sometimes coupled with government-imposed standards) are major factors in certain product categories. And although the Internet has opened opportunities for consumer and business marketing, it has also raised questions about privacy and security. Still, technology touches virtually every element of marketing, from digitally enhanced advertisements to packaging and beyond. As an example, Philips is designing computer chips that will bring mobile handset prices below €20, making mobiles affordable for consumers in developing nations as part of its overall marketing plan for growth.[16]

When examining technological factors to understand potential threats and opportunities, look at: how rapidly innovations are spreading or evolving; how technology is affecting customers and others in the marketing environment; how technology is affected by or affecting standards and regulations; what and when technology is prompting substitute or improved products; how much the industry and key competitors are investing in research and development; and how technology is affecting costs and pricing.

Ecological factors

Ecological factors can influence marketing in numerous ways. Manufacturers will be unable to achieve their objectives if vital raw materials such as water or minerals are unavailable for production. A steady source of non-polluting energy is problematic for businesses and non-governmental organizations in certain regions; in other areas, high energy costs pose a challenge. Further, government regulations and public attitudes are shaping how companies interact with the natural environment. Clearly, this is an area you must consider during marketing planning, especially as it relates to your products and your societal objectives.

Also be aware that public sentiment is pressuring companies to report on their progress toward sustainability, although disclosures are, for now, voluntary. The financial services provider HSBC Group, based in London, posts sustainability goals on its website and issues yearly reports describing its achievements. The bank also has a department specifically for sustainable development projects. These activities support HSBC's marketing plan to position itself as a leader in corporate social responsibility.[17]

Competitive factors

Every organization, not just businesses, faces competition. Charities compete with other charities for a share of donors' contributions; governments compete with each other when trying to attract businesses to create jobs in an area, for example. As a marketer, you should examine three sets of industry forces to gauge the competitive attractiveness of the industry before you prepare your marketing plan: (1) how easily competitors can enter or leave the market; (2) how much power buyers and suppliers have; and (3) whether substitutes are available for your products and the effect on industry rivalry (*see* Figure 2.4).

According to Michael Porter's model,[18] when rivals can easily enter the market, the industry may become suddenly and unpredictably become more competitive, which complicates the marketing planning process. When buyers and suppliers have relatively little power, the competitive environment is likely to be less pressured and the market may have more profit potential. When there are few rivals and few substitutes for the company's

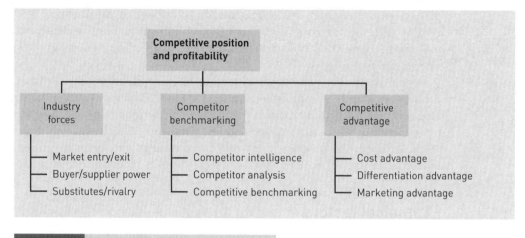

FIGURE 2.4   Competitive position and profitability

Source: Adapted from Roger J. Best, *Market-Based Management: Strategies for Growing Customer Value and Profitability*, 2nd edn (Upper Saddle River, NJ: Prentice Hall, 2000), p. 127.

product, the company will feel less pricing pressure and be better positioned for profit potential. Keep this in mind as you think about pricing and other competitive issues.

Next, gather information on rivals, analyse the data and use benchmarking to set targets for equalling or exceeding what competitors do in key areas. Consider what your customers value as well as what your organization needs to achieve its objectives and goals. Also be sure the measures you choose for monitoring your activities and competitors' activities can be tracked over time.[19]

The third set of competitive factors relates to how you plan for competitive advantage. Companies like Carrefour (retailing) and Acer (computers) strive for cost advantage, minimizing costs to keep their prices low. Companies like Luxottica (spectacles) derive competitive advantage from quality, style or another point of differentiation by positioning their offerings as superior in delivering features and benefits valued by customers. Companies like Shell (petrol and energy products) get a competitive edge from cost-effective marketing due to high brand awareness, extensive distribution and other efficiencies. Here's how Sweden's H&M builds competitive advantage worldwide.

MARKETING IN PRACTICE: H&M

Hennes & Mauritz – better known as H&M – built its global empire based on affordable fashion, minimizing overhead and operating costs to keep prices low. Staff designers choose from 900 outside suppliers and rotate suppliers to get better deals. The company shaves costs by speeding up cycle time from design to production to delivery of products. As a result, customers visit H&M's 1,300 stores and its website often to buy the very latest styles. H&M's competitive advantage is so powerful that its turnover and profits are soaring even as some retailers are struggling.[20]

Many marketers tend to focus on current competitors that follow marketing plans similar to their own, typically within the same industry. However, you also need to scan the environment for trends that might change the future competitive situation and for companies that might soon be able to satisfy customer needs in an entirely new or different way.[21] For example, the head of Travelplanet.pl, a large Internet travel agency in Poland, sees online purchases of travel services growing much faster than purchases made through traditional travel agencies. Citing the country's economic climate and greater interest in buying online, Travelplanet.pl reports that 60 per cent of its revenues come from purchases of tour packages, which is why its marketing plan emphasizes those offerings.[22]

PREPARING THE SWOT ANALYSIS

Once you have data from internal and external audits, you will prepare a SWOT analysis to make sense of what you have learned and interpret it in the context of the organization's situation, mission and goals. As discussed earlier, strengths and weaknesses are internal capabilities and factors that may support or hinder performance. The purpose of a SWOT analysis is to match key strengths with promising opportunities and see how strengths can guard against weaknesses and threats in supporting marketing decisions and programmes.

How can you determine whether a particular internal capability, resource or factor is a strength or a weakness? Four criteria can be used:[23]

1. *Previous performance*. How has the factor affected earlier performance, as measured by trends in turnover and profitability, market share, employee productivity or other appropriate standards? Are prior trends and performance likely to continue?

2. *Outcomes*. How has the factor contributed to specific outcomes defined by objectives and goals? Will the factor be likely to influence short- and long-term outcomes in the future?

3. *Competitors*. How does the factor compare with that of competitors, and is significant change likely to occur in the future?

4. *Management judgement*. How do organizational managers view the factor and what changes, if any, do they foresee in the coming months or years?

As shown in Figure 2.5, you should examine your major strengths and weaknesses to determine their sources and effect on opportunities or threats and the implications for your marketing plan. You can confirm the suitability of opportunities when you further analyse markets and customers in Stage 2 of the marketing planning process (*see* Chapter 3).

The point is not to analyse every capability, resource or factor but to single out the most important as strengths (to be employed) and weaknesses (to be counteracted). Opportunities cannot be profitably exploited unless the organization possesses strengths to take full advantage of the situation, as managers at Siemens' transport division found

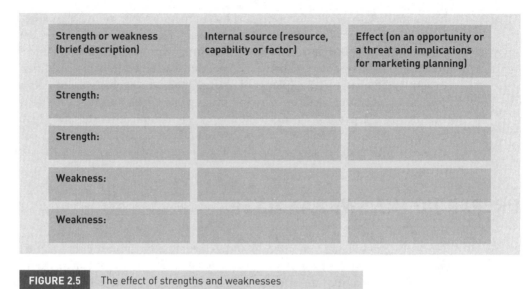

Strength or weakness (brief description)	Internal source (resource, capability or factor)	Effect (on an opportunity or a threat and implications for marketing planning)
Strength:		
Strength:		
Weakness:		
Weakness:		

FIGURE 2.5   The effect of strengths and weaknesses

out. Customers that bought its electrical systems for trains began expressing interest in buying fully assembled locomotives. Lacking the capabilities to manufacture locomotives, Siemens responded by acquiring companies in that industry so it could launch a major marketing initiative in this product category. This strength has helped the company win multi-million-euro contracts to supply locomotives for rail freight firms worldwide.[24]

ESSENTIAL MARKETING PLAN CHECKLIST NO. 3:
THE EXTERNAL ENVIRONMENT

As you prepare your marketing plan, you need to analyse how external factors affect your current marketing situation and how they might influence future marketing activities. Insert a tick mark by each question below as you note your answers in the space provided. If you're writing a marketing plan for a hypothetical business, use this checklist to list what you would focus on when analysing the external environment.

☐ Does the organization have appropriate human, informational, financial and supply resources for marketing?

_____

☐ What developments and changes in the political–legal environment can or will affect the organization and, specifically, its marketing decisions and actions?

_____

☐ How can local, regional, national and international economic conditions affect demand and customer buying power now and in the future?

_____

☐ In what ways are trends in demographics, social values, popular culture, customer attitudes and customer perceptions influencing demand, markets and segments?

_____

☐ How are technological innovations affecting customers, competitors, suppliers, channel partners, marketing and internal processes such as research and development?

_____

☐ What emerging and ongoing ecological concerns may affect the organization's materials, suppliers, energy access, processes, marketing programmes and public reputation?

_____

☐ What is the current competitive situation and how is it changing (or likely to change)?

_____

☐ What are each main competitor's market share, strengths, weaknesses, opportunities, threats, resources and competitive advantages?

_____

☐ What benchmarks can be used for competitive performance and on what basis can the organization achieve competitive advantage?

_____

☐ What lessons learned through the external audit can be applied to marketing planning?

_____

CHAPTER SUMMARY

Marketers use an internal audit to examine resources and capabilities, current offerings, past results, business relationships and key issues that affect marketing and performance. They use an external audit to examine political–legal, economic, social–cultural, technological, ecological and competitive factors and see how these might affect marketing. To gauge whether a market is competitively attractive, marketers look at: ease of market entry and exit; power of buyers and suppliers; availability of substitutes and the likely effect on industry rivalry.

After completing the internal and external audits, marketers analyse and distil the relevant data into a critique summarizing the organization's primary strengths, weaknesses, opportunities and threats, examined in the context of the mission and goals. Some marketers also prepare a SWOT analysis of key competitors. A SWOT analysis helps marketers match strengths with opportunities and understand how to guard against weaknesses and threats as they prepare the marketing plan.

CASE STUDY: MORE MARKETING CHALLENGES AHEAD FOR SONY

Sony's international entertainment empire stretches from movies and music to electronics, videogame consoles and beyond. For years, its reputation for innovativeness has translated into new technologies and category-defining products. In recent years, however, internal challenges and a highly volatile environment have slowed Sony's momentum and squeezed its profits.

For example, the worldwide launch of the PlayStation 3 game console had to be postponed as Sony's engineers struggled with the Blu-ray DVD format and revamped the software to play older PlayStation games. Because of high production costs, analysts estimate that Sony initially lost £100 or more on each console (although the firm expected to profit eventually from game sales). Another costly setback was the recall of 9 million lithium-ion laptop batteries. Moreover, Sony was slow to adopt flat-screen televisions, even as consumers enthusiastically adopted the technology. On the other hand, Sony's digital cameras have been big sellers. The bottom line is an estimated 5 per cent annual profit margin, slim even for the electronics industry.

Looking ahead, Sony's marketers are revising the marketing plan to revitalize profits. Taking advantage of core competencies, all divisions are being directed to leverage the firm's strength in software. In addition, Sony is considering the introduction of new products powered by the super-fast Cell microprocessor, developed jointly with IBM and Toshiba for game consoles. 'If realized, [the Cell] would be a highly important component that would make our consumer products as well as industrial products stand out among competitors', observes Sony's president. Where will marketing take Sony in the coming years?[25]

Case questions

1. Which internal factors have most influenced Sony's recent marketing performance?

2. Which external factors are likely to have the most effect on Sony's future marketing performance?

APPLY YOUR KNOWLEDGE

Research and analyse the forces shaping the industry of a company that is facing intense competitive pressure, such as a particular retailer or a consumer electronics firm. Then prepare a brief oral or written report summarizing your results.

- How powerful are suppliers to this industry? What are the implications for the company's business relationships?

- How powerful are buyers in this industry? What are the implications for the company's pricing decisions?

- Can customers substitute other goods or services for the company's offerings? What are the implications for customer loyalty to this company – and how can this be addressed through marketing?

- Can the company or competitors easily exit the industry? Can more rivals easily enter the industry? What are the implications for the company's marketing if environmental conditions threaten profitability?

- How do you think this competitive environment is likely to affect the chosen company's marketing plan for the coming year?

BUILD YOUR OWN MARKETING PLAN

Continue the marketing planning process using the concepts and tools from this chapter, including the two checklists. Start with an internal audit of resources, offerings, previous performance, business relationships and key issues. If the organization is a start-up, examine the recent performance of direct competitors and discuss what the trends might mean for your organization. Next, look at relevant political–legal, economic, social–cultural, technological, ecological and competitive factors in the external environment and how these factors might affect your marketing decisions (and your competitors' marketing activities).

On the basis of your internal and external audits, prepare a SWOT analysis explaining how the main strengths and weaknesses relate to specific opportunities or threats and their implications for marketing strategy. Before you record your conclusions, think about how these latest ideas will help you develop a practical, successful marketing plan. Then enter this data in your marketing plan, with as much detail as needed to support your conclusions.

STOP ENDNOTES

1. Quoted in Megan Barnett, 'Taking on Tech's Titans', *SmartMoney*, April 2006, pp. 29–30.

2. Based on information from: Leila Abboud and Vauhini Vara, 'SAP Trails Nimble Start-Ups As Software Market Matures', *Wall Street Journal*, 23 January 2007, p. C1; 'SAP Intends to Triple Customer Base in Four Years', *InformationWeek*, 5 December, 2006, n.p.; 'New Campaigns', *B to B*, 11 December 2006, p. 14; Barnett, 'Taking on Tech's Titans'; 'Bloggers' Corner Proves Successful at SAP Event', *PR Week*, 20 November 2006, p. 19.

3. Craig S. Fleisher and Babette E. Bensoussan, *Strategic and Competitive Analysis* (Upper Saddle River, NJ: Prentice Hall, 2003), pp. 269–83.

4. Matt Richtel, 'Console Sales Beat Goals, Makers' Early Reports Say', *New York Times*, 8 January 2007, p. C4; 'Sony Keeps PS3 Targets Despite Headwind', *eWeek*, 14 December 2006, n.p.; 'Sony to Delay Release of PlayStation 3', *New York Times*, 15 March 2006, www.nytimes.com.

5. Melanie Warner, 'In Defense of Soda and Gum', *New York Times*, 4 March 2006, p. C3.

6. Quote from Cadbury Schweppes website (www.cadburyschweppes.com/EN/ EnvironmentSociety/Consumer/ WhatWeAreDoing).

7. Jane Bussey, 'Wal-Mexico: Wal-Mart's Biggest Success', *Miami Herald*, 24 January 2006, www.herald.com; Kerry A. Dolan, 'It's Nice to Be Big', *Forbes*, 1 September 2003,pp. 84–5.

8. 'Pacesetters Collaboration: Procter & Gamble', *BusinessWeek*, 21 November 2005, p. 92; 'India Emerges as New Auto Hub', *Asia Africa Intelligence Wire*, 30 August 2005, n.p.; 'Focusing on the Big Picture: What's the Real Deal with Global Supply Chains?', *World Trade*, February 2006, pp. 28ff.

9. Mitch Betts, 'Unexpected Insights', *Computerworld*, 14 April 2003, p. 34.

10. 'Campaign Direct Awards 2006: The Ortus Award', *Campaign*, 7 April 2006, p. 8.

11. Quoted in Theresa Howard, 'Dove Ads Enlist All Shapes, Styles, Sizes', *USA Today*, 29 August 2005, p. 7B; Michelle Jeffers, 'Behind Dove's "Real Beauty"', *Adweek*, 12 September 2005, p. 34.

12. 'Metro Eyes Pakistan', *MMR*, 24 April 2006, p. 15; 'Vietnam: Competitor to Go Up Against Big C, Metro', *Thai Press Reports*, 31 January 2006, n.p.; 'Metro Vietnam Holds Supplier Conference', *Asia Africa Intelligence Wire*, 8 November 2005, n.p.; Catherine McKinley, 'Vietnam Has a Market for Superstores', *Wall Street Journal*, 13 August 2003, p. B3A.

13. Beth Carney, 'Home Design's House of Clues', *BusinessWeek*, 24 August 2005, www.businessweek.com.

14. Quoted in Sara Seddon Kilbinger, 'European Malls Keep Habits in Mind', *Wall Street Journal*, 14 September 2005, p. B3E.

15. Quoted in Nicholas Thompson, 'More Companies Pay Heed to Their "Word of Mouse" Reputation', *New York Times*, 23 June 2003, p. C4.

16. 'Calling an End to Poverty', *The Economist*, 9 July 2005, pp. 51–2.

17. 'Corporate Social Responsibility: Banks Told to Improve CSR Standards', *Europe Intelligence Wire*, 20 February 2006, n.p.

18. Discussion based on theories in Michael Porter, *Competitive Advantage* (New York: Free Press, 1985), pp. 11–26; and Roger Best, *Market-Based Management*, 4th edn (Upper Saddle River, NJ: Pearson Prentice Hall, 2005), Chapter 6.

19. Companies may want to analyse competitors using some of the metrics they apply to their own

performance. See Thomas J. Reynolds and Carol B. Phillips, 'In Search of True Brand Equity Metrics', *Journal of Advertising Research*, June 2005, pp. 171ff.

20. 'Hennes & Mauritz AB: Retailer Will Debut in Japan', *Wall Street Journal,* 12 December 2006, p. B7; Kerry Cappell, 'Hip H&M', *Business Week*, 11 November 2002, pp. 106–10; Robert Murphy, 'H&M Posts 6% Increase in Profits', *WWD,* 27 January 2006, p. 18.

21. Fleisher and Bensoussan, *Strategic and Competitive Analysis*, Chapter 11.

22. 'Internet Travel Boom', *Europe Intelligence Wire,* 15 January 2006, n.p.

23. Mary K. Coulter, *Strategic Management in Action* (Upper Saddle River, NJ: Prentice Hall, 1998), Chapter 4.

24. 'Siemens in 60-Loco Upgrade Deal', *International Railway Journal*, January 2006, p. 3; 'Rising Above the Sludge', *The Economist*, 5 April 2003, pp. 61–3.

25. Based on information from: Matt Richtel, 'Console Sales Beat Goals', *New York Times,* 8 January 2007, p. C4; 'PlayStation: Testing Times', *Marketing Week,* 14 December 2006, p. 22; 'Sony Keeps PS3 Targets Despite Headwind', *EWeek,* 14 December 2006, n.p.; 'New Leader for Sony's PlayStation Unit', *Business Week Online,* 13 December 2006, www.businessweek.com; Daren Fonda, 'How Sony Got Game?' *Time,* 27 November 2006, pp. 54+.

3 Analysing customers and markets

Comprehension outcomes

After studying this chapter, you will be able to:

- Understand why marketers examine markets according to definition, changes and share
- Explain the main influences on customer behaviour in consumer and business markets
- Describe how secondary and primary data are used in marketing planning

Application outcomes

After studying this chapter, you will be able to:

- Define and describe the market for a product
- Identify sources of information about consumer and business markets
- Calculate market share
- Analyse customer behaviour for marketing planning purposes

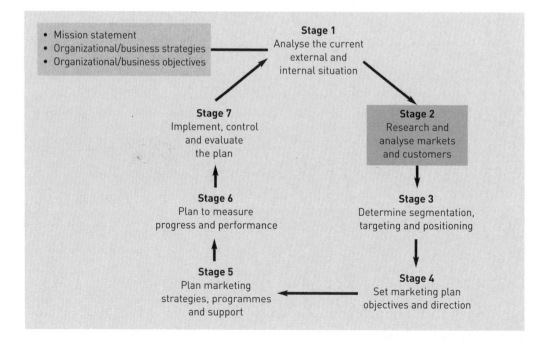

CHAPTER PREVIEW

'The better we know you, the more we can do' is ANZ Banking Group's slogan. But the bank can't serve everyone, everywhere, so to keep profits growing, its marketing plan focuses on specific markets and customers. Based in New Zealand, ANZ has a plan for expansion through alliances with banks in China, Vietnam, Cambodia and other Asian nations. It maintains bank branches and also offers online banking so business customers and consumers can check balances and transfer money at any hour. In addition, its rural managers are trained to meet farmers' financial needs. And a partnership with Woolworths in Australia enhances customer convenience by putting hundreds of automated teller machines in local shops, petrol stations and other retail locations.[1]

This chapter takes you into Stage 2 of the marketing planning process, starting with a look at how and why markets are defined as a first step toward choosing specific markets and segments to be targeted. Next you'll see how market share is calculated and used. This discussion is followed by a discussion of how to analyse customer behaviour in consumer and business markets. ANZ, for example, has thrived in the competitive world of financial services by recognizing that its customers would value the convenience of automated banking services in local stores. The final section explores the use of secondary and primary data to inform marketing decisions. Use the two checklists in this chapter to analyse customers in consumer and business markets.

ANALYSING CONSUMER AND BUSINESS MARKETS

People make a **market**, the group of potential customers for a good or service. The **consumer market** consists of individuals and families who buy goods and services for their own use. ANZ, for example, offers checking and savings accounts, credit cards, home loans and other banking services to one million consumers in New Zealand alone. The **business (organizational) market** consists of companies, institutions, non-governmental organizations and government agencies that buy goods and services for organizational use. In the case of ANZ, a broad range of financial services are offered for businesses of all sizes, including agribusinesses.

However, business marketers are not dealing with faceless organizations: buying decisions are, of course, made by people. Even when a company or institution develops an automatic system for reordering without human intervention, it still relies on a manager, employee or team to establish decision rules for when to buy, what to buy and from which supplier. As Figure 3.1 indicates, market analysis provides valuable background for understanding who might buy the product, what their needs are and what influences their buying behaviour – information you need to prepare an effective marketing plan.

Influences on consumer markets
• Customer characteristics and needs
• Cultural elements
• Social connections
• Personal elements

Analysis of consumer and business markets
• Market definition
• Market changes
• Market share

Influences on business markets
• Customer characteristics and needs
• Organizational considerations
• Internal and external relationships

FIGURE 3.1   Consumer and business market analysis

Consider how Panasonic sees the business market for 'ruggedized' laptop computers.

MARKETING IN PRACTICE: PANASONIC TOUGHBOOK

Not everyone needs or wants to pay for a notebook computer so well built that it can operate in extreme temperatures, resist repeated spills on the keyboard and start up after being dropped again and again. Panasonic's Toughbook notebook computers offer all these benefits and more. The firm, owned by Japan's Matsushita Electric Industrial Co., understands that the business market for such products is a tiny fraction of the overall market for notebook computers. Still, government agencies are willing and able to pay a bit more for reinforced notebooks that law enforcement officers and others can use even under the harshest conditions. This niche therefore represents a good marketing opportunity, which is why Panasonic's marketers have chosen to target it in their marketing plans for the past few years.[2]

During your preliminary analysis of consumer or business markets you will examine three things: (1) market definition, (2) market changes and (3) market share.

Market definition

Defining the market helps you narrow the marketing focus to consumers or businesses that are qualified to be or already are buyers of a particular type of product. Within a given market, the broadest level of definition is the potential market, which has four subsets: the available, qualified available, target and penetrated markets.[3] The **potential**

market is all the customers who may be interested in that good or service. However, some customers in this market may be unaware of the product; some may have no access to it; some may not require its benefits; some may not be able to use it; and some may not be able to afford it. Thus, the potential market represents the *maximum* number of customers who might be interested in the product – but not the number who will *realistically* buy.[4]

Part of the potential market is the **available market**, all the customers who are interested and have both adequate income and adequate access to the product. A subset of that is the **qualified available market**, all the customers who are qualified to buy based on product-specific criteria such as age (for alcohol and other products that may not legally be sold to under-age consumers). The **target market** is the segment of customers within the qualified available market that an organization decides to serve. The smallest market of all is the **penetrated market**, all the customers in the target market who currently buy or have bought a specific type of product. Figure 3.2 shows how a car-hire company might define its market according to these levels.

For planning purposes, define your potential market by more than the product. Many organizations use geography and customer description in their market definitions. 'The UK consumer market for credit cards' is a general description of one potential market for the British bank Abbey National. If offering credit cards beyond UK borders, the bank would define each new market geographically, such as 'the Western European consumer market for credit cards'. If the bank wanted to restrict its marketing to certain areas, it would describe each market more precisely: 'the London consumer market for credit cards' and 'the Manchester consumer market for credit cards'. And if the bank determined that one of its strengths was evaluating applications from consumers who had previously defaulted on loans, it might describe a market even more precisely: 'the higher-risk London consumer market for credit cards'.

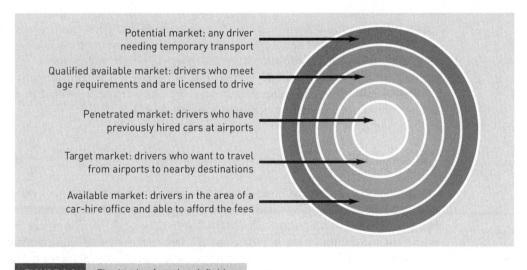

Potential market: any driver needing temporary transport

Qualified available market: drivers who meet age requirements and are licensed to drive

Penetrated market: drivers who have previously hired cars at airports

Target market: drivers who want to travel from airports to nearby destinations

Available market: drivers in the area of a car-hire office and able to afford the fees

FIGURE 3.2   Five levels of market definition

Source: After Marian Burk Wood, *The Marketing Plan: A Handbook* (Upper Saddle River, NJ: Prentice Hall, 2003), p. 39.

Now narrow your focus by researching customer needs and buying behaviour within the potential market, yielding a more specific definition of the available and the qualified available markets. Research will help you understand what your customers value and what marketing decisions will best support competitive differentiation in a given market. For example, marketers for Vespa motor scooters realize that consumers in the qualified available market need and want more than mere transportation. Style is therefore an important part of Vespa's competitive advantage, as are engineering, affordability and eco-friendly operation.[5]

Market changes

During the decades that Vespa scooters have been marketed, the company has tracked changes in its markets and responded accordingly. One change is increased interest in safety features; another is the desire for fuel efficiency. In response, company engineers have introduced advanced braking systems and engines that take riders further on a tank of petrol. Vespa is a good example of the rule that no market remains static for very long. Every day, consumers and business customers leave or enter an area; every day, consumers begin or stop buying a product. For this reason, you will need to research expert projections and track overall market trends.

Two key changes that affect the size and nature of a market are:

- *Number of customers.* Is the consumer population (or number of businesses) increasing or decreasing, and by how much?

- *Purchases.* How many products are all companies in the industry estimated to buy in the next year and later years? How has the trend in purchases changed?

The purpose is to determine how changes, trends and projections are likely to affect customers in the market and the implications for your marketing decisions. For example, the global market for computer chips designed to power medical devices is projected to grow to £2.5 billion by 2015. Such growth makes the market attractive to Philips Electronics and other chip manufacturers. If the market was expected to remain flat or shrink, companies would be much less eager to target it. [6]

Market share

Going beyond current and projected market size and trends, you will want to estimate your product's or brand's market share and the share held by competitors. Remember that your share will change as the market grows or shrinks and rivals enter, expand, reduce their presence or leave. Still, market share serves as a baseline against which you can track market dynamics and measure the progress of your marketing plan results.

Market share is defined as the percentage of sales within a market accounted for by a company, brand or product, as calculated in terms of units or money (or both, if the data can be obtained). The basic formula is: divide the company's or brand's unit or monetary sales by the entire market's unit or monetary sales of that type of product. Thus, if you sell 3 million units and overall market sales by all competitors selling that type of product are 12 million units, you hold a 25 per cent share. Your share would be 15 per cent if your product sales totalled £15 million or €15 million and overall sales of that type of product in that market totalled £100 million or €100 million.

Market share is one of the vital signs of a product or brand that you can track over time to spot potential problems and opportunities. You will want to calculate or at least estimate the share for each product in each market on a regular basis to detect any significant shifts. Examining both market changes and market share changes can give you a better picture of what customers are doing, what rivals are doing and where the market is going so your marketing plan does not involve attracting an increasingly large share of an ever-shrinking, less profitable market. You can also identify less-competitive markets and markets where purchases are projected to rise rapidly.

Sony, for instance, captured 70 per cent of the videogame market after introducing its PlayStation 2 in 2000. By the time PlayStation 3 was introduced in 2006, however, strong competition from Nintendo and Microsoft was already eroding Sony's market share.[7] Bear in mind that changes in share are not the only indicators – or the most important indicators – of competitive standing, nor do they necessarily warrant immediate attention. In the case of Sony, the PlayStation 3 was intended to advance the company's move to establish Blu-ray technology as the successor to DVD video; thus, share was important but not paramount. Companies usually include share among the standards for measuring progress in marketing programme implementation and to signal the need for adjustments, as discussed in Chapters 11 and 12.

ANALYSING CUSTOMERS IN CONSUMER MARKETS

Once you have a preliminary definition of the market, understand market changes and know your market share, you are ready to look more closely at customer demographics, needs, buying behaviour and attitudes. For example, the owner of Tuk-Tuk Foods has based her marketing decisions on observations of consumer behaviour in Sweden.

MARKETING IN PRACTICE: TUK-TUK FOODS

Sawanee Engblom was teaching in Stockholm when she observed that students returning from visits to Thailand craved Thai foods but had difficulty finding dishes prepared in the authentic manner. Understanding this behaviour convinced Engblom to start Tuk-Tuk Foods, a small business producing microwave-ready Thai foods based on her own recipes. Today Tuk-Tuk Foods has a daily output of 3,000 packaged dishes such as Panaeng Moo (pork curry). The foods are sold through grocery chains in Stockholm, with colourful labels featuring the founder in traditional Thai attire. Engblom has also expanded Tuk-Tuk Foods by opening a Thai restaurant and catering centre.[8]

As the Tuk-Tuk Foods example shows, what customers buy and how many customers buy can be influenced by different factors and experiences. Although you may start out with aggregated data to form a picture of the average customer, technology is available to help you identify and understand customer behaviour at the individual level. To understand consumers as a prelude to developing market targeting and programmes, you should analyse characteristics and needs as well as cultural elements, social connections and personal and psychological elements (*see* Figure 3.3).

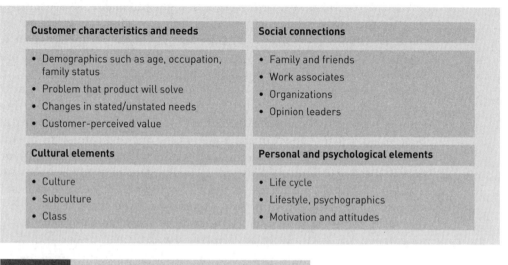

Customer characteristics and needs

- Demographics such as age, occupation, family status
- Problem that product will solve
- Changes in stated/unstated needs
- Customer-perceived value

Social connections

- Family and friends
- Work associates
- Organizations
- Opinion leaders

Cultural elements

- Culture
- Subculture
- Class

Personal and psychological elements

- Life cycle
- Lifestyle, psychographics
- Motivation and attitudes

FIGURE 3.3   Understanding behaviour in consumer markets

Characteristics and needs

Often some characteristic, such as gender, family status, age, education or ethnic background, affects what consumers need and buy. Gender, for example, is a key factor in marketing clothing and personal care products geared to women. Similarly, Huggies and other disposable nappies are marketed to families with babies. Before conducting extensive marketing research, try to learn more about the characteristics of particular consumer markets from a variety of secondary sources.

As you assess consumers' needs, ask: What problem do customers want to solve by buying a particular product? What are customers requesting now that they haven't requested in the past? What changes in need are suggested by developments revealed through internal and external audits? Do customers have unstated needs and wants (such as boosting status) that can be uncovered through marketing research and satisfied through marketing?

Closely related is the value that consumers receive when they buy products to satisfy their needs. **Value** is defined as the difference customers perceive between the benefits they derive from a product and the total price they pay for the product. Customers perceive more value from a good or service that seems to deliver more benefits for the money. For example, retailer WH Smith is opening stores in airports and railway stations to meet travellers' needs for books, snacks, stationery and other products. With more travellers spending more time in terminals and stations, the benefit of convenience adds value to such purchases.[9]

Cultural elements

The beliefs, customs and preferences of the culture in which consumers were raised – and the culture where they currently live – can have an influence on consumer buying behaviour. It is a mistake to assume that customers everywhere have the same wants, needs and buying patterns as you. Marketing research is a crucial way for marketers to avoid this misconception.[10] For example, marketers for the appliance manufacturer Daikin, based in Japan, cannot take for granted that consumers in France are just as interested in buying home air conditioners as consumers in Japan. In fact, French consumers buy fewer air conditioning units because of concerns about ecological effects, energy consumption and health. Understanding this cultural difference helps Daikin make better decisions about targeting and marketing activities.[11]

Within a larger culture are **subcultures**, each a discrete group that shares a particular ethnicity, religion or lifestyle. These groups can affect buying behaviour. As an example, many marketers see teens as a distinct global subculture. Consumers in this age group have much in common regardless of geography, including a shared interest in pop music and fashion. Television and the Internet – including popular sites such as YouTube, Second Life and Passado.com – have only intensified the commonalties of this subculture, which has an immense collective spending power. The Italian clothing retailer Benetton is one of many companies using their knowledge of this subculture to market to teenagers around the world.[12]

Class distinctions – more subtle in some cultures than in others – are yet another influence on consumer behaviour. Consumers in a certain class tend to buy and use products in similar ways. At the same time, consumers who want to emulate a different class – such as those who strive to move into a higher class – may adopt that class's buying or usage behaviours.

To illustrate, as part of BMW's research prior to marketing a new Rolls-Royce model, an engineer spent months driving a Rolls-Royce around Great Britain and talking with upper-class consumers about the brand. He learned that these consumers were concerned about car quality and wanted new Rolls-Royce models to perform in much the same way as older models. They stressed that new models, like older models, should be able to accelerate quickly and easily to high speed without any apparent strain. Understanding how these consumers think was essential to planning a suitable marketing plan. 'Rolls customers are almost invisible to start with', the engineer noted, 'and if you approach them in the wrong way they will just disappear.' Still, status remains an important part of the brand's appeal and drives its pricing strategy.[13]

Social connections

Social connections such as family members, friends, work associates and non-work groups can influence how, what and when consumers buy. You will want to determine whether any of these connections are relevant to a particular product's purchase or usage and how they affect buying behaviour. Just as some consumers follow the buying behaviour of another class to which they aspire, others follow the buying behaviour of the social groups to which they aspire. Youngsters often imitate the clothing and accessory choices of their older siblings; employees seeking job advancement may imitate the attire of higher-level managers.

Children and teenagers are becoming more influential in family car purchases, for instance.

MARKETING IN PRACTICE: MAZDA MOTOR

Do car-buying parents heed the brand preferences of their children? In one study, more than 25 per cent of mothers said they do pay attention to the car brand their children want. For this reason, many vehicle manufacturers are reaching out to children with advertising, product placement and special promotions. Mazda Motor Corp. has arranged for its cars to be featured in videogames and comic books targeted to teens not yet old enough to drive. 'If nothing else, when Mom or Dad are discussing at the family dinner table what kind of car they should look at, the kids might think Mazdas are cool and suggest a Mazda', explains a Mazda marketer. At the same time, Mazda's media advertising is based on the knowledge that 'consumers are buying for emotion, not for the price or the deal', says the director of marketing operations in North America. 'We want to be the most aspirational accessible brand.'[14]

People who are especially admired or possess special skills may be seen as **opinion leaders** in a social group and therefore exert more influence over the purchasing decisions of others. Sports figures are frequently viewed as opinion leaders for athletics wear and equipment. They are also considered opinion leaders for clothing and accessories, as are pop stars and actors, among others. Not surprisingly, marketers often single out opinion leaders for special marketing attention.

Increasingly, consumers and businesses are making social connections through **blogs,** short for *web logs*, informal online journals where people can exchange ideas and opinions (**vlogs** are blogs with mainly video content). Many organizations are launching blogs to build relationships and encourage dialogue with customers and prospects. For instance, Wensleydale Dairy Products started a blog to get public support for designating Real Yorkshire Wensleydale Cheese a Protected Designation of Origin in the European Union (*see* www.wensleydaleblog.co.uk/index.php).[15] Thus, blogs and vlogs are not only sources of information about consumers but also vehicles for communicating with them.

Personal elements

The fourth category of influences in consumer markets relates to personal elements such as life cycle, lifestyle, motivation and attitudes. An adult's *life cycle* is his or her changing family status over time. People may be single, single parents, single but co-habitating, engaged, married, married with children, divorced, divorced with children and so on. Consumers have different needs, behaviour patterns and buying priorities in each of these life-cycle phases – which, in turn, translate into marketing opportunities.

Lifestyle is the pattern of living reflecting how consumers spend their time or want to spend their time. Through research, you can learn more about how lifestyle influences what and when purchases are made in your market, how purchase transactions are planned and completed, who is involved in the purchase and other aspects of consumer buying behaviour. For example, the Joe Bloggs brand, owned by the UK-based Juice Corporation, markets urban-styled apparel to teenagers based on its knowledge of their lifestyle.[16] By analysing consumer behaviour using a complex set of lifestyle variables related to activities, interests and opinions – collectively known as **psychographic characteristics** – you can learn more about what drives consumer behaviour.

Psychological factors such as motivation and attitudes are also important influences on consumer buying. **Motivation** is the internal force that drives a consumer to act in a certain way and make certain purchases as a way of satisfying needs and wants. **Attitudes** are the consumer's assessment of and emotions about a product, brand or something else, which can affect actions. Understanding how such factors drive consumer behaviour gives you a solid foundation for making decisions about who to target, where a product should be distributed and so on.

ESSENTIAL MARKETING PLAN CHECKLIST NO. 4: ANALYSING CUSTOMERS IN CONSUMER MARKETS

This checklist will guide you through the stage of marketing planning in which you must research and analyse information about consumers. Answer the questions in the spaces provided, putting a tick mark next to each as you finish it. If your marketing plan is for a start-up or a hypothetical company, use this checklist to note where you might obtain the information you need and ideas about how to research appropriate details.

☐ What consumer needs must the product and product category address?

_____

☐ How can customers in each consumer market be described (by demographics, geography, etc.)?

_____

☐ How is customer behaviour affected by cultural elements such as subculture and class?

☐ How is customer behaviour affected by social connections such as family and friends?

☐ How is customer behaviour affected by personal elements such as lifestyle, motivation and attitudes?

☐ What do these influences mean for segmentation, targeting and marketing decisions?

ANALYSING CUSTOMERS IN BUSINESS MARKETS

Individuals or groups make buying decisions for businesses, government agencies and non-governmental organizations. Sometimes these decisions involve huge sums of money and months of internal review spanning multiple management layers. Business buying behaviour is generally influenced by: the organization's characteristics and needs; relationships inside and outside the organization; and considerations unique to each organization and its environment (*see* Figure 3.4).

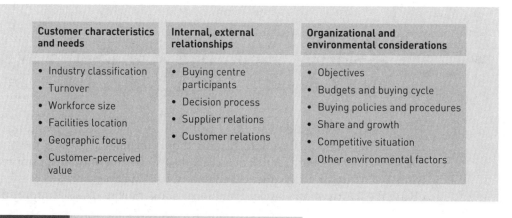

Customer characteristics and needs	Internal, external relationships	Organizational and environmental considerations
• Industry classification • Turnover • Workforce size • Facilities location • Geographic focus • Customer-perceived value	• Buying centre participants • Decision process • Supplier relations • Customer relations	• Objectives • Budgets and buying cycle • Buying policies and procedures • Share and growth • Competitive situation • Other environmental factors

FIGURE 3.4   Understanding behaviour in business markets

Characteristics and needs

Organizations with different characteristics have different needs and buying patterns, so gather general information about any business markets you are considering. Try to determine the common needs and concerns of organizations in each industry and see which characteristics affect these needs (and how). One way to do this is by categorizing organizations according to characteristics such as type of industry, annual turnover, number of employees, location of facilities and geographic focus.

The European Commission's Eurostat system provides a standardized method for researching, describing and categorizing statistics by industry. Similarly, the North American Industry Classification System (NAICS) provides a method for researching the characteristics of companies in specific industries in the United States, Mexico and Canada. Data organized according to UN industry standard classifications and other international and national industry standards systems is available as well.

To gather more data about industries, characteristics of businesses, non-profit organizations or government agencies and business products, you can consult numerous sources, including: national and international trade organizations; country consulates; multinational banks; university sources; magazines, newspapers and other publications that follow international business developments.

Organizational and environmental considerations

Although a few organizations buy without budgets, most plan ahead by budgeting for certain purchases during a specified period. Thus, after gathering and analysing general data about a business market, your next step is to learn something about the size of each organization's budget and the timing of its purchases, which can vary widely within an industry.

Think about the company's environmental influences, including its market share situation, its objectives and its competitive situation – all of which can influence what, when and how much the organization buys. Also research the buying policy and procedure, buying cycle and policies. If a multinational corporation's policy is to encourage decentralized or local buying, for example, you will have to plan for communicating with more buyers than if the policy is to centralize buying at the headquarters level. If a business insists on online buying, that policy must also be taken into account during the marketing planning process.

Budgeting and buying cycles are particularly important factors for business-to-business (B2B) marketers that sell to non-governmental organizations and government agencies. On the other hand, rapidly growing cities and countries tend to increase their annual budgets for infrastructure improvements, creating opportunities for construction companies, telecommunications firms and other suppliers.

Internal and external relationships

Many internal and external relationships can affect an organization's buying patterns. Particularly in large organizations, a group of managers or employees may be responsible for certain purchases. Different individuals within this **buying centre** play different roles in the buying process, as shown in Figure 3.5. Moreover, not every member of the buying centre will participate in every purchase. Each participant's individual situation (age, education, job position and so forth) also affects the buying

Buying centre participant	Influence on purchases
Users	Often initiate the buying process and help define specifications.
Influencers	Often define specifications and provide information for evaluating alternatives.
Buyers	Have the formal authority to select suppliers and negotiate purchases.
Deciders	Have the formal or informal power to select or approve suppliers.
Gatekeepers	Control the flow of information to other buying centre participants.

FIGURE 3.5   How buying centre participants influence purchases

Source: Adapted from Philip Kotler, Veronica Wang, John Saunders and Gary Armstrong, *Principles of Marketing*, 4th European edn (Harlow: Pearson Education, 2005), p. 309.

decision. Thus, you should investigate relationships within the buying centre, understand the participants and the decision process so you can market to the right participants at the right time. This is especially vital when the purchase represents a major commitment of money, time and changeover for a business customer.[17]

Check the organization's relations with current suppliers to find out whether long-term contracts are the norm; whether certain future purchases are already committed to current suppliers; what standards suppliers are expected to meet; and how suppliers are evaluated. In some cases, a company cannot become a supplier until it has met certain criteria and been approved. Even if prior approval is not needed, you should determine what criteria the business customer uses to select suppliers so you can plan accordingly.[18]

Clearly, cost is not the only criterion in a B2B buying decision. Staff expertise, quality, reliable delivery and other considerations can be important criteria by which buying centre participants choose among competing suppliers. In addition, by looking at how an organization deals with its customers, you can get a sense of the value you can add to help satisfy your customers' customers.

ESSENTIAL MARKETING PLAN CHECKLIST NO. 5: ANALYSING CUSTOMERS IN BUSINESS MARKETS

If you're preparing to target a business market, this checklist will guide you through the planning in which you research and analyse information about business customers. Simply put a tick mark by each question, one by one, as you write answers in the spaces provided. If your marketing plan is for a start-up or a hypothetical company, use this checklist to note information you can obtain and ideas about how to research additional details, including possible data sources.

☐ What customer needs must the product and product category address?

_____

☐ How can customers in each business market be described (by demographics, buying policies, etc.)?

_____

☐ Who participates in the buying centre and what is each participant's role?

_____

☐ How does each business customer solicit, qualify and assess suppliers?

_____

☐ How do current supplier arrangements affect competition for orders?

_____

☐ What other relationships and considerations affect buying behaviour in this business market?

_____

☐ What do these influences mean for your segmentation, targeting and marketing activities aimed at the business market?

_____

RESEARCHING MARKETS AND CUSTOMERS

When researching markets and customers, you will usually start by consulting **secondary data** – information previously collected for another purpose. You can glean basic facts and figures from secondary research more quickly and cheaply than through **pri-**

mary data, data from studies undertaken to address specific marketing questions or situations. When using secondary research, check that the information is current, comes from a legitimate and unbiased source, can be verified through another source and can be clarified (if necessary) through contact with sources.

Primary research is particularly useful for supporting the development of specific marketing activities. Heineken, the Netherlands-based brewing company, uses a variety of primary research methods to learn about customers' needs, unstated wants, attitudes and characteristics. Its marketers travel the world to sip beer and chat with the younger consumers they want to attract as well as the core customer base of middle-aged beer lovers who drink Heineken, Tiger and other company brands.[19]

Ethnographic research– observing customers' behaviour in real situations rather than in experimental surroundings– has become increasingly important for learning about needs and preferences not easily articulated.[20] Advertising expert Joseph Plummer notes that ethnography can lead to new customer behaviour insights, generate learning across cultures and spark product design ideas as well as advertising creativity.[21] China's Lenovo Group, for example, uses ethnographic software to interpret large quantities of visual and written observations of how consumers around the world use personal computers and laptops.[22]

Indicate any need for primary research in your marketing plan and allow for the time and money in your schedules and budgets. Also plan for research to test programmes and track marketing progress, including customer satisfaction surveys, market-share studies and promotion pre- and post-tests. These kinds of studies can yield insights to help you make decisions about segmentation, targeting, positioning and the marketing mix.

CHAPTER SUMMARY

Marketers examine markets to narrow their focus to a subset of customers qualified to buy (or currently buyers of) a particular type of good or service. The overall market consists of the potential market (all customers who may be interested in that product) and, inside that, the available market (those with income and access). A narrower definition is the qualified available market (those who meet product-related criteria for buying); narrower still is the target market (which the organization wants to serve) and, narrowest of all, the penetrated market (customers who buy or have bought that type of product). Then marketers dig deeper to research and analyse market changes and market share.

During marketing planning for consumer markets, look at: (1) needs stemming, in part, from characteristics such as age; (2) national or regional culture, subculture and class; (3) social connections; (4) personal and psychological elements. Three main influences on business markets are: (1) organizational characteristics; (2) organizational and environmental considerations; (3) internal and external relationships. Secondary data is information previously collected for a different purpose; primary data is collected to address specific questions or situations relevant to the marketing plan.

CASE STUDY: NESTLÉ'S PURINA PETCARE PLANS FOR PROFITS

The global pet food market is both large and lucrative: in the United Kingdom alone, pet owners buy nearly £2 billion worth of food yearly for their cats and dogs. Marketers at Nestlé's Purina PetCare division have used their knowledge of pet-owner behaviour to build profits by offering pet food brands for different segments and regions, including Felix (for cats) and Alpo (for dogs).

To keep its pet food brands in front of pet owners and build customer loyalty, Nestlé Purina uses a constant stream of promotions. For example, the company recently teamed up with Sainsbury's supermarkets to mail pet care tips and discount coupons to 200,000 pet owners. Knowing that owners worry about pet health, Nestlé Purina also introduced a range of natural pet foods. The company regularly advertises in print and electronic media, including web-based promotions. As a result, the company's Felix brand holds a sizeable share of the cat food market in the United Kingdom (where it is strongest) and in 12 other European countries.

In many parts of Africa, however, commercial pet food brands represent a tiny share of the overall market. One reason is that pet owners have little disposable income; another is that some brands are of lower quality, which affects pet health and inhibits overall market growth. The share of pet foods marketed through veterinary practices has been rising and now accounts for about one-third of all commercial pet foods sold in South Africa. To build brand image while educating pet owners about pet nutrition, Nestlé Purina has partnered with veterinary surgeons to operate six pet clinics in South Africa. This has raised awareness of the company's Alpo dog food among pet owners who can buy the brands locally. As the African market for commercial pet food grows, Nestlé Purina will be well positioned to compete and to increase its market share.[23]

Case questions

1. How does Nestlé Purina provide value with extra benefits for pet owners?

2. What specific questions about the influence of family and other social connections would you suggest that Nestlé's marketers seek to answer through primary research?

APPLY YOUR KNOWLEDGE

To reinforce your knowledge of Stage 3 of the marketing planning process, research the general definition of a particular market. You might focus on the consumer market for mobile phones, for instance, or the business market for laptop computers. Prepare a brief oral or written report summarizing your thoughts.

- How can your chosen market be described broadly in terms of product, geography and demographics?

- What characteristics relevant to the product might influence the behaviour of consumers or organizations in this market?

- What, specifically, are the main influences on buying behaviour in this market? Refer to the checklists in this chapter as you answer this question.

- What have you learned that would affect your decisions if you were preparing a marketing plan for this market?

BUILD YOUR OWN MARKETING PLAN

Continue the marketing planning process for a hypothetical organization or an actual organization you have chosen by broadly describing the market and the influences on customer buying behaviour. Use the two checklists in this chapter as you build your marketing plan. First, identify the five levels of market definition that apply, from the potential market to the penetrated market. Also determine the criteria by which you would consider customers to be in the available market and in the qualified available market.

Next, research the most important changes affecting this market. Also look at market share trends and the major influences on customer needs and behaviour in this consumer or business market. How do cultural elements, social connections, personal elements or psychological elements affect the consumer's buying behaviour? If your plan is for a business market, how do customer characteristics and needs, internal and external relationships and organizational/environmental considerations affect buying behaviour? Finally, list any primary and secondary data you would like to have to better understand your markets. Be sure to document what you have learned and the implications for your marketing-plan decisions.

ENDNOTES

1. 'ANZ Banking Group: Partnership with Woolworths to Offer ATMs in Australia', *Wall Street Journal*, 20 March 2006, p. 1; Morag Mackinson, 'Australian Bank Seeks to Expand in Asia-Pacific for Profit Bump', *Wall Street Journal*, 4 May 2005, p. 1; www.anz.com.

2. 'Next-generation Toughbook', *Fleet Owner*, 1 December 2006, n.p.; Peter Burrows, 'The Humvee of Laptops', *Business Week*, 21 April 2003, p. 74; Marc Spiwak, 'Panasonic Notebooks "Tough" It Out', *Computer Reseller News*, 10 March 2003, p. 41.

3. Based on Gary L. Lilien and Arvind Rangaswamy, *Marketing Engineering*, 2nd edn (Upper Saddle River, NJ: Prentice Hall, 2003), p. 159.

4. Roger J. Best, *Market-Based Management: Strategies for Growing Customer Value and Profitability*, 4th edn (Upper Saddle River, NJ: Pearson Prentice Hall, 2005), p. 69.

5. 'Vespa Sales Still Buzzing', *Europe Intelligence Wire*, 10 January 2007, n.p.; Meg Mitchell Moore, 'Paolo Timoni: CMO Strategy, The Innovators', *Advertising Age*, 2 October 2006, pp. 1–10; 'Design Choice – Vespa Granturismo', Marketing, 7 August 2003, p. 10.

6. Cliff Edwards, 'To See Where Tech Is Headed, Watch TI', *BusinessWeek*, 6 November 2006, p. 74.

7. Matt Richtel, 'Console Sales Beat Goals, Makers' Early Reports Say', *New York Times*, 8 January 2007, p. C4; 'Can the PlayStation 3 Revive the Ailing Electronics Giant?', *The Economist*, 18 November 2006, pp. 63–4.

8. Krissana Parnsoonthorn, 'Thai-Owned Producer of Food Business Set for Rapid Expansion in Scandinavia', *Bangkok Post*, 20 February 2003, www.bangkokpost.com.

9. Lorna Strickland, 'Spreading the Word', *Duty-Free News International*, 15 October 2006, pp. 127ff; Alison Smith, 'The Middle Road Gives WH Smith a Rough Ride', *Financial Times*, 29 August 2003, www.ft.com; Alison Smith, 'WH Smith Warns and Signals US Withdrawal', *Financial Times*, 28 August 2003, www.ft.com.

10. Andrew Gershoff and Eric Johnson, 'Avoid the Trap of Thinking Everyone Is Just Like You', *Financial Times*, 28 August 2003, www.ft.com.

11. John Tagliabue, 'Europe Decides Air-Conditioning Is Not So Evil', *New York Times*, 13 August 2003, pp. W1ff.

12. Amanda Kaiser, 'Benetton: Celebrating a Colorful History', *WWD*, 6 October 2006, p. 20.

13. Quoted in Scott Miller, 'British Blue Bloods Instruct BMW on Retooling the Rolls', *Wall Street Journal*, 11 October 2002, www.wsj.com; 'New Campaign: Rolls Royce', *Marketing*, 6 December 2006, p. 2; 'Rolls Will Add Smaller Car to Lineup in 2010', *Automotive News*, 15 January 2007, p. 8.

14. Quotes reported in Mark Rechtin, 'Mazda Marketer's Challenge', *Automotive News*, 25 December 2006, p. 22, and Jennifer Saranow, '"This Is the Car We Want, Mommy"', *Wall Street Journal*, 9 November 2006, p. D1; Rick Kranz, 'Mazda Exec: MPV Was Considered for a Redo', *Automotive News*, 29 January 2007, p. 97.

15. '2006: Year in Review – The Year of the Blog', *PR Week (UK)*, 8 December 2006, pp. 25ff.

16. 'Joe Bloggs Unveils Teen Interiors Range', *Marketing*, 7 August 2003, p. 2.

17. Allison Enright, 'It Takes a Committee to Buy into B-to-B', *Marketing News*, 15 February 2006, pp. 11–13.

18. William Band and John Guaspari, 'Creating the Customer-Engaged Organization', *Marketing Management*, July–August 2003, pp. 35–9.

19. Jack Ewing, 'Waking Up Heineken', *Business Week*, 8 September 2003, pp. 68–72.

20. Virginia Matthews, 'How to Dig Deeper in the Consumer Mind', *Financial Times*, 8 October 2003, www.ft.com.

21. Joseph T. Plummer, 'Up Close and Personal: the Value of Ethnography', *Journal of Advertising Research*, September 2006, p. 245.

22. Robert Berner, 'Design Visionary', *BusinessWeek Innovation*, June 2006, pp. 102–14.

23. Based on information from: 'Direct News: Purina in Mail Tie with Sainsbury's', *Marketing*, 8 November 2006, p. 11; 'Pet Care: Industry Overview', *Progressive Grocer*, 15 November 2006, p. 64; 'Nestlé Purina Sponsors Pet Smile Month', *Marketing*, 1 May 2003, p. 12; 'Nestlé Overhauls Felix Identity Across Europe', *Marketing*, 6 March 2003, p. 10; Larry Claasen, 'Nestlé Zooms in on Local Pet Food Market', *Africa News Service*, 17 January 2003, www.comtexnews.com.

4

Planning segmentation, targeting and positioning

Comprehension outcomes

After studying this chapter, you will be able to:

- Explain the benefits of segmentation, targeting and positioning
- Identify segmentation variables for consumer and business markets
- Describe undifferentiated, differentiated, concentrated and individualised target marketing
- Discuss the criteria for effective positioning

Application outcomes

After studying this chapter, you will be able to:

- Apply segmentation variables in consumer and business markets
- Evaluate segments for marketing attention
- Choose a targeting approach for market coverage
- Formulate a meaningful positioning for marketing planning purposes

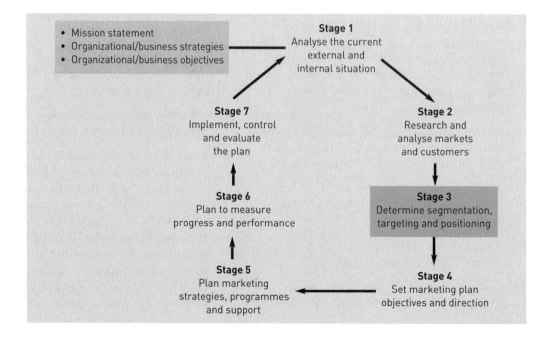

CHAPTER PREVIEW

What does the Virgin Group want its brand to stand for? According to one of its marketing executives: 'Value for money – but that doesn't mean cheap – and great customer service. The Virgin brand is challenging convention in existing markets. And there's an element of simplicity, an element of fun and an element of innovation.' Virgin's positioning must be consistent, even though it targets so many customer segments with an ever-changing portfolio of offerings from music and mobiles to travel and entertainment. Now Virgin's commitment to sustainability has added an ecological dimension to how the brand is perceived in the context of competing brands.[1]

Virgin's marketing plan is not to reach out to every customer, everywhere. Instead, the company studies the needs, attitudes, behaviour and buying patterns of different customer groups, then selects specific groups for marketing attention – as in Stage 3 of the marketing planning process. First, the chapter looks at the benefits of market segmentation, targeting and positioning. Next is an explanation of the segmentation process and how it applies to consumer and business markets. Following a section about targeting, the chapter concludes by examining the use of positioning for competitive power. Use this chapter's checklist as you prepare to evaluate segments for marketing attention.

BENEFITS OF SEGMENTATION, TARGETING AND POSITIONING

Market segmentation involves grouping consumers or business customers within a market into smaller segments based on similarities in needs, attitudes or behaviour that marketing can address. Virgin segments its markets on the basis of similarities in consumers' attitudes, including price sensitivity. By eliminating inappropriate markets and identifying appropriate segments for more thorough research, the company can better understand customers and more effectively respond to their needs. This also helps Virgin decide which segments to target for marketing activities, and in what order. Finally, it helps the firm determine how to create a meaningful and competitively distinctive position in the minds of the targeted customers (*see* Figure 4.1).

Segmentation is useful for marketing planning when:

- the customers within each segment have something identifiable in common
- different segments have different responses to marketing efforts
- the customers in segments can be reached through marketing
- competitive advantage can be gained by focusing on segments
- segments are sufficiently large or profitable to warrant attention.

A segment may consist of millions of people, yet still be a select subset of a much larger market. Customers within each segment will have similar behaviour and needs or be

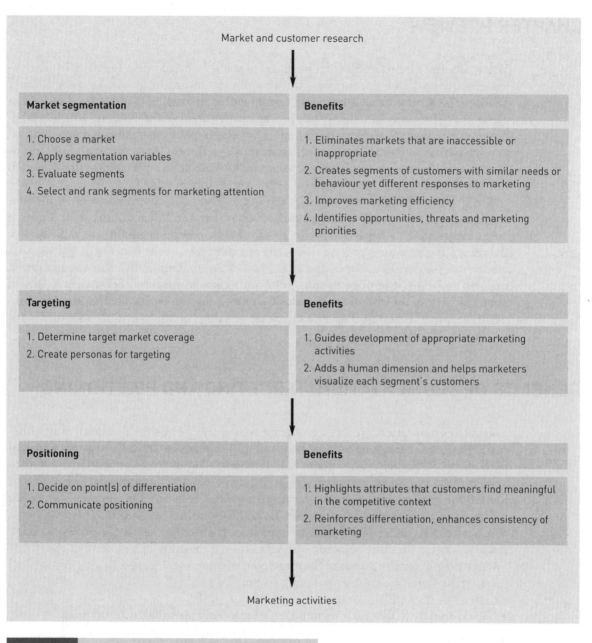

FIGURE 4.1 Applying segmentation, targeting and positioning

seeking the same benefits from a product. Taking segmentation one step further, you may be able to distinguish **niches**, small sub-segments of customers with distinct needs or requirements. Consider the success that many companies enjoy by focusing on soy milk niches.

MARKETING IN PRACTICE: SOY MILK

From Birmingham to Brisbane, a growing number of consumers have started buying soy milk during the past 25 years. One niche is consumers who cannot digest cow's milk or are allergic to it; a second is consumers seeking soy's health benefits; and a third is consumers interested in organic foods. In fact, the CEO of Canada-based So Good International sees soy milk outgrowing niche marketing: 'Now milk alternatives appeal to a much wider audience, our products are becoming less niche and more mainstream', he says.[2] In addition to flavour, companies such as So Good are varying their marketing mixes to appeal to niches created by preferences for refrigerated or long life, unrefrigerated packages and purchases at supermarkets or health-food stores.[3]

Taken to the extreme, you may be able to segment a market to create niches of one. In the past, marketing to such small niches would not be profitable. Now you can use technology to discern the specific needs, behaviours and responses of individual consumers or business customers. In some industries, the potential size of and profit from a single order make it worthwhile to segment and target single-customer niches or, in large markets, to individualize marketing on a mass basis.

THE MARKET SEGMENTATION PROCESS

You will follow three steps to segmenting a market, as Figure 4.1 indicates. The first is to choose the market to be segmented; the second is to apply appropriate segmentation variables and evaluate segments for marketing attention; and the third is to select your coverage approach for targeting chosen segments. Your decisions in all three steps depend on understanding your mission and long-term goals as well as on detailed, current information drawn from internal and external audits (*see* Chapter 2), plus your analyses of markets and customers (*see* Chapter 3).

Choose the market

With your market definitions as a starting point, you begin the segmentation process by determining which markets you will investigate further and which you will eliminate. Although the specific criteria differ from organization to organization, you may want to consider eliminating markets based on:

- formidable legal, political, social or competitive pressures

- extreme logistical difficulties

- lack of purchasing power or other serious economic challenges

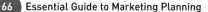

- troubling ethical controversies

- persistent ecological concerns.

For years, many marketers eliminated Vietnam from their list of viable markets because of trade barriers and other legal and regulatory difficulties. Once Vietnam simplified its business laws, joined the World Trade Organization and lowered trade barriers, however, the country rejoined the list of markets being considered by companies around the world. Now Vietnam's economy is thriving and wages are rising as Panasonic and other firms open factories, making the country an appealing market for many products. Shiseido and L'Oréal have already begun targeting Vietnamese buyers interested in high-end cosmetics.[4]

Apply segmentation variables

Once you have eliminated inappropriate markets, look for ways to distinguish meaningful segments in your chosen markets. The point is to form consumer or business segments that are internally homogeneous yet exhibit some differences (compared with other segments) that can be addressed through marketing. If you find no differences, segmentation is pointless, because you will not need to vary your marketing approach for each segment. You can segment consumer and business markets using a number of variables, as discussed in the following sections.

Consumer market variables

Customer characteristics and product-related behavioural variables can be used to group consumers into segments for marketing planning purposes (*see* Figure 4.2). You will rarely apply a single segmentation variable; for more specific segment definition, you should apply a combination of appropriate variables. User-based customer characteristics are easier to identify and apply. Yet behaviour-based, product-related approaches, which are not as easy to isolate and analyse, typically give you more insight into potentially effective marketing approaches for each segment.

The most appropriate variables for each consumer market may not be obvious or intuitive. For example, L'Oréal, the French beauty products company, uses price perceptions (specifically, interest in higher quality at a higher price for a luxury feeling) as one segmentation variable for hair colouring and other beauty products. A second variable is gender and a third is place of usage. By gearing its product features, packaging, promotion and distribution strategies to different segments – women willing to spend a bit more to pamper themselves at home, men using skin-care products for a sense of well-being, women having their hair dyed at salons and so on – L'Oréal has become the global market leader in its industry.[5]

Customer characteristics – consumer

One reason to apply consumer segmentation variables, which describe the buyer or user in some way, is because they are easy to identify within a market. L'Oréal's marketers

Customer characteristics – a user-based approach that asks, 'Who purchases what?'

Demographic
- Age
- Family size
- Marital status
- Gender

Socioeconomic
- Income
- Class
- Vocation
- Education
- Religion
- Ethnicity

Geographic
- Global, hemispheric, national, state, city, postal code
- Climate
- Rural vs. urban

Lifestyle/personality
- Attitudes/opinions
- Interests
- Avocations
- Tastes and preferences

Product-related approaches – a behavioural approach that asks, 'Why do they purchase?'

User types
- Regular
- Non-user
- First-time
- Potential

Price sensitivity
- Low-cost orientation
- Higher-cost quality/differentiation focus

Consumption patterns/usage frequency
- Low
- Medium
- Strong

Perceived benefits
- Performance
- Quality
- Image enhancement
- Service

Brand loyalty
- Loyal/satisfied
- Experimenters
- Unsatisfied/Defectors
- Unaware

Application

Purchase occasion/buying situation

Media exposure

FIGURE 4.2   Variables for segmenting consumer markets

Source: Adapted from Craig S. Fleisher and Babette E. Bensoussan, *Strategic and Competitive Analysis* (Upper Saddle River, NJ: Prentice Hall, 2003), p. 173.

apply the demographic variable of gender as a segmentation variable for cosmetics. Marketers for LVMH Moët Hennessy–Louis Vuitton and for Richemont (parent of Cartier and Montblanc) apply the socioeconomic variables of income and class to segment the market for their luxury brands. Geographic and lifestyle variables are also important to LVMH, which has selected segments of wealthy consumers who live in Japan and Canada and are not frequent travellers.[6]

You can also apply geographic variables when you want to enter or increase sales in specific regions or climates; avoid specific countries or regions because of competitive challenges or other threats; or leverage your organization's strengths for competitive advantage in those areas. Remember, however, that people are more complex and buying is motivated by numerous factors; even those who share a particular characteristic will not necessarily respond in the same way to the same marketing activities. Thus, applying non-geographic variables such as gender or vocation can reveal viable segments across geographic boundaries. And, because consumer reactions are often heavily influenced by product-related variables, you should apply those in addition to characteristics and other variables during your marketing planning.

For example, Starwood Hotels uses a number of variables to segment the market for hotel accommodation. One segment it has identified consists of consumers who (1) own dogs, (2) prefer driving holidays and (3) are not price-sensitive. Despite these similarities, people in this segment may have few other characteristics in common. Starwood communicates how it meets the needs of this segment by publicizing that it welcomes dogs at more than 700 hotels worldwide. This is not just good public relations: the company's research shows that dog owners will be loyal to a hotel chain that accepts their pets.[7]

Product-related variables – consumer

On the most basic level, you can segment a market according to users and non-users, such as those who use insect repellent and those who do not. You should look deeper to determine how and why a consumer uses or does not use a product – behaviour related to the product – which helps you identify signs of underlying wants or needs that may be addressed through marketing strategies.

One advantage to using variables such as consumption patterns and purchase occasion is that they are easily observed, measured and analysed. For example, fast-food restaurants such as McDonald's and Burger King see significant profit potential in selling breakfasts, especially for takeaway. Starbucks is also starting to offer breakfast sandwiches along with its signature coffees.[8]

Here is how Zespri International applied the variable of purchase occasion/ buying situation when entering a new market.

MARKETING IN PRACTICE: ZESPRI INTERNATIONAL

Zespri International, owned by New Zealand farmers, has segmented by geography, ethnicity, purchase frequency and taste preferences to establish its Zespri Gold brand of golden kiwi fruit. Through geographic segmentation, Zespri's marketers chose to market in Europe, Japan, South Korea, Taiwan and the United States. For US markets, they also applied product-related variables and customer characteristics. Through research, they learned that Latino consumers in the United States shop for fruits and vegetables twice as often as other consumers, and these consumers like sweet tropical fruits. In response, Zespri's initial Spanish-language campaign ran in US cities with high Latino populations; it was so successful that demand temporarily outstripped supply.[9]

Note that different segmentation variables are appropriate for different markets and products. In the Korean market for mobile phone services, for instance, some companies are successfully identifying segments using the variable of variety-seeking behaviour. The companies have noticed that Korean teenagers (like their counterparts in many countries) use their mobiles to download the latest ring tones, music, television programmes, avatars and more. Thus, variety-seeking behaviour is a good segmentation variable for phone companies and content providers who offer fee-based music, ring tones and other extras.[10]

Business market variables

As in consumer markets, business markets can be segmented using both customer characteristics and product-related approaches that probe behaviour (*see* Figure 4.3).

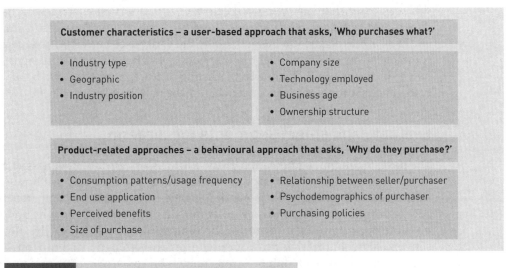

FIGURE 4.3   Variables for segmenting business markets

Source: Adapted from Craig S. Fleisher and Babette E. Bensoussan, *Strategic and Competitive Analysis* (Upper Saddle River, NJ: Prentice Hall, 2003), p. 174.

Customer characteristics describe the organization from the outside, whereas behavioural variables look at activities and dynamics below the surface. Generally marketers apply both types of variables to form segments of organizational customers that are internally homogeneous but have different needs or different responses to marketing when compared with other segments.

Customer characteristics – business

You can apply demographics such as industry type, geography and annual turnover to narrow the dimensions of a business market before you apply behavioural variables. For example, the anti-plagiarism service Turnitin.com uses industry (such as colleges and universities) and geography (country by country) to sharpen its focus. It also segments by the specific need for anti-plagiarism services. Trinity College, University of Toronto and National University of Singapore are among Turnitin.com's international customers.[11]

Business customers typically have different needs and responses from those of non-profit organizations and government agencies; likewise, larger or older organizations tend to have different needs and responses from those of smaller or newer organizations. Some organizations rely more heavily on certain technologies (such as e-commerce or customer contact software) than others, another indicator that can help you segment your market. In general, look carefully at how certain characteristics reveal differences that you can build on when planning marketing activities.

Product-related variables – business

You can use frequency, size, timing and method of purchasing to segment business markets, along with variables reflecting purchasing policies and authorized buyers. When you segment a business market by product-related variables, especially in combination with customer characteristics, you can uncover important customer needs and buying patterns. Mitsubishi Fuso Truck and Bus Corp., one of Japan's largest truck manufacturers, had success segmenting its market by the variable of perceived benefits. It found that commercial truckers were eager to buy new trucks before the government implemented new vehicle emissions standards. Marketing to truckers seeking this benefit boosted the firm's annual turnover by 25 per cent before the new standards took effect.[12]

Evaluate and select segments for targeting

The next step in the segmentation process is to assess the attractiveness of each segment in terms of opportunity, environment, reach and response and see how each fits with internal considerations such as mission, image, strengths, core competencies, resources and performance. The purpose is to eliminate undesirable segments and evaluate the possible opportunities inherent in the remaining segments. Ideally, you want to be active in segments that play to your organization's strengths and capabilities but do not stretch your resources too thin. At this point, you can screen out segments with insufficient profit potential, intense competition or other complications.

Top managers of the Fast Retailing chain, for instance, decided against continuing to focus on certain geographic segments after experiencing increased competition and lower profits in those segments. On the basis of this decision, the Japanese retailer closed several of its UK Uniqlo stores but retained stores in Japan and London as well as opening new stores in Seoul, Hong Kong, Shanghai and metropolitan New York. Uniqlo stores' positioning is based on offering stylish apparel at reasonable prices.[13]

After you drop unattractive or unsuitable segments from consideration, you are ready to rank the remaining segments in priority order for marketing attention, on the basis of research and analysis. You can do this in several ways. For example, you might assign relative weights to each of the evaluation criteria and calculate the total scores segment by segment. The sample ranking shown in Figure 4.4 shows how you might score three segments based on the four criteria categories, along with a total score per segment. As in this sample, a segment may merit a high score for opportunity yet have a much lower score for environment or another of the criteria.

To decide which segment should be your top priority, look at the total score and, if necessary, set minimum scores for individual criteria. In the sample ranking, Segment A has the highest total score and, if the organization does not require a minimum score of 5 or higher on all criteria, would be the highest priority. Note that Figure 4.4 is a very simplified, fictitious example; organizations vary widely in their evaluation criteria, weighting and ranking systems.

Different companies use different criteria to rank segments. One criteria used by some marketers is **customer lifetime value**, the total net revenue (or profit) a particular customer relationship represents to the organization over time. The choice of criteria depends on your unique situation, your chosen market and your customer knowledge.

	Segment A	Segment B	Segment C
Opportunity	8	6	5
Environment	3	5	5
Reach and response	6	4	7
Internal considerations	9	7	4
Total score	26	22	21

FIGURE 4.4   Sample segment ranking

Note: Weighted scores range from 1 (extremely unattractive) to 10 (extremely attractive).

If possible, use sensitivity analysis to adjust criteria weights under differing forecasts and confirm priority rankings by testing prospective strategies before moving ahead with full-scale marketing plans.

Among the criteria you can use to select and rank segments for marketing attention are:

- fit with the firm's strengths and core competencies

- advantageous competitive environment

- advantageous pricing or supply costs due to relative power of buyers or suppliers

- sizeable profit and growth potential

- significant potential for building long-term customer relationships.

This chapter's checklist offers specific questions to ask when evaluating and selecting segments for marketing attention.

ESSENTIAL MARKETING PLAN CHECKLIST NO. 6:
EVALUATING MARKET SEGMENTS

Before you can set objectives and plan marketing programmes, you must determine which customer segments you want to reach. This checklist will help you evaluate the various segments identified within the overall market. After you write your answers in the spaces provided, put a tick mark next to the questions you've answered. If your marketing plan is for a hypothetical firm, you can use this checklist as a guide to the data you'll need to gather to be able to evaluate segments.

☐ What is the current size of the segment and how is it changing?

_____

☐ What current and future sales and profit potential do you see for this segment?

_____

☐ Would marketing to this segment yield an appropriate payback in customer lifetime value?

_____

☐ What is the competitive situation like in this segment?

_____

☐ Can the organization realistically capture or defend market share in this segment?

_____

☐ How much power do buyers and suppliers in this segment have?

_____

☐ What threats exist or could emerge to prevent success in this segment?

☐ Can customers in the segment be reached through appropriate marketing activities?

☐ Does the organization have the strengths, competencies and resources to serve this segment?

☐ Does the segment fit with the organization's mission, image and overall goals?

Once you've selected segments for marketing attention, you're ready to make decisions about targeting.

THE TARGETING PROCESS

To plan for targeting, you must consider the market coverage approach you want to take. As shown in Figure 4.5, you can use one of four coverage approaches: undifferentiated marketing, differentiated marketing, concentrated marketing or individualized marketing.

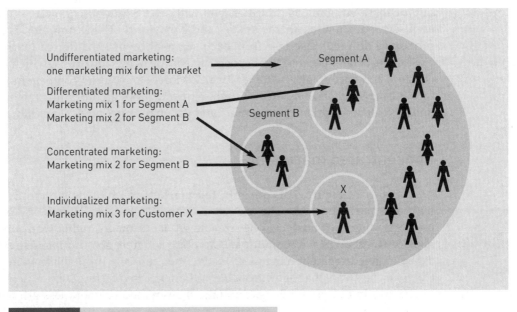

FIGURE 4.5   Segment targeting coverage strategies

Undifferentiated marketing

Essentially a mass-marketing approach, **undifferentiated marketing** means targeting the entire market with the same marketing mix, ignoring any segment differences. This assumes that all customers in a particular market, regardless of any differences in characteristics or behaviour, will respond in the same way to the same marketing attention. Undifferentiated marketing is less expensive than other coverage strategies, due to the lower costs of developing and implementing only one marketing mix. However, today's markets are rarely so homogeneous; even slight differences can serve as clues to underlying needs in segments where an organization can gain competitive advantage, encourage customer loyalty and ultimately return profits.

Consider the increasingly fragmented market for salt. Industry giants Cargill (owner of the Diamond Crystal brand) and Morton (owned by Rohm & Haas) have segmented what was once assumed to be a homogeneous market according to type of customer (consumers, restaurants and institutional customers) and specific cooking uses and occasions. Now products such as sea salt, coarse crystal salt, natural mineral rock salt and other variations are marketed differently to different segments. Meanwhile, brands such as La Baleine and small, family-owned businesses such as Quoddy Mist are marketing gourmet salts for smaller niches. Any marketer in this industry would avoid undifferentiated marketing because the mass market for salt no longer exists.[14]

Differentiated marketing

With **differentiated marketing**, you formulate a separate marketing mix for the two or more segments you choose to target. You may not target all segments in a given market, but for those you rank as priorities, you will need different marketing mixes geared to each segment's unique characteristics and behaviours. The assumption is that you can provoke a different response from each segment by using different marketing mixes. Customers benefit because their specific needs are being addressed, which increases satisfaction and encourages customer loyalty. Moreover, you can compete more effectively by tailoring the marketing mix for each segment, although this is much more costly than undifferentiated marketing and may overburden resources if not carefully managed.

Concentrated marketing

As you saw in Figure 4.5, **concentrated marketing** involves targeting one segment with one marketing mix. The idea is to compete more effectively and efficiently by understanding and satisfying one sizeable set of customers, rather than spreading organizational resources across multiple marketing activities for multiple segments. As long as the targeted segment remains attractive, this can be a profitable coverage approach. However, be aware that uncontrollable and unexpected factors such as new competition or changes in customer needs can make the targeted segment less attractive or even unfeasible over time.

Ryanair has profited from its concentrated marketing approach to targeting.

MARKETING IN PRACTICE: RYANAIR

Based in Dublin, Ryanair targets one big segment: price-sensitive customers who respond to low, low fares. 'You want luxury? Go somewhere else', states CEO Michael O'Leary. Ryanair saves money by using smaller airports, getting planes on the ground and into the air very quickly, flying limited schedules to selected European destinations and selling 98 per cent of all tickets online. Customers pay for every extra, from checked baggage to bottled water – even seat assignments carry a price tag. Ryanair's targeting is paying off with a healthy net profit margin of 18 per cent.[15]

Individualized marketing

You may be able to tailor marketing offers to individuals within certain targeted segments, a coverage approach known as **individualized** (or **customized**) **marketing**. Airbus, for example, can identify all the potential buyers for passenger jets and cargo planes, get to know their needs and specifications, then develop a separate marketing mix for each. The markets for passenger jets and cargo planes are not so large that this is impractical, and the potential profit from each order is so great that individualized marketing makes sense for Airbus, especially in its competitive battle with arch-rival Boeing.[16]

If you have the right technology, you can opt for **mass customization** and create products and/or communications tailored to individual customers' needs on a larger scale. New Zealand, Canada and the United States are doing this with personalized postage stamps. Other products being marketed to individual customers through mass customization are personalized candies (such as M&Ms chocolates) and condiments in personalized bottles (such as Heinz catsup).[17]

Segment personas

Unilever and other marketers are adding a human dimension to targeting by constructing **personas,** fictitious yet realistic profiles representing how specific customers in targeted segments would typically buy, behave, and react in a marketing situation. The idea is to think about how customers actually interact with a product (and competing products), what influences and motivates those customers and how their needs and preferences affect their buying and consumption behaviour.

With assistance from its marketing agencies, Unilever constructed the persona of Katie, a 25-year-old single woman who represents a targeted consumer segment for its Sunsilk haircare products. Being able to envision Katie as a real person helped Sunsilk's marketers and agencies think about how specific marketing activities might fit into her life. What television programmes would Katie watch? How would she tend to react to marketing communications? 'It's about being in her world', explains the Sunsilk brand manager.[18]

THE POSITIONING PROCESS

With positioning, you use marketing to create a competitively distinctive position for your product in the minds of targeted customers. You need marketing research to understand how your targeted customers perceive your organization, product or brand and your competitors. Research can also help determine which attributes matter most to the targeted customers. Regardless of how you see your products, it is the customer's view that counts.

Altering a brand's positioning – even slightly – can be difficult. Consider the case of Montblanc, the German company famous worldwide for its premium writing instruments. In the early 1990s, Montblanc began **repositioning** – using its marketing plan to change the competitively distinctive positioning of its brand in the minds of the targeted customers. Montblanc wanted its brand perceived as super-luxury and it wanted to expand beyond pens. As a result, it needed to influence how customers thought and felt about its brand in relation to other super-luxury brands. One way Montblanc did this was by creating limited-edition pens embellished with precious metals and gems. Wealthy collectors took notice and soon were vying for the privilege of buying these very special pens, the world's most expensive. Montblanc's super-luxury positioning ultimately enabled the company to launch new products and enter new markets.[19]

Deciding on differentiation

Montblanc's experience illustrates the importance of deciding on a point of difference that is not only competitively distinctive but also relevant and believable. The limited-edition pens were nothing like ordinary pens – they were extremely high quality, beautifully designed and in quite short supply. Montblanc thus differentiated itself from rivals in ways that were credible, desirable and important to the targeted customer segment. Today Montblanc holds a solid 70 per cent of the world market for upmarket pens.[20]

In general, you can differentiate your offering along the lines of product, service, image, personnel or value. Whatever your choice, a product's positioning must be based on criteria that are meaningful and desirable from the customer's perspective yet competitively distinctive. Here are three examples of effective positioning based on desirable differentiation criteria:

- Mercedes-Benz: well-engineered, well-appointed luxury vehicles (product differentiation)
- Ryanair: low-cost, no-frills air travel (value differentiation)
- Vision Express: spectacles ready in one hour (service differentiation).

Applying positioning

In addition to satisfying the three desirability criteria, you must actually carry through the positioning in your product's marketing and performance. Determine first whether your organization can, realistically, develop and market a product that will live up to meaningful points of difference. Second, consider whether the points of difference can be communicated to the targeted segments. And third, determine whether you can sustain the product's performance and continue to communicate a meaningful point of difference over time. Montblanc has been so successful at repositioning itself as a super-luxury brand that it has been able to implement marketing plans for expanding into leather goods, wristwatches, eyewear and even fragrances.[21]

Positioning is basically the driver behind all the marketing activities you will include in your marketing plan. With differentiated marketing, you develop a positioning appropriate to each segment and apply that positioning through your marketing decisions for each segment. With concentrated marketing, you establish one positioning for the single segment you target. Remember that positioning is not a one-time decision: as markets and customers' needs change, you must be prepared to reposition a product, if necessary, for desirability and deliverability.

CHAPTER SUMMARY

Segmentation helps marketers rule out inappropriate markets, identify specific segments for more study and better understand customers in those segments so the organization can more easily respond to their needs by providing value. Evaluating segments enables the organization to decide which to target and in what order. The process also provides a basis for creating a meaningful and competitively distinctive position in the minds of each target segment's customers.

Marketers can segment consumer markets by user-based characteristics (demographic, geographic, socioeconomic and lifestyle/personality) and product-related behavioural variables (user types, consumption patterns and usage frequency, brand loyalty, price sensitivity, perceived benefits and more). Business markets can be segmented using customer characteristics (industry type, geographic, industry position, company size and more) and product-related behavioural variables (consumption patterns/usage frequency, end use application, perceived benefits and more). Target-market coverage strategies include undifferentiated, differentiated, concentrated and individualized (customized) marketing. Effective positioning and repositioning must be competitively distinctive, relevant and credible as well as feasible, able to be communicated and sustainable.

CASE STUDY: GROUPE DANONE: MORE THAN YOGHURT

Although yoghurt, water and biscuits are entirely different products, Groupe Danone competes effectively in all three categories. The French company is the world's largest maker of yoghurt products. In addition, it markets bottled water (under Evian and other brands) and biscuits (under LU and other brands). Danone's marketers study the needs that drive consumer behaviour and reach out to targeted segments through differentiated marketing. The five geographic markets where they see the highest growth potential are China, India, Russia, Mexico and the United States.

In the yoghurt market, company marketers identified segments based on a diversity of needs and wants: some consumers want health benefits, some want a low-calorie snack, some prefer a fruity or creamy taste and so on. In response, Danone makes dozens of varieties of yoghurts with higher or lower levels of active cultures, sweetener, flavourings, fruits and other ingredients. Its yoghurt packages come in different sizes and shapes to accommodate buyers who want portable snacks, or eat yoghurt at home and who display other consumption behaviours.

Seeking growth, Danone bought a majority interest in China's Hangzhou Wahaha Group, which makes dairy drinks. With Danone's backing, Wahaha expanded capacity and used its brand and distribution system to break into the bottled water market. Now China is Danone's largest market for water, with annual purchases of more than four billion bottles.

Like their counterparts in other countries, some consumers in China prefer to support local businesses. This worked to Danone's advantage when the government asked the parent to assist Wahaha in developing a cola soft drink, Future Cola, positioned as 'the Chinese people's own cola'. The drink quickly became the number-three cola behind Coca-Cola and Pepsi-Cola, although its share is far less than the 24 per cent held by Coca-Cola. Danone's future marketing plans will continue to cover more than just yoghurt.[22]

Case questions

1. Which of the customer characteristics and product-related variables shown in Figure 4.2 does Danone appear to be using to segment the yoghurt market?

2. How has positioning contributed to the success of Future Cola? What are the implications for Danone's future marketing plans in China?

APPLY YOUR KNOWLEDGE

Research the segmentation, targeting and positioning of a particular company active in consumer or B2B marketing, using its products, advertising, website and other activities as clues. Prepare a brief written or oral report summarizing your conclusions.

- Based on the organization's marketing, what market(s) and segment(s) appear to be targeted?

- Is this company using differentiated, undifferentiated, concentrated or individualized marketing?

- What benefits are highlighted by the company's marketing, and what customer needs are they designed to satisfy?

- What product-related variables do you think this company is using to segment its market(s), apart from benefits sought?

- In one sentence, how would you describe the positioning of the firm or one of its products?

BUILD YOUR OWN MARKETING PLAN

Proceed with the marketing plan you've been preparing. During the segmentation process for this organization, what markets would you eliminate from consideration, and why? What specific segmentation variables would you apply to the remainder of the market, and how would you expect them to create segments that make sense from a marketing perspective? What further research would support this segmentation? What criteria would you use to evaluate the segments you identify? Given the organization's overall goals, strengths and resources, what targeting approach would you choose? Finally, on what basis would you differentiate your offering for the customers in each targeted segment? Be sure that these ideas are appropriate in light of your earlier decisions, then document your choices in your marketing plan.

STOP ENDNOTES

1. Quote reported in Lucy Barrett, 'Protecting the Purity of the Virgin Brand', *Marketing Week,* 25 July 2002, p. 22. Also: 'Rebel Grown Up: Katherine Salway, Group Brand Director, Virgin', *Marketing,* 25 October 2006, p. 24; Terry Keenan, 'Virgin Group Chairman – Interview', *The America's Intelligence Wire,* 6 July 2003, n.p.; 'Profile: Policing Growth', *Marketing,* 25 July 2002, p. 18; Jeremy Lee, 'Close-up: Newsmaker Ashley Stockwell', *Campaign,* 26 July 2002, p. 15.

2. Quoted in Jaq Bayles, 'It's an Age of Intolerance', *Grocer,* 9 September 2006, p. S66.

3. Christina C. Berk, 'Health-Food Maker Hain Faces Rivals', *Wall Street Journal,* 13 August 2003, pp. 1ff.; Dina ElBoghdady, 'Soy Milk Spilling into the Mainstream', *Washington Post,* 15 March 2003, pp. E1ff.; 'New Soy Milk Products from Tully's and Others', *New Food Products in Japan,* 25 May 2003, n.p.

4. Ben Stocking, 'Vietnam Officially Becomes WTO Member', *Associated Press,* 11 January 2007, www.businessweek.com; Keith Bradsher, 'Vietnam's Roaring Economy Is Set for World Stage', *New York Times,* 25 October 2006, pp. A1, C4; Clay Chandler, 'Vietnam Vroooom', *Fortune,* 11 December 2006, pp. 147ff.

5. Kenneth Maxwell, 'L'Oréal CEO Sees New-Product Boost', *Wall Street Journal,* 10 September

2003, p. B4A; 'The Colour of Money: The Beauty Business', *The Economist*, 8 March 2003, p. 59.

6. Alan Cowell, 'Luxury Wobbles on Legs of Dollars and Yen', *New York Times*, 25 May 2003, sec. 3, p. 4.

7. Lauren Mack, 'Is "Lassie" on TV?', *Newsweek*, 26 June 2006, n.p.; Jane Engle, 'Starwood Opens Its Doggie Door', *Los Angeles Times*, 31 August 2003, p. L3.

8. Julia Moskin, 'The Breakfast Wars', *New York Times*, 10 January 2007, pp. F1, F7.

9. 'Tropical Treat', *Restaurants & Institutions*, 15 March 2005, p. 6; Debbi Gardiner, 'Selling Kiwis Without Tears', *Business 2.0*, October 2002, p. 62.

10. Richard Siklos, 'How Much Profit Is Lurking in That Cellphone?', *New York Times*, 5 March 2006, sec. 3, p. 3; Mark Russell, 'Musical Mobiles', *Newsweek*, 9 September 2003, p. 12.

11. 'Do Your Own Work: OSU Right to Go After Students Who Steal Others?', *Columbus Dispatch*, 24 January 2006, n.p.; Michael Hastings, 'Cheater Beaters', *Newsweek*, 8 September 2003, p. E16.

12. James B. Treece, 'Japan's No. 3 Truckmaker Sees a Surge in Profits', *Automotive News*, 21 July 2003, p. 20.

13. Elizabeth Wyoke, 'Hipster Appeal, Mall Prices', *BusinessWeek*, 12 February 2007, p. 68; Koji Hirano, 'Uniqlo Sets Sights on Big Markets', *WWD*, 8 December 2006, p. 18; Bayan Rahman, 'Fast Retailing Lifted by Better News at Uniqlo', *Financial Times*, 6 May 2003, www.ft.com; Bayan Rahman, 'Fast Retailing Makes Fast Exit from UK Market', *Financial Times*, 7 March 2003, www.ft.com.

14. Sharon Kiley Mack, 'From the Sea: Salt from Maine Proving Itself in National Market', *Bangor Daily News*, 10 January 2007, www.bangordailynews.com; Allison Askins, 'Salt Has an Ancient History and a Bright Future', *The State* (Columbia, S.C.), 2 June 2003, www.thestate.com; Michael J. McCarthy, 'Little Umbrella Girl Watches Her Back in Kosher Salt War', *Wall Street Journal*, 10 June 2002, pp. A1ff.

15. Quote in Kerry Capell, '"Wal-Mart with Wings"', *Business Week Online*, 4 December 2006, www.businessweek.com. Also: 'Michael O'Leary', *Newsweek International*, 23 June 2003, pp. 64ff; 'Ryanair Blasted over Christmas Bags Cost', *Irish Post*, 10 January 2007, www.irishpost.co.uk.

16. David Gow, 'Boeing Sales Soar Ahead of Rival Airbus', *Guardian*, 5 January 2007, p. 27.

17. 'New Zealand Post Tries Personalized Stamps', *ePostal News*, 10 October 2005, p. 2; Alicia Henry, 'You Oughta Be In . . . Stamps?', *Business Week*, 25 August 2003, p. 14; 'Heinz Anniversary Efforts Push Personalized Labels', *PR Week*, 11 September 2006, p. 2.

18. Todd Wasserman, 'Unilever, Whirlpool Get Personal with Personas', *Brandweek*, 18 September 2006, p. 13.

19. Pranay Gupte, 'Hand Candy', *Forbes Global*, 8 January 2007, p. 76; William George Shuster, 'Montblanc Celebrates Its Centenary', *Jewelers Circular Keystone*, May 2006, pp. 226ff.

20. Gupte, 'Hand Candy'.

21. Julie Bosman, 'Venerable Maker of Pens Turns to Young Designers', *New York Times*, 7 August 2006, p. C6.

22. Based on information from: David Gauthier-Villars, 'Water Fight in France Takes a Dirty Turn', *Wall Street Journal*, 1 February 2007, p. B7; Carol Matlack, 'Investors Like the Taste of Groupe Danone', *BusinessWeek Online*, 22 November 2006, www.businessweek.com; Julie Chao, 'China's Homegrown Cola Sees Future in "Fashionable" Drinks', *Taipei Times*, 20 June 2004, p. 12; David Haffenreffer, 'Danone Restructures Products Portfolio', *America's Intelligence Wire*, 30 July 2003; Hannah Booth, 'Bloom Researchers Yoghurt to Update Its Pack-Shape', *Design Week*, 6 February 2003, p. 5; Sherri Day, 'Yoghurt Makers Shrink the Cup, Trying to Turn Less into More', *New York Times*, 3 May 2003, pp. C1ff.

5

Planning direction, objectives and strategy

Comprehension outcomes

After studying this chapter, you will be able to:

- Explain the three broad directions that can shape a marketing plan
- Describe the characteristics of effective objectives
- Understand how financial, marketing and societal objectives work together in a marketing plan

Application outcomes

After studying this chapter, you will be able to:

- Set a direction for your marketing plan
- Formulate your marketing plan objectives

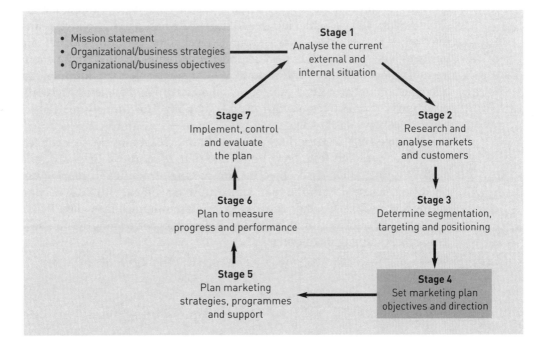

CHAPTER PREVIEW

Toyota believes in setting ambitious objectives. When planning the fuel-efficient Prius, the company pushed its engineers and designers to develop the car in only two years. An instant success, the Prius has polished Toyota's global image as an innovator. Toyota also set a goal of selling 1.2 million cars annually in Europe by 2010, despite competition from European, US, Japanese and Korean car manufacturers. To meet demand, Toyota's plant in Valenciennes, France, assembles small Yaris cars day and night. As a result, Toyota's European market share has risen to 5.7 per cent and it will reach its 2010 goal early, despite problems with vehicle recalls. Because sales in Japan are barely growing, Toyota's ability to reach future turnover targets depends on higher sales in Europe, Asia and the Americas.[1]

Toyota's marketing plans for each market are driven by its desire for rapid, profitable growth. This chapter discusses marketing plan objectives and direction, which make up the fourth stage in the marketing planning process. First, the chapter examines how direction and objectives guide the marketing plan and help the organization achieve longer-term goals. Next is a discussion of marketing plan direction, covering both growth and non-growth strategies. Finally, the chapter explains how to set effective marketing, financial and societal objectives.

DIRECTION AND OBJECTIVES DRIVE MARKETING PLANNING

No marketing plan is developed in isolation. Toyota's marketing plan for Europe is influenced by its corporate priorities as well as top management's expectation of how the plan should contribute to achieving overall goals. As noted in Chapter 1, plans are made at three levels in the organization. Corporate-level plans are supported and implemented by business-level plans and, in turn, supported and implemented by functional-level plans for marketing, operations and so forth. As a marketer, you will formulate strategy, determine the optimal marketing-mix tools, and make programme-level decisions based on the direction and objectives of your marketing plan. The strategy pyramid illustrated in Figure 5.1 shows this linkage.

If the objectives in your marketing plan are explicit and clearly connected to higher-level objectives and long-term goals, the plan is more likely to produce the desired performance.[2] Thus, each objective, marketing strategy and marketing programme must be consistent with the plan's direction as well as with both organizational and business objectives. Consider how the UK telecommunications giant BT Group is using marketing to pursue growth after divesting underperforming businesses, reducing its debt and expanding its offerings.

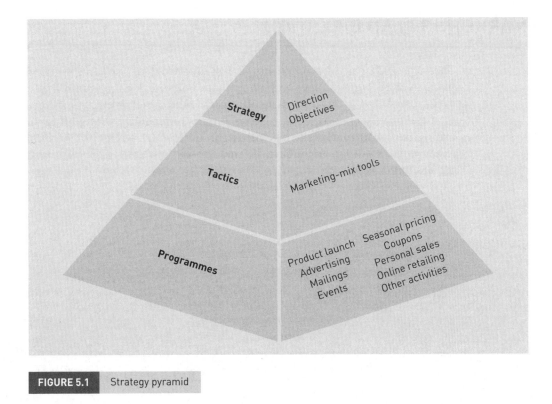

FIGURE 5.1   Strategy pyramid

Source: After Tim Berry and Doug Wilson, *On Target: The Book on Marketing Plans*, 2nd edn (Eugene, OR: Palo Alto Software, 2001), p. 107.

MARKETING IN PRACTICE: BT GROUP

BT Group, with annual turnover of £19.5 billion and profit of £2 billion, has made broadband the centrepiece of its UK marketing plan for growth. In 2002, the telecommunications company set a goal of establishing 5 million broadband connections before 2007. Despite intense competition, the company's marketing focus on communicating broadband's benefits was so effective that the firm had 10 million broadband connections by the end of 2006. BT has also acquired technology service firms and expanded its electronic networking capabilities to better serve the lucrative corporate market. Now the marketing plan calls for doubling annual revenue from China-based multinational firms by 2010; it includes objectives for corporate philanthropy and eco-friendly activities, as well.[3]

MARKETING PLAN DIRECTION

These days, BT has, like many companies, set growth as the direction for its marketing plans. Not all organizations pursue growth. Some seek to maintain their current position, postponing growth because of adverse economic conditions, fierce competition, financial problems or for other reasons. Others retrench by selling off units or products, exiting particular markets or downsizing in other ways – often for survival purposes or to prepare for later growth. Growth and non-growth strategies, summarized in Figure 5.2, are discussed next.

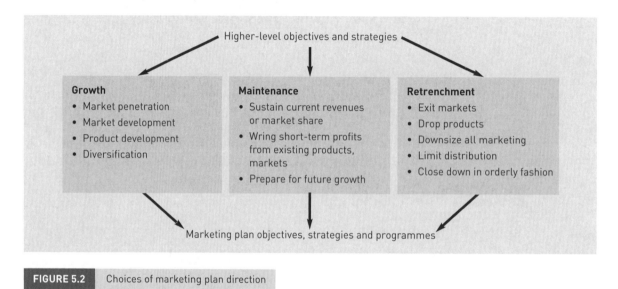

FIGURE 5.2   Choices of marketing plan direction

Growth strategies

If your organization wants to grow, you will choose among the four main growth strategies proposed by H. Igor Ansoff: market penetration, product development, market development and diversification.[4] With **market penetration**, you offer existing products to customers in existing markets. This increases unit and/or monetary sales and simultaneously reinforces the brand or product's strength in each market. It also strengthens relationships by connecting customers to the organization with more product ties.

With **product development**, you market new products or product variations to customers in existing markets. This only works when you can develop a steady stream of product innovations appropriate for the needs of customers in those markets. Lamborghini has done this by designing new sports cars, offering limited-edition designer versions of its existing models and licensing its famous logo for clothing and accessories.[5]

With **market development**, you pursue growth by marketing existing products in new markets and segments. Such a strategy builds on the popularity of established products and allows firms to expand their customer base either geographically or by segment. Korea's LG, for example, has leveraged its strength in appliance technology and styling to market more washing machines and refrigerators to consumers in Europe and North America. As a result of higher efficiency, LG earns a higher profit margin on its appliances than its competitors earn on their appliances.[6]

The fourth growth strategy is **diversification**, which means marketing new products in new markets or segments. You can diversify by (1) distributing new products in new markets through existing channel arrangements, (2) initiating new marketing activities in new markets or (3) acquiring companies to gain access to new products and new markets. London-based Hanson, once part of a conglomerate, has been growing through diversification within the building materials industry. By buying brick companies in North America, cement companies in Australia and related businesses elsewhere, the company can offer a wider range of construction products in Europe, the Americas, Australia and the Pacific.[7]

Non-growth strategies

Sometimes growth is not an appropriate direction. Pressured by severe economic or competitive conditions, insufficient resources, ambitious expansion, lower demand or stagnant revenues and profits, organizations may follow a maintenance strategy or even retrench. You might therefore create a maintenance marketing plan to keep revenues, market share or profits at current levels, if possible, or at least defend against deterioration. Rather than invest in improving products, targeting new markets, developing new promotions or other marketing activities, your organization could try to harvest short-term profits from existing products and markets as a way of conserving resources and building a stronger foundation for later growth.

Organizations that cannot maintain their current levels may be forced into making marketing plans to retrench or, in the extreme, to shut down entirely. As shown in Figure 5.2, some common choices here are to withdraw from certain markets, eliminate particular products, downsize all marketing efforts, shrink distribution or go out of business. And, if the retrenchment goes well, the company will soon be able to start planning for a turnaround through a new growth strategy.

Brio's retrenchment strategy is a good example.

MARKETING IN PRACTICE: BRIO

Sweden's Brio has long been known for high-quality, expensive toys such as wooden trains as well as prams and other items for children. Besides designing and producing its own products, it eventually owned a regional toy chain, distributed toys in Scandinavian countries and marketed board games, among other activities. Then IKEA, Tesco and other large retailers began selling wooden trains at lower prices, just as the number of independent toy stores – a key distribution channel – plummeted in many markets. Brio's sales and profits suffered. Finally, management decided on retrenchment. By outsourcing production, divesting unprofitable subsidiaries, focusing product development and cutting costs, Brio planned to become, in a few years, 'a smaller company but profitable', said one of the company's owners.[8]

Clearly, the marketing plan for Brio's retrenchment strategy will be completely different from the marketing plan for any growth strategy. Guiding the organization in a particular direction requires specific marketing plan objectives keyed to that situation, which in turn will lead to different marketing strategies and programmes.

MARKETING PLAN OBJECTIVES

Marketing plan objectives are short-term targets that, when achieved through implementation of appropriate action programmes, will bring the organization closer to its longer-term goals. Some companies use the **Balanced Scorecard**, broad performance measures used to align strategy and objectives as a way to manage customer relationships, achieve financial targets, improve internal capabilities and attain sustainability. In such cases, the marketing plan objectives have to be structured appropriately to support these broader measures of performance.[9]

To be effective, your marketing plan objectives should be:

- *Relevant.* Be sure your objectives relate to the chosen direction and higher-level strategies and goals. Otherwise, the programmes you implement to achieve your plan's objectives will not support organizational needs. Although most businesses set objectives for revenues and profits, non-financial objectives such as those relating to corporate image are also important because they build and strengthen connections with other stakeholders.

- *Specific and measurable.* Vague targets will not help you determine what you need to accomplish and how. Simply calling for 'growth' is not enough. To be effective, your objectives should indicate, in quantitative terms, what the marketing plan is being developed to achieve.[10] To illustrate, HSBC Bank Malaysia's marketing plan for growth sets an objective of increasing the number of credit cards issued by 20 per cent each year, which means opening 500,000 new accounts. The bank's marketing managers can check progress toward this objective at any time by counting the number of accounts opened and cards issued.[11]

- *Time defined.* What is the deadline for achieving the objective? You will plan differently for objectives that must be achieved in six months compared with objectives to be achieved in 12 months. Setting an open-ended objective is like setting no objective at all, because you will lack a schedule for showing results – and will not be accountable. During one recent year, the Swiss food company Nestlé set an objective of raising annual sales volume by 4 per cent over the prior year. Knowing the deadline, the company had time to adjust its marketing plans when it found that six-month growth was 3.5 per cent.[12]

- *Realistic.* A marketing plan geared to attaining market dominance in six months is unlikely to be realistic for any business – especially for a start-up. Thus, your marketing plan objectives should be realistic to provide purpose for marketing and to keep organizational members motivated. One of LG's marketing objectives, for instance, is to increase its US appliance sales so quickly that it will hold a 10 per cent share of the US market for refrigerators and washing machines within three years.[13]

- *Challenging*. Realistic objectives need not be easy to attain. In fact, many marketers set aggressive yet realistic marketing plan objectives so they can expand more quickly than if their objectives resulted in incremental growth. Objectives that are too challenging, however, may discourage the marketing staff and tie up resources without achieving the desired result. LG's market-share objective is quite challenging because the company faces strong competition from Whirlpool, observes one of LG's US marketing managers.[14]

- *Consistent*. Is the objective consistent with the organization's mission, goals, strengths, core competencies and interpretation of external opportunities and threats? Are all objectives consistent with each other? Inconsistent objectives can confuse staff members and customers, detract from the marketing effort and result in disappointing performance. In the case of LG, its market-share objective makes sense in the context of the company's product development expertise, investment in customer service support and manufacturing capacity.

When G.R. Gopinath launched Air Deccan, he set specific, challenging and time-defined objectives to guide the new company's marketing.

MARKETING IN PRACTICE: AIR DECCAN

'We're going to connect cities that are poorly connected by roads and trains', founder and managing director G.R. Gopinath said in introducing his no-frills airline, Air Deccan.[15] The company sees a profitable opportunity to serve India's growing middle-class segment of price-sensitive business travellers, families and sightseers. One of its first-year objectives was to attract 700,000 passengers. Three years after its founding, Air Deccan had exceeded its objectives and was carrying nearly 7 million passengers annually. Now Air Deccan has ambitious objectives for its new executive charter division. Will the airline reach its objectives and continue to fly high as competition intensifies?[16]

You can set marketing plan objectives in three categories. **Financial objectives** are targets for achieving financial results through marketing strategies and programmes. **Marketing objectives** are targets for achievements in marketing relationships and activities, which in turn directly support attainment of financial objectives. **Societal objectives** are targets for accomplishing results in areas related to social responsibility; such objectives indirectly influence both marketing and financial achievements. The choice of marketing plan objectives and specific targets will, of course, be different for every organization.

Financial objectives

Companies usually set objectives for external results such as unit, monetary, product and channel sales plus internal requirements such as profitability, return on investment and break-even deadlines. Figure 5.3 shows the focus and purpose of financial objectives commonly used by businesses. Non-governmental organizations (NGOs) typically set objectives for short-term and long-term fund-raising as well as other financial targets. To achieve the organization's financial objectives, you will need to coordinate other compatible objectives dealing with relationships between buyers and sellers as well as suppliers and distributors.

A company might set a financial objective for external results such as: *to achieve a minimum weekly sales volume of £1,000 for each new product.* Notice that this objective is relevant (for a profit-seeking organization); specific; time-defined; and measurable. Whether it is realistic, challenging and consistent depends on the company's particular situation. A financial objective related to internal requirements might be: *to achieve an average annual profit margin of 13 per cent across all products.*

Because such objectives are measurable and time-defined, you can check progress, adjust your targets or change your marketing if necessary. Mercedes-Benz, for example, originally set an objective of selling 1,000 Maybach cars in its introductory year, at a price of €250,000 each. When unfavourable economic conditions dampened demand for super-luxury vehicles, the company lowered its first-year objective to 800 cars and set 1,000 cars as the second-year objective. Increased competition then became a factor. Two years later, Mercedes said annual sales of Maybachs stood at about 400.[17]

Focus of financial objective	Purpose and examples
External results	**To provide targets for outcomes of marketing activities such as:** • Increasing unit or monetary sales by geographic market • Increasing unit or monetary sales by customer segment • Increasing unit or monetary sales by product • Increasing unit or monetary sales by channel • Other objectives
Internal requirements	**To provide targets for managing marketing to meet organizational requirements such as:** • Achieving break-even status • Achieving profitability levels • Achieving return on investment levels • Other objectives

FIGURE 5.3 Focus and purpose of financial objectives

Marketing objectives

Connections with customers and channel members are particularly critical to organizational success, which is why every marketing plan should include objectives for managing these external relationships. Looking at the life cycle of a customer relationship, the organization would begin by approaching the customer to explore a possible relationship; establishing a relationship and adding more ties to strengthen it; reigniting customer interest if purchases plateau or loyalty wavers; saving the relationship if the customer signals intention to switch to another product or brand; and restarting the relationship if the customer is open to switching back. This life cycle applies to relations with channel members, as well.[18]

Consider Toyota's marketing objectives. Knowing that many car buyers begin to develop brand preferences years before they're old enough to drive or buy, the company has set objectives for starting relationships with young teens. Translating those objectives into action, it has become involved with Whyville.net, an online community. Participants are invited to use their avatars (the people or characters they create to depict themselves on the site) to 'drive' Toyota cars around the virtual world. The company hopes this will raise awareness of, and build preference for, its brand.[19]

Many businesses establish explicit objectives for building their customer base; enhancing customers' perceptions of the brand, product or company; holding on to existing customers; increasing customer loyalty; boosting or defending market share; strengthening ties with key distributors; improving customer satisfaction; and so on, as in Figure 5.4. The US conglomerate General Electric sets objectives for customer satisfaction and then examines the processes it must improve in order to meet those objectives. To boost satisfaction, GE's business financing division needed to process loan applications more quickly. After eliminating some steps in the process and working on some simultaneously instead of sequentially, GE was able to approve loans in just five days and improve its satisfaction ratings.[20]

In practice, you need to avoid conflicts between your marketing objectives and your financial objectives. It can be difficult to dramatically increase both market share and profitability at the same time, as one example. Therefore, marketers must determine the organization's priorities and formulate the marketing plan accordingly.

Non-profit organizations also set marketing objectives for attracting contributors, sponsors and other key relationships. For instance, the Canadian office of Doctors Without Borders set a one-year marketing objective of adding 1,000 new donors who would contribute at least once – and possibly more than once – to the organization's cause. The related financial objective was to break even on fund-raising costs within four months or less.[21]

In conjunction with objectives aimed at external relationships, you may formulate objectives covering internal activities such as increasing the accuracy or speed of order fulfilment; adjusting the focus, output or speed of new product development; and arranging the resources for entering new segments or markets. Planning for these activities helps lay the groundwork for achieving relationship objectives and the financial objectives that depend on those relationships.

Focus of marketing objective	Purpose and examples
External relationships	To provide targets for managing relations with customers and other stakeholders such as: • Enhancing brand, product, company image • Building brand awareness and preference • Stimulating product trial • Acquiring new customers • Retaining existing customers • Increasing customer satisfaction • Acquiring or defending market share • Expanding or defending distribution • Other relationship objectives
Internal activities	To provide targets for managing specific marketing activities such as: • Increasing output or speed of new product development • Improving product quality • Streamlining order fulfilment • Managing resources to enter new markets or segments • Conducting marketing research • Other objectives

FIGURE 5.4   Focus and purpose of marketing objectives

Societal objectives

Because businesses are increasingly mindful of their responsibilities to society – and the way their actions are viewed by stakeholders – a growing number are setting societal objectives to be achieved through marketing. Such objectives are addressed in marketing plans because they indirectly help the company strengthen ties with customers (achieving marketing objectives) and increase or maintain sales (achieving financial objectives). As shown in Figure 5.5, societal objectives may relate to ecological protection or to social responsibility and stakeholder relations. The UK grocery chain Tesco, for example, has set an objective of reducing the average energy use in its facilities by 50 per cent within four years, part of its drive for environmentally friendly operations.[22]

Many businesses fulfil their societal objectives by donating money, goods or services to charities or good causes. This helps polish their image and demonstrates their commitment to the community and to society at large. Meralco (formerly the Manila Electric Co.) offers free computer literacy training to teachers in the Philippines. The company also sponsors an annual book drive in which employees donate reference books and

Focus of societal objective	Purpose and examples
Ecological protection	**To provide targets for managing marketing related to ecological protection and sustainability:** • Reducing pollution with natural or 'greener' products, ecologically friendly processes • Doing business with 'greener' suppliers and channel members • Reducing waste by redesigning products and processes for recycling, other efficiencies • Conserving use of natural resources • Other objectives
Social responsibility and stakeholder relations	**To provide targets for managing marketing related to social responsibility and stakeholder relations:** • Building a positive image as a good corporate citizen • Supporting designated charities, community projects, human rights groups and others, with money and marketing • Encouraging volunteering among employees, customers, suppliers, channel members • Communicating with stakeholders to understand their concerns and explain societal activities • Other objectives

FIGURE 5.5   Focus and purpose of societal objectives

other educational materials to local schools. Surveys confirm that customers notice and appreciate the energy company's activities. 'This definitely inspires us to work even harder and have more projects for social and national development', says CEO Manuel M. Lopez.[23]

Some companies set specific societal objectives for **cause-related marketing**, in which the brand or product is marketed through a connection to benefit a charity or other social cause. Experts say the chosen cause should have value for both stakeholders and the company.[24] Properly implemented social responsibility initiatives have a positive effect on customer satisfaction and the company's market value, research shows.[25]

To communicate their societal objectives, activities and results to stakeholders, some companies distribute information to the media and post social responsibility and sustainability reports on their websites. For example, Royal Dutch/Shell posts its annual corporate social responsibility report on the corporate website, along with details about how it gathers data, the global principles and codes it follows and what external experts think of its sustainability reports. Shell has, in fact, been recognized for its management's use of external experts and the mechanisms it uses for fostering dialogue with stakeholders.[26]

Two starting points for more information about societal objectives are the UK government site on corporate social responsibility (www.csr.gov.uk/) and CSR Europe (www.csreurope.org/).

ESSENTIAL MARKETING PLAN CHECKLIST NO. 7:
EVALUATING OBJECTIVES

You must set appropriate objectives if you are to develop suitable marketing programmes for your organization's chosen direction and current situation. This checklist will help you evaluate the marketing, financial and societal objectives you have formulated for your marketing plan. Note your responses in the spaces provided, then put a tick mark next to the questions as you answer each one.[27]

☐ Is the objective relevant to the organization's direction and long-term goals?

_____

☐ Is the objective consistent with the organization's mission, strengths and core competencies?

_____

☐ Is the objective appropriate for the market's opportunities and threats?

_____

☐ Is the objective specific?

_____

☐ Is the objective time-defined?

_____

☐ Is the objective measurable?

_____

☐ Is the objective realistic yet challenging?

_____

☐ Is the objective in conflict with any other objective?

_____

FROM OBJECTIVES TO MARKETING-MIX DECISIONS

The objectives you set during this stage of the marketing planning process are the targets to be achieved by implementing the decisions you make about the various marketing-mix elements. This is the point at which your earlier work comes together: on the basis of your situational analysis, your market and customer research and your segmentation, targeting and positioning decisions, you will be creating product, place, price and promotion strategies and action programmes for the who, what, when, where and how of marketing. Your objectives will also guide the development of customer service and internal marketing strategies to support the marketing mix.

Be aware that designing programmes to achieve some of your objectives may require marketing research support. To illustrate, Procter & Gamble, the US-based consumer packaged goods company, is already using social networking websites to promote certain brands. Its Herbal Essences shampoo page on MySpace.com invites consumers to upload photos of their latest hairstyles, for instance. Now P&G is sponsoring social networking sites such as Capessa (health.yahoo.com/capessa) to engage consumers and learn more about their concerns and preferences. The insights gained will help P&G set more appropriate objectives and plan programmes that more closely fit what its target markets want and need.[28]

Chapters 6, 7, 8 and 9 discuss planning for the four marketing-mix elements; Chapter 10 covers customer service and internal marketing. All of these are part of Stage 5 in the marketing planning process.

CHAPTER SUMMARY

Higher-level strategies and goals set the direction for marketing plans that outline objectives to be achieved through marketing strategies, tactics and programmes. Many organizations prepare marketing plans for growth through market penetration (offering existing products to existing markets), product development (offering new products or variations to existing markets), market development (offering existing products to new markets or segments) or diversification (offering new products to new markets or segments). Non-growth strategies include maintenance (to sustain current levels of revenues, share or profits) and retrenchment (to prepare for a turnaround into growth or to close down entirely).

Effective objectives must be relevant, specific, time-defined, measurable, realistic yet challenging, and consistent with the current situation. Financial objectives are targets for attaining financial results such as profitability through marketing strategies and programmes. Marketing objectives are targets for achievements in marketing relationships and activities. Societal objectives are targets for ecological protection or other areas of social responsibility. These objectives indirectly support the organization's ability to achieve financial and marketing objectives.

CASE STUDY: GROWTH IS ON McDONALD'S MARKETING MENU

In an ongoing quest to increase sales and market share, McDonald's has spread its red-and-yellow logo far and wide. Using marketing plans keyed to local conditions, the company encourages customers to try menu items as diverse as Ebi Filet-O shrimp burgers in Japan and Bigger Big Mac burgers in Britain. It also sets marketing objectives for building relationships with customers in a number of ways. For example, it invites people with mobile phones to sign up for special late-night offers delivered via text-message.

Responding to public interest in healthier foods, McDonald's now offers yoghurt, apple juice and other healthy foods in children's Happy Meals packages. The company has successfully introduced organic foods and reduced transfat levels in cooking oils. These initiatives also fit into McDonald's marketing plan for meeting societal objectives. Sustainability is a major focus, which is why all European McDonald's restaurants brew only coffee from Rainforest Alliance-certified growers and more than 30 per cent of the fish used in McDonald's menu items come from sustainable fisheries. In addition, the company sets societal objectives for charitable contributions and community-based efforts such as improving literacy.

Europe is a very lucrative market for McDonald's, contributing nearly 40 per cent of the company's annual profit. The marketing budget is far from unlimited, however. Thus, the company's marketers must decide on specific growth objectives for each year's marketing plan. Spending heavily to open new outlets has not produced the kind of profit impact that McDonald's expected. As a result, the CEO now has company marketers putting more emphasis on increasing the turnover of existing restaurants.[29]

Case questions

1. Not long ago, McDonald's decided to close 25 UK restaurants. How do you think this decision might have affected its UK marketing plan?

2. To set consistent and realistic yet challenging objectives, what internal and external factors should the marketers at McDonald's consider?

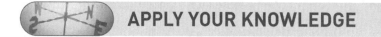 **APPLY YOUR KNOWLEDGE**

Research the direction, marketing, financial and societal objectives of a particular company by examining its website, media coverage, products, advertising, packaging, financial disclosures, social responsibility reports and other aspects of its operation. Based on your findings, write a brief report or make a brief oral presentation to the class.

- Is the company pursuing a growth, maintenance or retrenchment strategy? How do you know?

- Does the company disclose any specific objectives? If so, what are they and how do they relate to the company's direction?

- Identify one specific marketing, financial or societal objective that this company has set and compare it to the characteristics in this chapter's checklist. What changes would you recommend to make this objective more effective as a target for performance?

- Look for clues about whether the objective you have identified was actually achieved (and if not, why).

BUILD YOUR OWN MARKETING PLAN

Continue working on your marketing plan. Looking at the organization's current situation, environment, markets, customers and mission statement, what is an appropriate direction for your marketing plan? What marketing, financial and societal objectives will you set to move in the chosen direction? If any of these objectives conflict, which should take priority, and why? How will these objectives guide your planning for the marketing mix and marketing support? What might cause you to rethink your objectives? Take a moment to consider how the direction and objectives fit with the information already in your marketing plan and how practical they are in terms of marketing implementation. Then record your thoughts in your marketing plan.

STOP   ENDNOTES

1. Ian Rowley, 'Even Toyota Isn't Perfect', *BusinessWeek*, 22 January 2007, p. 54; Micheline Maynard, 'Now Playing in Europe: The Future of Detroit', *New York Times*, 29 October 2006, sec. 3, p. 1; Yoshio Takahashi and Andrew Morse, 'Toyota Is Posed to Surpass GM as the Top Car Maker Next Year', *Wall Street Journal*, 23 December 2006, p. A4; Alex Taylor III, 'The Birth of the Prius', *Fortune*, 6 March 2006, pp. 111ff.

2. Tim Ambler, 'Set Clear Goals and See Marketing Hit Its Target', *Financial Times*, 29 August 2002, p. 8.

3. 'British Telecommunications Beats Connectivity Goal by Double', *InformationWeek*, 3 January 2007, n.p.; 'BT Buys U.S. Anti-Hacking Specialist Counterpane', *eWeek*, 25 October 2006, www.eweek.com; 'BT Group PLC: U.K. Telecom Aims to Boost Annual Revenue from China', *Wall Street Journal*, 6 September 2006, n.p.; Dominic O'Connell, 'BT's 10-point Plan Becomes a Masterclass in Recovery', *Sunday Times*, 18 September 2005, p. 12.

4. H. Igor Ansoff, 'Strategies for Diversification', *Harvard Business Review*, September–October 1957,

pp. 113–25; Philip Kotler, *Kotler on Marketing* (New York: Free Press, 1999), pp. 46–8.

5. Gail Edmondson, 'A Burst of Speed at Lamborghini', *BusinessWeek*, 15 January 2007, p. 44.

6. Moon Ihlwan, 'Korea: Red-Hot White Goods', *BusinessWeek*, 30 October 2006, p. 48.

7. 'Hanson Charters New Business Unit', *Concrete Products*, 1 April 2006, n.p.; Abby Ellin, 'Building a Brand, One Brick at a Time', *New York Times*, 15 June 2003, sec. 3, p. 13.

8. Quote reported in Nicholas George, 'Brio's Toy Trains Hit the Buffers', *Financial Times*, 29 August 2003, www.ft.com; also: www.brio.net; 'BRIO AB Divests Polish Operations', *Nordic Business Report*, 19 December 2006, n.p.

9. For more about applying these performance measures, see Andrew Likierman, 'The Balanced Scorecard: Lots of Firms Have Got One, But Has It Done Them Any Good?', *Financial Management*, November 2006, pp. 29ff.

10. Tim Ambler, 'Awards Scheme Highlights the Need for Data-Driven Marketing', *Marketing*, 21 March 2002, p. 16.

11. Leon Harris, 'HSBC Targets More Than 20 pc Growth', *Business Times*, 18 August 2003, n.p.

12. 'Nestlé: A Dedicated Enemy of Fashion', *The Economist*, 31 August 2002, pp. 47–8.

13. Ihlwan, 'Korea: Red-Hot White Goods.'

14. Ibid.

15. Quoted in Ray Marcelo, 'Deccan Aspires to Soar Above Rivals', *Financial Times*, 12 September 2003, www.ft.com.

16. 'Deccan Lures India's New Jet Set with Executive Charters', *Flight International*, 17 October 2006, n.p.; Marcelo, 'Deccan Aspires to Soar Above Rivals'; Rasheed Kappan, 'Air Deccan to Link "Unconnected" Towns in South', *The Hindu*, 13 August 2003, www.thehindu.com; www.airdeccan.net.

17. 'Mercedes Car Group Unit Sales Rise 3.2 pct in 2006', *Reuters*, 5 January 2007, www.reuters.com; Neal E. Boudette and Joseph B. White, 'Car Sales Get Chilly at Altitudes of $150,000', *Wall Street Journal*, 11 September 2003, www.wsj.com.

18. *See* Sandy D. Jap and Erin Anderson, 'Testing the Life-Cycle Theory of Inter-Organisational Relations: Do Performance Outcomes Depend on the Path Taken?', *Insead Knowledge*, February 2003, www.insead.edu.

19. Jean Halliday, 'Marketer of the Year: Toyota', *Advertising Age*, 13 November 2006, p. M-1.

20. Kathryn Kranhold, 'Theory & Practice: Client-Satisfaction Tool Takes Root', *Wall Street Journal*, 10 July 2006, p. B3; Craig Smith, 'Marketers Still Lost in the Metrics', *Marketing*, 10 August 2000, p. 15.

21. Tom Pope, 'Fundraising Ideas from North of the Border', *The Non-profit Times*, 15 January 2003, pp. 1ff.

22. David Pinto, 'Environment as a Retail Priority', *MMR*, 30 October 2006, p. 17.

23. Quoted in 'Power Distributor Cited for Social Responsibility', *Business World*, 23 July 2003, n.p.

24. Paul B. Brown, 'Strategic Corporate Altruism', *New York Times*, 23 December 2006, p. C5.

25. Xueming Luo and C.B. Bhattacharya, 'Corporate Social Responsibility, Customer Satisfaction and Market Value', *Journal of Marketing*, October 2006, pp. 1–18.

26. Telis Demos, 'Beyond the Bottom Line', *Fortune International*, 30 October 2006, p. 72; Howard Stock, 'U.K. Large Caps Hone Social Reporting Online', *Investor Relations Business*, 9 June 2003, n.p.

27. *Source*: After Marian Burk Wood, *The Marketing Plan Handbook, 3rd edn* (Upper Saddle River, NJ: Pearson Prentice Hall, 2008), Chapter 5.

28. Suzanne Vranica, 'P&G Boosts Social-Networking Efforts', *Wall Street Journal*, 8 January 2007, p. B4.

6 Planning for products and brands

Comprehension outcomes

After studying this chapter, you will be able to:

- Explain how product mix, product line and product life cycle affect product planning
- Understand the steps in new product development
- Discuss how product attributes provide value for customers
- Describe how to analyse and enhance brand equity

Application outcomes

After studying this chapter, you will be able to:

- Analyse a product's position in the product mix and the life cycle
- Make planning decisions about products
- Make planning decisions about brands

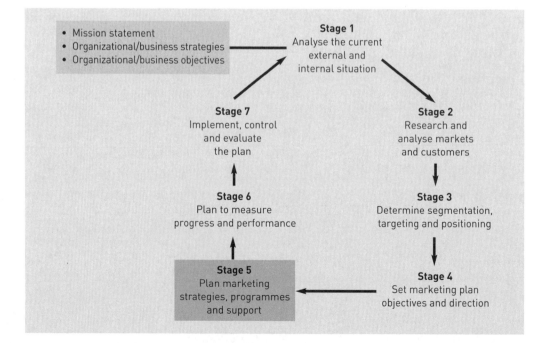

- Mission statement
- Organizational/business strategies
- Organizational/business objectives

Stage 1
Analyse the current external and internal situation

Stage 2
Research and analyse markets and customers

Stage 3
Determine segmentation, targeting and positioning

Stage 4
Set marketing plan objectives and direction

Stage 5
Plan marketing strategies, programmes and support

Stage 6
Plan to measure progress and performance

Stage 7
Implement, control and evaluate the plan

CHAPTER PREVIEW

Trainers for toddlers? Germany's Adidas makes a wide variety of sports footwear, apparel and accessories for global markets. In addition to the Adidas brand, the company owns the Reebok, TaylorMade and Rockport brands. Now it has joined with Mattel, a well-known US toy manufacturer, to co-brand infant clothing and dolls. It is also testing some new product ideas online in Second Life, the virtual community that attracts consumers from all over the world. Although turnover is rising, will Adidas gain enough market share to overtake industry leader Nike?[1]

Adidas is seeking to achieve financial and marketing objectives through product and brand planning, part of stage 5 in the marketing planning process. This chapter opens with a discussion of product mix, product lines and the product life cycle, followed by an examination of new product development. Next, you will learn how to use different attributes in devising a tangible good or intangible service that will meet your customers' needs, your organizational targets and the marketplace realities. The final section looks at planning for brands and brand equity. Chapters 7, 8, 9 and 10 continue with activities during stage 5.

PLANNING FOR PRODUCTS

At this point in the planning process, you understand your current situation and what each product means to the organization in financial and marketing terms. Now you're ready to plan your marketing mix, starting with the product. If you are creating a marketing plan for a company, your product may be a physical item (such as Adidas trainers), a service or a combination of tangible and intangible elements. If you work for a non-governmental organization, your product may be an idea such as better health; if you are marketing a geographic region, your product may be a place such as a tourist destination.

For any specific product you market or plan to market, look closely at:

- the customer segment being targeted

- the needs satisfied and value provided

- trends in pricing, unit sales, market share, revenues and profits

- age and performance over time, by segment, channel and geography

- sales connections between products

- current or potential opportunities and threats related to each product

- competitive strengths, weaknesses, position

- customers' perceptions of competing products.

The point of these analyses is to determine how each product provides value to customers and your organization. As a visual summary, you can create a grid matching each product to the intended target market, detail the need each product satisfies and indicate the value delivered from the customer's and organization's perspectives (*see* Figure 6.1). In addition, you may want to include information about each product's competitive position and strength.

	Customer segment A (briefly describe)	Customer segment B (briefly describe)	Customer segment C (briefly describe)
Product 1 (identify)	Customer need: Value to customer: Value to organization:	Customer need: Value to customer: Value to organization:	Customer need: Value to customer: Value to organization:
Product 2 (identify)	Customer need: Value to customer: Value to organization:	Customer need: Value to customer: Value to organization:	Customer need: Value to customer: Value to organization:
Product 3 (identify)	Customer need: Value to customer: Value to organization:	Customer need: Value to customer: Value to organization:	Customer need: Value to customer: Value to organization:

FIGURE 6.1   Product/segment analysis grid

Next you face decisions about managing the product mix and product lines; the product life cycle; new product development; and product attributes including quality and performance, features and benefits, design, packaging, labelling and brand. Figure 6.2 shows the four categories of product planning decisions.

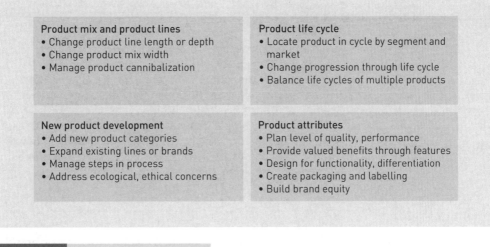

Product mix and product lines
- Change product line length or depth
- Change product mix width
- Manage product cannibalization

Product life cycle
- Locate product in cycle by segment and market
- Change progression through life cycle
- Balance life cycles of multiple products

New product development
- Add new product categories
- Expand existing lines or brands
- Manage steps in process
- Address ecological, ethical concerns

Product attributes
- Plan level of quality, performance
- Provide valued benefits through features
- Design for functionality, differentiation
- Create packaging and labelling
- Build brand equity

FIGURE 6.2 Product planning decisions

Product mix and product line decisions

When planning for products, you will face choices about managing the **product mix** (the assortment of product lines offered by an organization), **product line length** (the number of individual items in each line of related products) and **product line depth** (the number of variations of each product within one line). Your marketing plan can cover one or more of the following:

- introduce new products in an existing line under the existing brand name (**line extensions** that lengthen the line)
- introduce variations of existing products in a product line (deepening the line)
- introduce new brand names in an existing product line or category (**multibrand strategy**)
- introduce new products under an existing brand (**brand extensions** that widen the mix)
- introduce new lines in other product categories (**category extensions** that widen the mix)
- eliminate a product (shortening the line)
- eliminate or add a product line (narrowing or widening the mix).

Each decision about the product changes the way you satisfy customers in targeted segments, address opportunities, avert threats, allocate marketing resources and achieve marketing objectives. Consider the product decisions made by London-based Cadbury Schweppes.

MARKETING IN PRACTICE: CADBURY SCHWEPPES

Several years ago, Cadbury Schweppes' marketers noticed that more consumers were watching their weight and buying lower-calorie snacks. Until that time, the company's sales and profits had come primarily from chocolate sweets and soft drinks. Since then, Cadbury's marketers have invested heavily in lengthening and deepening chewing gum product lines to serve the needs of weight-conscious consumers. Recently Cadbury introduced sugar-free Trident gum, one of its most successful US gum brands, to European markets. It has also purchased gum brands in other countries to lengthen the gum product line and gain local customers. Despite a costly chocolate contamination scandal, Cadbury's timely product innovation and management have increased annual turnover beyond £6 billion and increased profit margins as well.[2]

Adding new products by extending a familiar, established line or brand can minimize the risk that customers and channel partners may perceive in trying something new. Because of this familiarity, the product's introductory campaign is likely to be more efficient and may even cost less than for an entirely new brand or product in a new category. Your development costs may also be lower if you base a new product on an existing product.

Extensions that are well received will reinforce the brand, capture new customers and accommodate the variety-seeking behaviour of current customers. Extensions are not without risk, however. If you extend a line or brand, customers or channel members may become confused about the different products you offer. For example, will a co-branded Adidas/Mattel doll be successful? Remember that channel members with limited shelf or storage space may be reluctant to carry additional products. And if the product does not succeed, perceptions of the brand or the remaining products in the line may be affected.[3]

In particular, look closely at whether you are spreading your resources too thinly and at how each product or line will contribute to organizational objectives. Be ready to cut products or lines that do not perform as desired, as Heinz did by eliminating a line of unusually coloured and flavoured frozen chips – even as its green catsup was gaining popularity. The company is also reducing the number of product variations offered in European markets to make better use of the shelf space stores allot to its brands.[4]

Also manage your products with an eye toward minimizing product **cannibalization**, which occurs when one of your products takes sales from another of your products. A line extension may attract customers who previously purchased other products in the same line, for example. Still, marketers sometimes decide they can attract new customers, retain current customers or achieve other objectives only by cannibalizing their own products rather than risk having competitors lure customers away.

Product life-cycle decisions

As you plan, you must make decisions about how to manage the **product life cycle**, a product's movement through the market as it passes from introduction to growth, maturity and eventual decline. Although no individual product's life cycle is entirely pre-dictable or even necessarily sequential, the typical life cycle pictured in Figure 6.3 shows how sales and profitability can change in each part of the cycle. Corporate giants such as Heinz, Cadbury Schweppes and Unilever tend to have numerous products in targeted markets at one time, and each could very well be in a different part of its life cycle.

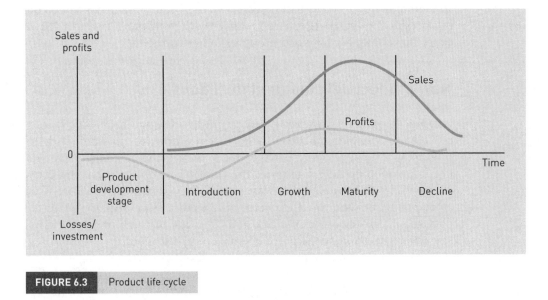

FIGURE 6.3 Product life cycle

Source: Philip Kotler, Veronica Wang, John Saunders and Gary Armstrong, *Principles of Marketing*, 4th edn (Harlow: Pearson Education, 2005), p. 604.

Analysing a product's life-cycle situation and using marketing activities actively to manage the cycle can help you plan to take advantage of anticipated ups and downs. Where is the product within its life cycle, how quickly is it progressing through each part of the cycle and what can marketers do either to alter the cycle or to get the most out of each part? As Figure 6.3 suggests, profitability is highest during the growth part of the life cycle and tends to decrease with maturity. This is why many companies plan strategies to extend or at least reinvigorate product growth.

Moreover, some products are reaching maturity much faster, compressing their life cycle. The DVD player, for instance, matured extremely quickly because of standardized components and technology; as more competitors entered the market and volume sky-rocketed, the average price dropped to little more than 10 per cent of the introductory price in only six years. Now manufacturers are extending the life cycle by introducing high-definition DVD players, even as a standards battle rages between Blu-ray and HD-DVD technology. Looking ahead, will wider availability of downloadable movies and television programmes push DVD players into decline?[5]

Be aware that product life cycle can vary by segment and by market. For instance, research shows that sales of new household products and foods tend to increase more rapidly and reach maturity earlier in the United Kingdom and the Netherlands than in France and Spain. Knowing this, marketers targeting UK and Dutch consumers would push for wide distribution by the launch date to build growth momentum early in a product's introduction stage.[6] On the other hand, home appliances and consumer electronics products tend to move into the growth stage earlier in Denmark, Norway and Sweden – in about four years – than in France, the United Kingdom and Greece, where accelerating growth takes more than six years. Thus, marketers should consider launching products in markets where faster growth is possible early in the life cycle, and expect to wait longer for rapid growth in other markets.[7]

New product development decisions

Having discovered promising opportunities during earlier stages of the planning process and analysed the life cycle of current products, you may decide to change your product mix by developing new products for targeted customer segments. Some products may open up new categories for your organization; other products may extend existing lines or brands. Either way, product development details are usually shown in an appendix or separate document, not in the main marketing plan. However, your plan should outline the major decisions, include research or other evidence, highlight key actions and outline the product development schedule.

Here is an overview of the new product development process:

1. *Generate ideas* from inside the organization and from customers, sales representatives, channel partners, suppliers, competitive materials and other sources. To do this, IBM invites 100,000 employees, customers and consultants to join a yearly online Innovation Jam.[8]

2. *Screen ideas* to eliminate those that are inappropriate or not feasible, given the organization's strengths, core competencies and resources.

3. *Develop and test product concepts* to find out whether customers (and perhaps influential channel members) perceive value in the remaining ideas and respond positively to them.

4. *Develop the marketing strategy* to clarify targeting, positioning and specific marketing plan objectives for the new product. Also outline the proposed marketing mix and project sales and profits.

5. *Analyse the business case* for introducing each new product, including associated costs, sales and profits, to gauge the contribution toward achieving organizational objectives.

6. *Develop the product* to see whether the concept is practical, cost-effective and meets customers' needs and expectations.

7. *Test market the product*, with associated marketing strategies, to assess the likelihood of market acceptance and success. Try different marketing activities, evaluate cus-

tomer response, anticipate competitors' reactions and adjust the product and marketing as needed.

8. *Launch the product commercially*, applying the lessons learned from test marketing and from previous product introductions.

New product development doesn't end with commercialization. You must monitor market response, including the reactions of customers, channel members and competitors. If you see that the product is not selling as well as projected, you will want to change the product or other elements of the marketing mix as needed. Research shows that the most successful new product innovations result from need identification, solution identification and marketing research. At the same time, the rate of new product failure is so high that you must carefully screen ideas to avoid investing in unpromising or unneeded products.[9]

Sweden's Electrolux approaches new product development from the perspective of meeting observed yet unstated consumer needs.

MARKETING IN PRACTICE: ELECTROLUX

Known for household appliances such as dishwashers and cookers, Electrolux visits consumers at home to learn how, when and why they use appliances. Design chief Henrik Otto and his team use four personas to represent distinct customer segments defined by personality and lifestyle, benefits expected, usage patterns and similar elements. Working with marketing experts, sales staff and engineers, the designers create a new product and ask consumers to try out the prototype. Otto notes that 'people want their personalities to be reflected by their appliances', which is why Electrolux pays close attention to both aesthetics and functionality. As a result, its newer products earn higher profit margins than products that have been in the product mix much longer. The company also holds a yearly contest to honour creative appliance ideas from design students.[10]

Don't forget the ecological and ethical issues related to your product. Can ecofriendly supplies and processes be incorporated? Will the product's production or use adversely affect the natural environment? How will the new product serve your organization's societal objectives? What ethical questions might arise (such as whether to test products on animals) and how can you address these in a satisfactory way? Thinking about water conservation, Electrolux created countertop dishwashers that small families can use to clean a few dishes without wasting a lot of water.

Whether you are developing new products or improving existing ones, you will seek the optimal combination of quality and performance, features and benefits, design, packaging, labelling and brand (*see* Figure 6.4). You want your product to be competitively distinctive, attractive and valuable to customers while returning profits to the organization. Be sure your product is competitively superior on features and benefits valued by

	Product 1	Product 2	Product 3
Quality (customers' view) and **performance** (objective measures)			
Features (and benefits delivered to satisfy customer needs)			
Design (for performance differentiation)			
Packaging (protect, store, facilitate use) and **labelling** (information, marketing communication)			
Brand (identity, differentiation, provoke response)			

FIGURE 6.4   Planning product attributes

customers; also check that the product supports your marketing plan objectives. At W.L. Gore, a US company known for innovation, executives assess product ideas by asking: 'Is the opportunity real? Is there really somebody out there that will buy this? Can we win? What do the economics look like? Can we make money doing this? Is it unique and valuable? Can we have a sustained advantage [such as a patent]?'[11]

Quality and performance decisions

Quality means different things to different people; this is why you should define a product's **quality** in terms of how well it satisfies the needs of your customers. From this perspective, a high-quality product is one that satisfies needs better than a poor-quality product. You can certainly use objective performance measures to demonstrate a product's functionality, reliability, sturdiness and lack of defects. In the marketplace, however, customers are the final judges of quality and decide for themselves what level of quality they want and will pay for.

Extremely affluent consumers may be satisfied only by exceptionally high performance and quality. Or, as Hewlett-Packard found out, far superior quality may not be necessary.

MARKETING IN PRACTICE: HEWLETT-PACKARD

At one time, Hewlett-Packard, the US marketer of printers, computers and related equipment, routinely designed printers to exactingly high standards, even though this drove up costs and prices. As lower-priced competing printers gained popularity, however, HP's marketers realized they were missing the segment of customers who want reasonable quality at a reasonable price. They redesigned HP's printers to eliminate non-essential features and incorporate lighter materials. Now the expanded product line includes smaller and lower-priced printers based on innovative, cost-effective technologies that provide value to consumers and business buyers. Even the ink cartridge packages have been redesigned with earth-friendly recycled materials.[12]

B2B marketers know that quality is essential to products such as computer chips, which are the heart of many technology products. For example, Intel is aware that business customers require consistently high performance so it meticulously controls its manufacturing process to maintain the same high quality whether its chips are made in Ireland, Vietnam or Arizona.[13] Before you introduce or even begin developing a new product, you have to ensure that the entire organization is capable of consistently delivering the expected quality, given the available resources and schedule. This, too, is part of the marketing planning process.

Feature and benefit decisions

Customers buy a product not only for the **features**– specific attributes that contribute to functionality– but also for the **benefits**– the need-satisfaction outcomes they want or expect. Hewlett-Packard's customers want quickly printed, clear documents; some may even quantify the benefits sought in terms of number of pages printed per minute. Those customers would want to know that HP's product line includes inkjet printers that can produce 71 pages per minute. When evaluating competing printers, customers look at whether each model has the features that provide the benefits they value. In practice, you should plan for features that deliver the benefits that you know your customers value (based on marketing research).

As Hewlett-Packard discovered, not all customers want or are willing to pay for the benefits provided by a particular product's features. In fact, too many features can make a product too complex or expensive for the targeted audience.[14] Different segments often have different needs and different perceptions of the value of features and benefits. Figure 6.5 shows, in simplified form, how Groupe Michelin, the French tyre maker, might match features to benefits that satisfy the needs of specific customer segments. You can see how Michelin could offer value and differentiate its tyres from those of competitors such as Goodyear.[15] Creating a similar matrix can help you pinpoint each segment's needs and identify features and benefits to satisfy those needs.

Customer segment and need	Feature and benefit
Lorry fleet owners who need to monitor tyre pressure and track the location of all tyres	Sensor patch on each tyre electronically transmits pressure and identification data to owners
Farmers who need to drive tractors over fields and in uneven terrain	Large, deep tyre patterns provide more secure road grip
Professional sports car drivers who seek winning performance	Special composition tyres for speed and handling

FIGURE 6.5   Matching features and benefits to needs

Features are as important for services as for physical goods. Jinjiang International, China's largest hotel chain, matches the features and furnishings of each of its 263 hotels with the needs of the targeted travellers, and then prices the accommodations accordingly. Before the Beijing Olympics and the Shanghai World Expo, Jinjiang opened new, no-frills, low-price hotels to accommodate thousands of budget-conscious travellers. It also renovated and updated its upmarket hotels for wealthy and executive travellers and raised the average room rate to 1,800 yuan (about €179).[16]

Design decisions

Directly or indirectly, customers' perceptions and buying choices are influenced to some degree by design. Moreover, your design decisions can affect the ecology as well as product performance. Therefore, as with all other product decisions, you should be sure that a product's design is consistent with your organization's marketing, financial and societal objectives and that it fits with your other marketing mix decisions. Ideally, design decisions should create a bridge to your future vision of how the product will benefit the target market. To illustrate, Nokia's senior consumer vision manager is responsible for guiding product designers toward a future in which consumers will use new-generation mobiles to connect, entertain and communicate at all times. Moreover, Nokia's designs are planned with fashion as well as functionality in mind.[17]

Your company may develop designs internally or hire outside design specialists. Denmark's Bang & Olufsen generates new product ideas and hires specialists to come up with designs that are aesthetically pleasing and technologically advanced as well as functional. 'If we have designers in-house, they tend to come too close to the technicians', explains the design and concepts director. 'That means they begin solving technical problems rather than focusing on the design.'[18] Bang & Olufsen also collaborates with other companies on product design; working with Korea's Samsung, it recently designed a stylish, premium-priced mobile for the luxury market.[19]

Product design has become such a prime point of differentiation, especially for mature products like household appliances, that everyday products need not be ordinary-looking. The sleek design lines of refrigerators made by China's Haier Group, for example, attract customers and help the company compete in the domestic market and internationally. In fact, the pressure of global competition has prompted many marketers to devote more time and resources to product design.[20]

Packaging and labelling decisions

Good packaging protects tangible goods, makes their use or storage more convenient for customers and, ideally, serves societal objectives such as ecological protection. For instance, Nike is reducing excess packaging and shipping costs by packaging some of its trainers in moulded cardboard containers that exactly fit the shoes, rather than in uniform rectangular shoeboxes.[21]

When planning for any product to be sold in a store, think carefully about how labelling can serve marketing functions. Labels are more than informative: they can capture the shopper's attention, describe how product features deliver benefits, differentiate the product from competing items and reinforce brand image.

Marketing functions aside, your labels must meet applicable laws and regulations. Cigarette marketers in the European Union, for instance, are required to devote 30 per cent of the front label and 40 per cent of the back label to health warnings. Also, labelling cannot use terminology implying that one type of cigarette is safer than others.[22] In Canada's Quebec province, multilingual labels must include a French equivalent for every word, printed in type that is as big as or bigger than the type used for other languages.

Use the following checklist as you proceed with product planning.

ESSENTIAL MARKETING PLAN CHECKLIST NO. 8:
PLANNING FOR PRODUCTS

Now that you've set specific objectives for your marketing plan, you need to begin planning for your products. This checklist will help you think through the main issues and decisions. Write your answers in the spaces provided and put a tick mark next to the questions as you complete each one. If your marketing plan is for a product not yet on the market, use this checklist to consider the key decisions you'll face in planning for a successful introduction.

☐ What is the current situation of each product within its line and the overall product mix?

☐ Would customers' needs and the organization's interests be served by changing the product mix, product lines or line depth?

☐ Where is each product in its life cycle and what are the implications for product planning?

☐ What new products can be developed to take advantage of promising opportunities in targeted segments?

☐ If you're planning a new product, how can you improve the odds of success as you move through each step in the development process?

☐ How might cannibalization be minimized following new product introductions?

☐ What are the ecological and ethical considerations associated with each product?

☐ How can you change quality and performance, features and benefits, design, packaging or labelling to provide more value for customers and your organization?

PLANNING FOR BRANDS

Branding is a pivotal aspect of product planning because it provides identity and competitive differentiation to stimulate customer response. An unbranded product is just a commodity, indistinguishable from competing products except in terms of price. A branded product may have the same attributes as competitors yet be seen as distinctly different (and provoke a different customer response) because of the rational or emotional value the brand adds in satisfying the customer's needs and wants.[23]

In planning for a brand, you should identify ways to increase **brand equity**, the extra value customers perceive in a brand that ultimately builds long-term loyalty. Higher brand equity contributes to sustained competitive advantage, attracts new channel partners and reinforces current channel relationships. It also enhances marketing power, allowing you to wring more productivity out of your marketing activities as customers (1) become aware of your brand and its identity, (2) know what the brand stands for, (3) respond to it and (4) want an ongoing relationship with it. The brand equity pyramid in Figure 6.6 illustrates these four levels leading to strong brand equity.

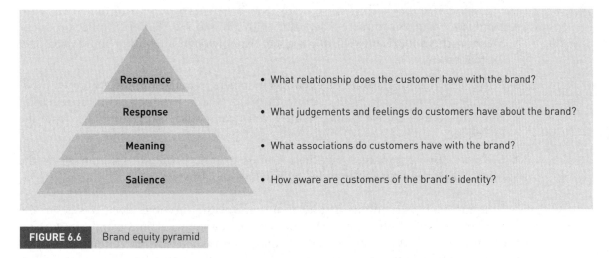

| **FIGURE 6.6** | Brand equity pyramid |

Source: After Kevin Lane Keller, *Strategic Brand Management*, 2nd edn (Upper Saddle River, NJ: Prentice Hall, 2003), p. 76.

Be aware that customers in the targeted segment may know the brand, understand what it stands for and respond to it – but not want the kind of ongoing relationship that the organization would like. The ultimate objective of brand planning is to move customers upward through the levels of brand equity and encourage them to remain at the top. This raises the customer's lifetime value to the organization and helps achieve your objectives. It is important to remember that companies benefit financially from brand equity, but the identity, meaning, response and relationships all derive from customer interaction with the brand.[24]

Brand identity

Here, you want to make customers in the targeted segment aware of your brand's identity. A brand can consist of words, numbers, symbols and/or graphics to add salience, such as the Nike name combined with its swoosh symbol or the Nestlé name combined with the nesting bird logo. You can develop or license a brand using one or more of the following approaches:

- *Company brand*. The company name becomes the brand, such as Sony and Starbucks. This associates the company's image with the product. If the company's image suffers, however, the brand is likely to feel the effect. Company brands are also known as *manufacturers' brands* or *national brands.*

- *Family or umbrella brand.* Each product in one or more lines or categories is identified as belonging to that particular brand family (or being under that brand umbrella). For example, Toyota puts the Lexus brand on a family of vehicles; Anheuser-Busch puts the Budweiser brand on a family of beers.

- *Individual brand.* A product is identified with a brand not shared by other products. The household lubricant WD-40 is a good example of an individual brand used only for that product.

- *Private brand.* Retailers and other channel members frequently brand their own products for differentiation from manufacturers' branded products. The supermarket chain Tesco uses Finest as its private brand; competitor Sainsbury uses Taste the Difference.

- *Co-brand.* Two companies put their brands on one product. An example is the MasterCard credit card co-branded by Barclays and Travelocity.

Bringing customers to this first level of brand equity involves decisions about the brand itself as well as other product attributes and marketing actions. For example, how can you use product packaging and labelling to convey a distinctive brand identity? Coca-Cola (ranked by some as the world's most valuable brand) uses hourglass bottles and red-and-white labelling to set its colas apart from other soft drinks. You can also build customers' awareness of the brand through advertising, in-store promotions, websites and other marketing activities that reinforce the differentiation. Customers who are unaware of a brand will not think of it when purchasing, which is why organizations often set marketing objectives for awareness. Establishing a brand identity and making customers aware of it is a prelude to creating brand meaning.

Brand meaning

The second level of brand equity is to shape the associations that customers have with your brand. What do you want the brand to stand for? What image or personality does the brand have, and is it the same as what you want to create? This is an especially important point when considering brand extensions. For example, the motorcycle manufacturer Harley-Davidson earns about 20 per cent of its revenues from extensions such as leather jackets. But experts doubt that its Xtreme Image cake-decorating kit reflects the brand's image of hard-driving independence, even though the kit is intended to appeal to women motorcycle riders.[25]

Once customers understand a brand's meaning, they come to rely on it as a shortcut when making buying choices, which expedites the buying process and reduces the perceived risk. You can mould brand meaning through positioning and through favourable associations backed up by product performance, features that deliver value through need satisfaction, distinctive design and so on. As with brand identity, other marketing activities are involved, as well.

Brand response

The third level of brand equity relates to customer response. Once customers are aware of the brand's identity and understand its meaning, they can make up their minds about the brand. Ideally, you want your customers to believe in your brand, trust it and perceive it as embodying positive qualities. You also want customers to see the brand as competitively superior and, just as important, have an emotional connection to it. Determining customer response requires marketing research, followed up by action steps either to reinforce positive responses or to turn negative (or neutral) responses into positive ones through marketing activities.

Marketers for Campbell's Soup recently faced the problem of a less enthusiastic response to the company's tinned condensed soups. 'I've got millions of households every week buying the product, despite the fact that we've priced too aggressively, that we haven't innovated, that we've allowed the quality gap between ourselves and alternatives to shrink', says Campbell's CEO.[26] To reignite brand perceptions of quality and competitive superiority, the company has devised new cooking methods, improved its recipes, created new easy-open packaging and added lower-sodium selections for health-conscious consumers.[27]

Brand relationship

The fourth level of brand equity deals with customers' relationship to the brand. They know about the brand, know what it means to them and how they feel about it. But are they sufficiently attached to remain loyal buyers? You want to encourage strong and enduring brand relationships because loyal customers tend to buy more, resist switching to competing brands and be willing to pay a premium for the brand and recommend it to others.[28] The issue is therefore how you can use your product plan, along with other marketing-mix activities, to reinforce customers' brand preference and loyalty.

One approach is to improve or at least maintain product quality and performance to avoid disappointing customers, tarnishing the brand and discouraging customer loyalty. Another is to add products or features that better satisfy current customers' needs. A third is to continue introducing innovative or upgraded product designs, packaging and labelling consistent with the brand image. Finally, your marketing plan should allow for research to see how effective you have been in moving customers up the brand equity pyramid toward sustained customer loyalty. Use the following checklist as you plan for your brand.

ESSENTIAL MARKETING PLAN CHECKLIST NO. 9:
PLANNING FOR BRANDS

Planning for brands must be carefully coordinated with planning for products. This brief checklist can help you think about your branding decisions and about how your product will support your brand. Note your answers in the spaces provided, putting a tick mark next to the questions as you answer them.

☐ How is the brand identified and what are the implications for its image?

_____

☐ How is the brand positioned for competitive differentiation?

_____

☐ How do product attributes support the brand image?

_____

☐ Are customers aware of the brand? If so, what does it mean to them? How can brand awareness be expanded through marketing?

_____

☐ What do customers think and feel about the brand? What relationship do they have or want with it?

_____

☐ How can brand preference and loyalty be encouraged through marketing?

_____

Source: Adapted from Kevin Lane Keller, *Strategic Brand Management*, 2nd edn (Upper Saddle River, NJ: Prentice Hall, 2003), Chapter 2.

CHAPTER SUMMARY

Planning for products includes decisions about the product mix (the assortment of product lines being offered), product line length (the number of items in each line) and product line depth (the number of product variations within a line). The product life cycle is a product's market movement as it progresses from introduction to growth, maturity and decline. In new product development, marketers: (1) generate ideas; (2) screen ideas; (3) research customer reaction to ideas; (4) develop the marketing strategy; (5) analyse the business case; (6) develop the product to determine practicality; (7) test market the product; (8) commercialize it. Then they monitor market response.

Decisions must be made about product quality and performance, features and benefits, design, packaging and labelling, and branding. Quality should be seen in terms of how well a product satisfies customer needs. Features are attributes that contribute to product functionality and deliver benefits. Design is especially important for differentiation. Packaging protects products and facilitates their use or storage. Labels provide information, attract attention, describe features and benefits, differentiate products and reinforce brand image. Branding identifies a product and differentiates it from competing products to stimulate customer response. Brand equity is the extra value customers perceive in a brand that builds long-term loyalty and boosts competitive advantage.

CASE STUDY: PHILIPS REFINES ITS BRAND IMAGE

Philips Electronics, based in the Netherlands, is rethinking its brand image to compete more effectively in the consumer and business markets. Philips' product mix consists of consumer and professional lighting products; home appliances and home entertainment products; and medical systems for hospitals and clinics. In the past, many of the company's strongest brands were individual brands, such as Norelco. Now the company name is being added to some product lines, resulting in brands like Philips Norelco, to strengthen brand salience.

Although research indicates that the targeted segments have a positive image of the brand, Philips also wants to sharpen its differentiation by refining the brand's associations. 'Philips already has an image of being reliable and trustworthy, and that gives us a great base on which to build', notes the head of global management. 'But we're not perceived as exciting or innovative in the minds of our consumers, even though we are constantly innovating. So we need to change that perception.'[29]

At the same time, Philips' marketers recognize that many products are overburdened with features that confuse customers. In response, the company is using customer-friendly design to heighten the 'sense and simplicity' of its products. Its four-member Simplicity Advisory Board, which consists of a fashion designer, an architect, a professor and a graphic designer, is on call to keep Philips focused on stylish yet easy-to-use functionality. Innovation is still a priority, but in the interest of simplicity rather than for the sake of new technology and complex features. The chief marketing officer explains: 'In the past, companies just developed the technology and hoped someone would buy it. Now we are starting from the point of discovering what exactly consumers want a product to do.'[30]

Case questions

1. What are the arguments for and against Philips adding the company brand to its individual brands (as in Philips Norelco)?

2. How is Philips integrating product and brand planning – and why?

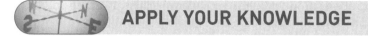

APPLY YOUR KNOWLEDGE

Select an organization offering a branded good or service with which you are familiar and research its product and brand. Summarize your findings in a brief oral presentation or written report.

- From a customer's perspective, how would you describe the product's quality and performance? Do you think this perception of value matches what the marketer intended?

- How do the features deliver benefits to satisfy needs of the targeted customer segments?

- How do design, packaging and labelling contribute to your reaction, as a customer, to this product?

- Where does this product appear to be in its life cycle? How do you know?

- How would you describe this product's brand? What is the organization doing to build brand equity?

BUILD YOUR OWN MARKETING PLAN

Going back to the marketing plan you've been preparing, is your product a tangible good or an intangible service? What level of quality is appropriate (and affordable) to meet the needs of the targeted customer segments? What needs do customers satisfy through products such as yours and what features must your product have in order to deliver the expected or desired benefits? What can you do with design, packaging and labelling to add value and differentiate your product? What brand image do you want to project? How do you want customers to feel about the brand and react toward it? What can you do to encourage brand loyalty? Think about your answers in the context of your earlier ideas and decisions, then draft the product and brand sections of your marketing plan.

STOP ENDNOTES

1. 'Mattel Dolls to Wear Adidas Brand', *Marketing Week*, 11 January 2007, p. 10; Christopher C. Williams, 'Barron's Insight: Adidas Is Pushing Its Game', *Wall Street Journal*, 12 November 2006, p. 2; Richard Siklos, 'A Virtual World But Real Money', *New York Times*, 19 October 2006, p. C1.

2. Matthew Boyle, 'Chew on This', *Fortune*, 4 September 2006, pp. 41ff; Kate Norton, 'A Bubbly 2007 for Cadbury Schweppes?', *BusinessWeek Online*, 6 December 2006, www.businessweek.com.

3. Kevin Lane Keller, *Strategic Brand Management*, 2nd edn (Upper Saddle River, NJ: Prentice Hall, 2003), pp. 582–91.

4. James Durston, 'Has Heinz Bottled It in Europe?', *Grocer*, 3 June 2006, pp. 32ff; Kevin O'Donnell, 'Green Ketchup Works, But Not on Blue Fries', *Brandweek*, 1 September 2003, p. 17; Sian Harrington, 'Sharper NPD at Heinz', *Grocer*, 21 June 2003, pp. 10ff.

5. Dylan McGrath, 'High-Def DVD War Is High-Stakes Fight', *Electronic Engineering Times*, 15 January 2007, pp. 1ff; Adam Lashinsky, 'Shootout in Gadget Land', *Fortune*, 10 November 2003, pp. 74ff.

6. Caroline Parry, 'New! Nouveau! Nieuw!', *Marketing Week*, 19 June 2003, p. 30.

7. 'When Will It Fly?', *The Economist*, 9 August 2003, p. 51.

8. Jessi Hempel, 'Big Blue Brainstorm', *BusinessWeek*, 7 August 2006, p. 70.

9. 'Expect the Unexpected', *The Economist*, 6 September 2003, p. 5.

10. Quoted in Ariane Sains and Stanley Reed, 'Electrolux Redesigns Itself', *BusinessWeek IN*, November 2006, pp. 12ff; also: Michael Rudnick, 'Electrolux's Sales in Major Appliances Slip 3.5 Percent in Third Quarter', *HFN*, 6 November 2006, p. 22; 'Electrolux Design Lab Announces Winning Product', *Appliance*, January 2007, p. S3.

11. Ann Harrington, 'Who's Afraid of a New Product?', *Fortune*, 10 November 2003, pp. 189ff.

12. Patrick Hoffman, 'HP Rolls Out Eco-Friendly Ink Cartridge Packaging', *eWeek*, 9 February 2007, http://www.eweek.com/article2/0,1759.2092886, 00.asp; 'Hewlett-Packard Co.: Firm Unveils New Technology Allowing High-Volume Inkjets', *Wall Street Journal*, 4 October 2006, p. B18; Noshua Watson, 'What's Wrong with This Printer?', *Fortune*, 17 February 2003, pp. 120C–120H.

13. 'The Problem with Made in China: Manufacturing in Asia', *The Economist (US)*, 13 January 2007, p. 68ff; Eric Pfeiffer, 'Chip Off the Old Block', *Business 2.0*, July 2003, pp. 54–5.

14. Roland T. Rust, Debora Viana Thompson and Rebecca W. Hamilton, 'Feature Bloat: The Product Manager's Dilemma', *Harvard Business School Working Knowledge*, 8 May 2006, hbswk.hbs.edu.

15. 'In-Tire Sensor Redesigned', *Fleet Owner*, 1 December 2006, n.p.; Ian Morton, 'Michelin System Will Check, Inflate Tyres', *Automotive News*, 21 July 2003, p. 22; 'Keeping Michelin on a Roll', *Business Week*, 7 July 2003, p. 46.

16. 'Jinjiang to Use IPO Funds for Hotel Facelift', *Business Daily Update*, 30 November 2006, n.p.; 'China's Budget Hotels Fill Up', *Wall Street Journal*, 27 November 2006, p. C8.

17. Cassell Bryan-Low, 'Nokia Aims at Rivals with Slimmer Phone', *Wall Street Journal*, 8 January 2007, p. A3; Jack Ewing, 'Staying Cool at Nokia', *BusinessWeek*, 17 July 2006, pp. 62–5.

18. Quoted in Poul Funder Larsen, 'Better Is . . . Better', *Wall Street Journal*, 22 September 2003, pp. R6, R11.

19. Evan Ramstad, 'The Cellphone Wears Prada', *Wall Street Journal*, 19 January 2007, p. B5.

20. Michael Rudnick, 'Sanyo Teams With Haier to Produce Refrigerators', *HFN*, 13 November 2006, p. 31; Michael Winnick, '5 Secrets to a Successful Launch', *Business 2.0*, September 2006, pp. 93ff; Frederick Balfour, 'China's Dream Team', *BusinessWeek*, 1 September 2003, pp. 50–1.

21. Nancy Einhart, 'Are Your Competitors Packing?', *Business 2.0*, July 2003, p. 52.

22. 'EU's Tobacco Clamp Upheld', *Grocer*, 14 December 2002, p. 9.

23. This section draws on concepts discussed in Keller, *Strategic Brand Management*, Chapters 1 and 2 (see note 3).

24. Don E. Schultz, 'Branding Geometry', *Marketing Management*, September–October 2003, pp. 8–9.

25. Lucas Conley, 'When Brand Extensions Go Bad', *Fast Company*, October 2006, p. 38; Kenneth Hein, 'Brand Extensions Can Go Too Far', *Adweek*, 5 December 2005, p. 8.

26. Quoted in Sarah Ellison, 'Inside Campbell's Big Bet: Heating Up Condensed Soup', *Wall Street Journal*, 31 July 2003, pp. B1–B2.

27. Adrienne Carter, 'Lighting a Fire Under Campbell', *Business Week*, 4 December 2006, pp. 96ff; see note 26 – Ellison, 'Inside Campbell's Big Bet: Heating Up Condensed Soup'.

28. 'New Customer Research on Customer Referrals, Commitment, Loyalty', *Report on Customer Relationship Management*, August 2003, pp. 2ff.

29. Quote reported in: Rina Chandran, 'Philips to Rework Brand Positioning', *Asia Africa Intelligence Wire*, 23 August 2003, n.p.

30. Quote reported in: Kerry Capell, 'Thinking Simple at Philips', *BusinessWeek*, 11 December 2006, p. 50. Also: Nelson D. Schwartz, 'Lighting Up Philips', *Fortune International*, 22 January 2007, p. 43ff; 'Cover Story: The Simple Life', *PR Week*, 29 January 2007, p. 15.

7

Planning for pricing

Comprehension outcomes

After studying this chapter, you will be able to:

- Explain how customers' perceptions of value affect price decisions
- Identify external and internal influences on pricing
- Understand pricing for new products
- Describe how to adapt prices

Application outcomes

After studying this chapter, you will be able to:

- Analyse the influences on your pricing decisions
- Set appropriate pricing objectives
- Make planning decisions about product pricing

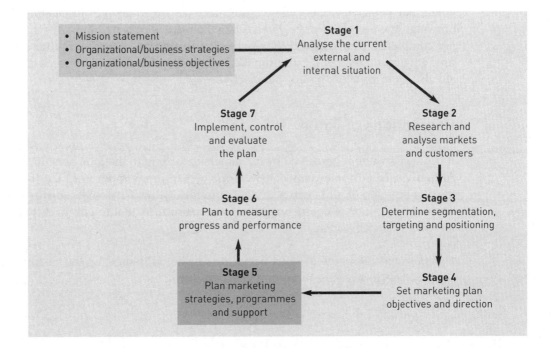

CHAPTER PREVIEW

The global market leaders in personal computers are Hewlett-Packard, Dell, Lenovo and . . . Acer. Based in Taiwan, Acer has emphasized pricing in its marketing plan to boost turnover and spread its brand around the world. It's already the top-selling laptop brand in Europe but is seeking a higher share in China and other markets by pricing its PCs at least 5 per cent below competing PCs. Acer's success shows how price can be used to achieve such marketing objectives as increasing market share and strengthening competitive position. Price is also the key to achieving financial objectives such as sales and profitability targets. Despite its low prices, Acer is profitable, although its margins are much lower than those of the top three market leaders.[1]

Whereas the company spends money on other marketing-mix elements, it actually makes money through pricing. Nonetheless, ultimately it is the consumer or business customer who determines whether the price of an offer represents real value. Therefore, this chapter begins with a discussion of how customers perceive value and the difference between cost-based and value-based pricing, which is essential to planning for effective pricing. The next section explains the various external and internal influences on pricing that you must consider when preparing a marketing plan. The final section discusses how to handle specific pricing decisions, including setting pricing objectives, pricing new products, pricing multiple products and adapting prices.

UNDERSTANDING PRICE AND VALUE

Whether the price is a pound sterling, a euro or a bag of rice, customers will buy only when they perceive value – when a product's perceived benefits in meeting their needs outweigh the perceived price. Even when the price is collected in barter, customers will not complete a transaction if they perceive insufficient value. No matter what type of product you market, you cannot make planning decisions about price without looking at value from your customers' perspective.

Perceptions of value

A product's value is perceived by customers according to the total benefits they receive. An individual customer may consider one benefit more important than the others, but the combination of all benefits is what provides value. Customers form value perceptions in the context of competing or substitute products that might meet their needs, on the basis of benefits such as:

- *Performance*. Does the product perform as it should in meeting the customer's needs? Does it perform better than competing products?

- *Features*. Does the product have all the features expected or desired to meet current needs and future or unspoken needs? How do the features compare with those of competing products?

- *Quality*. Is the product defect-free, reliable and durable, compared with competing products?

- *Service*. Does the service meet customers' expectations? Is it faster, more convenient or more personalized than that offered by competitors?

- *Personal benefits*. Does the product deliver personal benefits such as status or self-expression?

- *Availability*. Is the product available whenever needed? Does the price change according to availability? How does this compare with that of competing products?

Against the total perceived benefits, customers weigh the total perceived costs (time and money) associated with the product, including:

- *Initial purchase price*. What time and money must the customer spend to obtain the product initially? How does the purchase price compare with competing products?

- *Maintenance and repair costs*. What is the estimated cost of maintenance over the product's life? How often is maintenance or repair generally required and how much time or money might the customer lose while waiting for repairs or maintenance?

- *Ongoing fees*. Does the product require an annual usage charge or other fees after the initial purchase? Must the customer pay a tax to continue using or possessing the product?

- *Installation*. Does the product require installation? What is the cost in time and money for installing this product compared with competing products?

- *Training*. Do customers need training to use the product properly and if so, what is the cost in time and money compared with competing products?

- *Ancillary products*. Does the product require the purchase of ancillary products, and at what cost? How does this compare with competing products?

- *Financing*. If applicable, what is the cost of financing the purchase of this product, what is the monthly payment (if any) and how do such costs compare with those of competing products?

Pricing based on value

Through research, you can determine how customers in your targeted segment(s) perceive the value of your product's total benefits and costs and the value of competing products. Then you can use this understanding of the customer's perspective to plan your pricing as well as your costs and your product design (*see* Figure 7.1a). This is not the way marketers have traditionally planned for pricing. In the past, most started with the product and its cost, developed a pricing plan to cover costs and then looked for ways to communicate value to customer (*see* Figure 7.1b).[2]

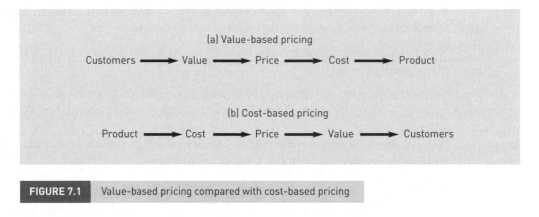

| **FIGURE 7.1** | Value-based pricing compared with cost-based pricing |

Source: Adapted from Thomas T. Nagle and John E. Hogan, *The Strategy and Tactics of Pricing*, 4th edn (Upper Saddle River, NJ: Pearson Prentice Hall, 2006), p. 4.

Consider how IKEA uses value-based pricing.

MARKETING IN PRACTICE: IKEA

Illustrating the trend toward value-based pricing, the Swedish furniture retailer IKEA starts by identifying a customer problem, such as the need for affordable, stylish, smaller-size furniture suitable for entertaining visitors in the kitchen. Its marketers examine value perceptions and competitive pricing, then set a target price lower than rivals. After estimating costs and setting product specifications appropriate for the target price, they consult with suppliers and come to agreement on costs. Finally, they design the product, have it manufactured, then pack and ship the furniture to stores as inexpensively and expeditiously as possible. Thanks to careful pricing, IKEA has been able to expand to more than 250 stores in 34 nations and sell products online as well.[3]

ANALYSING INFLUENCES ON PRICING DECISIONS

Notice how IKEA looks closely at customer needs and at the competition (external influences) as well as its costs (an internal influence). As you prepare your marketing plan, you must consider a number of external and internal influences on pricing decisions.

External influences

Among the major external influences on pricing are: (1) customers; (2) market and demand; (3) competition; (4) channel members; and (5) legal, regulatory and ethical considerations.

Customers

Not all customers can or want to compare prices; not all customers are interested in buying the lowest-priced alternative. Research shows that consumers will accept a price if it is within what they consider an acceptable range for that good or service.[4] Customers may decide against buying a product that is priced unusually low because they suspect poor quality yet be willing to spend more if a product appears to offer value-added benefits, such as a prestige brand or special service.

Business buyers in particular may feel pressure to acquire raw materials, components or services at the lowest possible prices, which in turn affects their suppliers' pricing strategies. Some business buyers and consumers constantly switch brands or suppliers in search of bargains, especially now that they can quickly and easily compare prices online. Your challenge as a marketer is to communicate your product's benefits so customers recognize the differentiation and perceive the value in relation to the price.

If your product is particularly innovative or meets unspoken customer needs, you may have to go against long-established traditions of pricing and service levels. For example, the founder of Japan's QB Net barbershops was accustomed to paying 3,000 yen or more for a traditional hour-long haircut with personal service. In a hurry during one such haircut, he wondered how many men shared his need for speed. When he asked people if they would be interested in a 10-minute haircut for 1,000 yen, he got such a positive reaction that he started QB Net. Today the chain has grown to 375 stores around Asia and serves 10 million customers annually in Japan alone.[5]

Market and demand

You also need to research the **demand** for your product in the target market – how many units are likely to be sold at different prices – and the effect of price sensitivity, or the **elasticity of demand**. When your research reveals **elastic demand**, a small percentage change in price will usually produce a large change in quantity demanded. On the other hand, if your research reveals **inelastic demand**, a small percentage change in price will usually produce a small percentage change in quantity demanded (*see* Figure 7.2).

Note that you can actually maintain or increase revenues by raising the price when demand is inelastic or by cutting the price when demand is elastic. Still, if you price a product excessively high you risk reducing demand; price it too low and you may spark strong demand that you cannot profitably satisfy. Yet it can be difficult to research the exact elasticity of demand for a particular product, even though you can conduct pricing experiments and analyse previous sales history to get data for estimating the elasticity of demand. Remember that elasticity of demand can vary widely from one segment to another and one market to another.

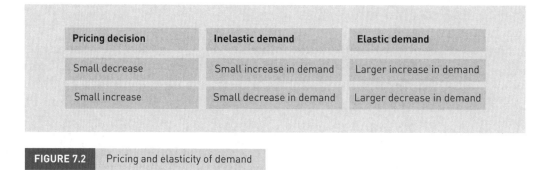

Pricing decision	Inelastic demand	Elastic demand
Small decrease	Small increase in demand	Larger increase in demand
Small increase	Small decrease in demand	Larger decrease in demand

FIGURE 7.2 Pricing and elasticity of demand

Competition

Whether the product is furniture or haircuts, competition exerts a strong influence on pricing decisions. Customers look at the costs and benefits of competing products when thinking about value, so be aware of what competitors are charging. However, it's risky to imitate another organization's pricing simply for competitive reasons, because your organization probably has very different costs, objectives and resources from those of your rival.

Should you become involved in a price war, your profit margins and prices will fall lower and lower. Another risk is that your product could face price competition from products that meet customers' needs in different ways, as when travellers can choose between air travel and train travel. In the planning process, therefore, you should consider any substitutes your customers might choose to meet their needs and how these choices could affect your pricing decisions.

Channel members

When making channel arrangements, you must ensure that wholesalers and retailers can buy at a price that will allow profitable resale to business customers or consumers. Channel members have to be able to cover the costs they incur in processing customer orders, repackaging bulk shipment lots into customer-size lots, product storage and other operations. To make this work, you have to think carefully about the costs and profit margins of all channel participants, along with the price perceptions of the targeted customer segment, when setting your product's price.

Even your choice of intermediaries depends on your product's price. If you market high-quality, high-priced products, you will have difficulty reaching your targeted segment through intermediaries known for stocking low-quality, low-priced products. If you market lower-quality, low-priced products, upmarket stores will not stock your products because of the mismatch with their target market. In short, carefully coordinate your channel decisions with your price decisions.

Legal, regulatory and ethical considerations

You will have to abide by local, national and regional laws and regulations when pricing your products. Among the issues are:

- *Price controls and price fixing.* Some countries control the prices of products such as prescription drugs, which limits pricing choices. Some areas also forbid the use of price fixing and other actions considered anti-competitive.

- *Resale maintenance.* Companies in the United Kingdom, the United States and some other nations are generally not allowed to insist that channel members maintain a certain minimum price on their products. This paves the way for more competition and reinforces the need to consider pricing throughout the channel.

- *Industry regulation.* Government regulators can affect pricing in some industries by allowing or blocking the sale of certain products or bundles.

- *Government requirements.* Legal and regulatory actions can affect pricing by mandating product standards, tests or labelling; these requirements add to the costs that you will seek to recoup through product pricing.

- *Taxes and tariffs.* Prices for products sold in certain countries must include value-added tax (VAT) or sales taxes, which vary from nation to nation. In addition, import tariffs also raise the price that customers pay for some products.

Going beyond legal and regulatory guidelines, look at the ethical implications. For example, is an airline or bank acting ethically when it promotes a special price without fully and prominently explaining any restrictions and extra fees? Is a pharmaceutical manufacturer acting ethically when it sets high prices for a life-saving drug that patients in some areas cannot afford? As challenging as such issues may be, building a reputation for ethical pricing ultimately enhances your brand's image and reinforces long-term customer loyalty.

Internal influences

Your pricing decisions will be affected by these major internal influences: (1) organizational and marketing plan objectives; (2) costs; (3) targeting and positioning; (4) product decisions and life cycle; and (5) other marketing-mix decisions.

Organizational and marketing plan objectives

Price and every other marketing-mix element must tie back to the objectives of the organization and the marketing plan. Because price generates revenue, it is a particularly important ingredient for achieving sales and profitability targets as well as for meeting societal objectives. If growth and market share are your key objectives, you might lower the product's price and reduce its perceived benefits or develop an entirely new product with fewer benefits that can be marketed at a lower price. Or you might develop a new product designed to sell for less as a way of meeting customer needs, as Nokia did by creating basic handsets for first-time mobile phone customers in India and other markets.[6]

Costs

Most companies price their products to cover costs, at least over the long run. In the short term, however, you may be willing to price for little or no profit when establishing a new product, competing with aggressive rivals or seeking to achieve another objective. When you have limited control over the **variable costs** that vary with production and sales, such as the cost of raw materials and parts, you will find pricing for profit even more challenging. For example, the sweets manufacturer Hershey recently experienced an increase in cocoa costs. Although the company had not raised the price of its chocolate candy bars for years, it finally decided on an 11 per cent increase. To pave the way for customer reception of this increase, the company promoted special 'limited edition' versions of Kit-Kat and other candy bars. As a result, sales increased 3 per cent during the three months following the price hike.[7]

If you compete primarily on the basis of price, you will be particularly concerned with managing variable costs and **fixed costs** (such as rent, insurance and other business expenses, which do not vary with production and sales). This keeps prices low and protects profit margins, as illustrated by Colruyt.

MARKETING IN PRACTICE: COLRUYT

Franz Colruyt, the Belgian discount food chain, looks for every possible way to minimize costs so it can keep grocery prices low. Its 165 stores have no fancy decorations, background music or shopping bags for customers to use. Instead of spending heavily on advertising, Colruyt invites customers to sign up to receive notices of forthcoming sales. To keep its prices competitive, 15 employees check prices at rival stores every day. The chain also publicizes a special hot-line number for customers to call if they find an item is being sold elsewhere for less. This reassures shoppers that Colruyt's prices are the lowest and encourages customer loyalty. Now Colruyt plans to open new stores in the Netherlands and Luxembourg.[8]

Although you may have difficulty determining a product's exact costs – especially if it has not yet been launched in the marketplace – you need cost information to calculate the **break-even point**. This is the point at which a product's revenues and costs are equal and beyond which the organization earns more profit as more units are sold. Unless you make some change in price (which will affect demand) or variable cost, your product will not become profitable until unit volume reaches the break-even point. The equation for this calculation is:

$$\text{break-even point} = \frac{\text{total fixed costs}}{\text{unit price} - \text{variable costs per unit}}$$

If, for example, a product's total fixed costs are €100,000, and one unit's variable costs are €2, the break-even point at a unit price of €6 is:

$$\frac{€100,000}{€6 - €2} = 25,000 \text{ units}$$

Using this break-even point, the organization will incur losses if it sells fewer than 25,000 units priced at €6. Above 25,000 units, however, the company can cover both variable and fixed costs and increase its profits as it sells a higher quantity. Figure 7.3 is a graphical depiction of break-even analysis, which does not take into account any changes in demand; how competitors might respond; how customers perceive the product's value; or other external influences on pricing. Nor does break-even analysis reflect how the cost per unit is likely to drop as you produce higher quantities and gain economies of scale. Still, it provides a rough approximation of the unit sales volume that you must achieve to cover costs and begin producing profit, which is important for planning purposes.

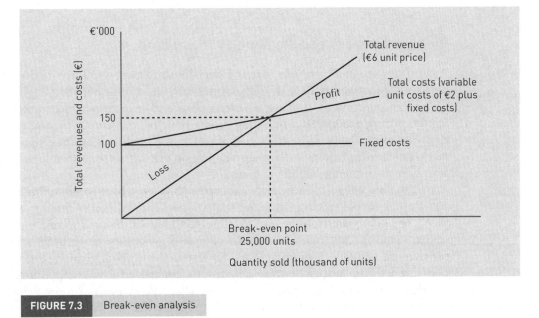

FIGURE 7.3　Break-even analysis

Targeting and positioning

Any pricing decisions should be consistent with your targeting and positioning decisions. For example, the grocery chain Aldi targets price-conscious consumers but positions itself as marketing good-quality food products for less. In line with this targeting and positioning, the retailer sets low prices and adjusts all its activities to keep costs as low as possible. When Aldi opened a city centre store in Manchester, its marketing plan targeted affluent shoppers in particular, because this segment is interested in upmarket foods at discount prices.[9]

Of course, if you're targeting non-price-sensitive customer segments and your positioning is upmarket, you will plan your pricing very differently.

MARKETING IN PRACTICE: VERTU

Vertu, a division of Finland's Nokia, sells a line of expensive mobile phone handsets that are both chic and functional. The limited edition Signature Cobra, encrusted with rubies, diamonds and emeralds, carries a price tag of more than £160,000. Vertu handsets are positioned as upmarket fashion accessories for celebrities and other wealthy customers, with a special service component. Users can reach Vertu's concierge staff with one button and request help (in five languages) with restaurant reservations, airline tickets and other arrangements anywhere in the world. The high prices support the brand's luxury positioning and exclusivity.[10]

Product decisions and life cycle

As you can see in Figure 7.1a, pricing decisions are closely intertwined with product decisions. More companies are developing new products after they have determined customers' perceptions of value, set target costs and set a target price, rather than starting the pricing process after initiating production. Of course your pricing decisions will change during the product life cycle. As discussed below, you may start with either market-skimming pricing or market-penetration pricing when launching a new product and then make changes in other stages.

By the time your product reaches the growth stage where competition is increasing, you should choose pricing strategies that support more differentiation in targeted segments or pricing strategies geared to stimulating higher demand for more economies of scale and lower costs (or a combination of both).[11] As one example, BMW's Mini Cooper car remains so well differentiated as it matures through its growth stage that the car does not need drastic price cuts to sell, despite intense industry competition.[12]

Sales of a product in maturity will grow less rapidly even as more competitors are vying for the attention of customers, which necessitates another change in your pricing plan. Figure 7.4 shows five options for pricing mature products, suggested by pricing experts Thomas Nagle and John Hogan.

Pricing alternatives	Purpose
Unbundle and price products individually	Compete by pricing goods and services individually rather than as a bundle
Re-examine customer price sensitivity and change price accordingly	Maintain or improve revenue and profits
Set prices based on better understanding of costs and capacity	Reflect realistic costs and earn more profit at times when demand outstrips capacity
Add related products	Leverage success of an existing product by adding related goods or services at a profit
Change channel pricing	Expand channel coverage while reducing channel margins

FIGURE 7.4 Pricing mature products

Source: Adapted from Thomas T. Nagle and John E. Hogan, *The Strategy and Tactics of Pricing*, 4th edn (Upper Saddle River, NJ: Pearson Prentice Hall, 2006), pp. 275–7.

Use the following checklist as you consider pricing decisions during marketing planning.

ESSENTIAL MARKETING PLAN CHECKLIST NO. 10:
PRICING THROUGH THE PRODUCT LIFE CYCLE

Whether your marketing plan is for a new product or an existing product, you will face pricing decisions as it moves through its life cycle. The following questions are a good starting point for considering key issues in pricing at each point in the life cycle. Place a tick mark alongside the questions that apply to your situation as you note your answers in the space provided.

☐ At introduction, how can pricing be used to encourage channel acceptance of a new product?

_____

☐ At introduction, what pricing approach will stimulate product trial and repeat purchasing among customers?

_____

☐ At introduction, how can pricing be used to manage initial supply and demand?

_____

☐ During growth, how can pricing be used for competitive purposes?

_____

☐ During growth, what pricing approach will lead to break-even and profitability?

_____

☐ In maturity, how can pricing encourage customer loyalty and defend market share?

_____

☐ In maturity, what pricing approach will achieve sustained profitability and other objectives?

_____

☐ In maturity, what pricing approach will support expanded channel coverage?

_____

☐ In decline, what pricing approach might slow the slide of unit sales and protect profits?

_____

☐ In decline, how can pricing be used for profit as competitors withdraw from the market?

_____

Other marketing-mix decisions

In addition to product decisions and channel arrangements, planning for pricing is influenced by (and influences) planning for marketing communications. Obviously, many producers and channel members feature pricing in their promotions to attract customer attention and compete with direct rivals. Although marketers of luxury products may not make price as visible a part of their promotion activities, their pricing decisions will be affected by the benefits and value they emphasize in their marketing communications. In short, be sure your pricing fits with the other decisions you include in your marketing plan.

MAKING PRICING DECISIONS

Once you understand the external and internal influences on pricing, you can set pricing objectives for the period covered by the marketing plan. If your product is new, you will decide between market-skimming and market-penetration pricing. As your product line expands, you will face decisions about pricing multiple products and you may need to plan to adapt your product's price.

Setting pricing objectives

Your objectives for pricing will be based on your organization's objectives and those of the marketing plan. There are three categories of pricing objectives:

- *Financial objectives for pricing.* You may seek to maintain or improve profits; maintain or improve revenues; reach the break-even point by a certain date; support another product's revenues and profitability; or achieve a certain return.

- *Marketing objectives for pricing.* Here, you set relationship targets for pricing that will attract or retain customers; build or defend market share; build or change channel relations; or build brand image, awareness and loyalty.

- *Societal objectives for pricing.* You may set targets for covering the cost of using ecologically friendly materials and processes; providing reverse channels for recycling; generating cash for charitable contributions; or achieving other non-business objectives.

To illustrate, London is one of a growing number of cities that has set the societal objective of using pricing to reduce traffic jams and pollution. London charges drivers a fee of £8 to take their vehicles into central districts during weekdays. Local residents receive a discount, and certain vehicles (such as ambulances and taxis) pay nothing. The fee has cut traffic by 15 to 20 per cent, increased the average speed during peak times and raised money to pay for public transportation improvements.[13]

Pricing new products

A new product presents a special pricing challenge because you must decide whether to use **market-penetration pricing** and price relatively low for rapid acquisition of market share or use **market-skimming pricing**, setting a relatively high price to skim maximum revenues from the market, layer by layer. With market-penetration pricing, the price may be so low that the product is unprofitable and/or priced lower than competing products in the short term. Yet such pricing may be effective in the long run, if you are determined to boost volume and gain efficiencies that will lower costs as a foundation for future profitability.

Toyota, for example, introduced its Yaris subcompact car in Europe using market-penetration pricing. To build sales, the carmaker packed the car with extra features that enhance value perceptions and accepted smaller profit margins than it earns on luxury cars under the company's Lexus brand. Toyota sees the Yaris as competing with the top European brands (Volkswagen, Renault, Opel/Vauxhall and Ford) rather than with low-priced cars from Hyundai and Kia. In the growth stage of its life cycle, the Yaris has been redesigned and sells more than 250,000 units in Europe every year.[14]

Market-penetration pricing is not appropriate for every product, which is where internal and external influences come into play. Your customers may perceive less value in a luxury product that is launched with market-penetration pricing, for example. Also, market-penetration pricing may be inappropriate for the kinds of channel members you need to use to reach targeted customer segments. Finally, such pricing may not be consistent with your promotion decisions.

You should consider market-skimming pricing for innovative or top-quality products, to make an upmarket impression on selected customer segments that are less price-sensitive and place a premium on innovation. Market-skimming pricing is common with products employing new technology such as digital radio receivers, for example. Not only do you take in more money to help cover costs with this approach, you have the flexibility to lower prices as you monitor competitive response, attain volumes that yield economies of scale and shift to targeting more price-sensitive segments. On the other hand, if your initial price is too high, you may set customer expectations too high, slow initial sales and lower repeat sales if the product does not fulfil those expectations.

Pricing multiple products

Your plan for pricing should take into account more than one product in the line or mix, any optional or complementary products and any product bundles. The way you price each product sets it apart from other products in your mix, reflecting or reinforcing customer perceptions of each product's value. You can then balance prices within the product line or mix to reach your total revenue or profit objectives. As an example, price competition among lower-priced models of car may produce slimmer profits for a carmaker even as prices on upmarket vehicles boost profit margins for those products.[15] In services, a hotel company may market deluxe hotels, convention hotels and modestly priced tourist hotels, each with its own target market, pricing objectives and room rates in line with the perceived value.

If you offer a bundle of goods or services you must determine how to price that bundle, given the competition and customers' perceptions of the bundle's value. One advantage of bundling is that competitors can't easily duplicate every aspect of a unique, specially priced bundle. If customers do not want everything in your bundle at the price set, however, they may buy fewer products individually or look at competitive bundles. And later in a product's life cycle, you may get more benefit by unbundling and pricing each part separately.

Adapting prices

Your plan should allow for adapting prices when appropriate, either by increasing perceived value or by reducing perceived cost. Depending on local laws and regulations – and the rest of your marketing plan – some ways in which you can adapt prices include:

- *Discounts*. You can plan special discounts for customers who buy in large quantities or during non-peak periods; pay in cash; or assume logistical functions such as picking up products that would otherwise be delivered.

- *Allowances*. You can invite customers to trade-in older products and receive credit toward purchases of newer products; you may also offer customers refunds or rebates for buying during promotional periods.

- *Extra value*. To encourage intermediaries to carry your products, you may offer small quantities free when resellers place orders during a promotional period. For consumers, you may temporarily increase the amount of product without increasing the price.

- *Periodic mark-downs*. Retailers, in particular, plan to mark down merchandise periodically, at the end of a selling season, to attract or reward shoppers or to stimulate new product trial.

- *Segmented pricing*. Depending on your segmentation decisions, your pricing can be adapted for customers of different ages (such as lower prices for children and older customers); members and non-members (such as lower prices for professional association members); different purchase locations (such as lower prices for products bought and picked up at the main plant); and time of purchase (such as lower prices for mobile phone service during non-peak periods).

Internal or external influences may prompt you to raise or lower a product's price. For example, you can use a price cut to stimulate higher demand or defend against competitive price reductions. You may want to use a price increase to deal with rising costs or product improvements that raise perceived quality and value. Whether such price adaptations achieve their objectives will depend on customer and competitor reaction.

Although you will usually fix most prices, the final price for a product is sometimes reached by negotiation with customers, as in the way consumers buy cars or airlines buy jet planes. And more organizations and consumers are allowing prices to be set through online auctions and *reverse auctions* (in which customers set the price at which they want to buy). Auction pricing can be a good way to market excess or out-of-date stock to price-sensitive customers without affecting the fixed price set for other segments.

CHAPTER SUMMARY

Customers perceive a product's value according to the total benefits weighed against the total costs, in the context of competitive products and prices. During the planning process, marketers must research how customers perceive the value of their product and the value of competing products and, ideally, work backwards using the perceived value to make price, cost and product decisions. External influences on pricing decisions are: customers; market and demand; competition; channel members; and legal, regulatory and ethical considerations. Internal influences on pricing decisions are: organizational and marketing plan objectives; costs; targeting and positioning; product decisions and life cycle; and other marketing-mix decisions.

Two approaches to pricing new products are market-penetration pricing (to capture market share quickly) and market-skimming pricing (to skim maximum revenues from each market layer). Depending on local laws and regulations and the rest of the marketing plan, marketers can adapt prices using discounts, allowances, extra value, periodic mark-downs or segment pricing. Also, prices may be increased or decreased according to internal or external influences; negotiated; or influenced by customers in online or reverse auctions.

CASE STUDY: TATA GROUP'S 'ONE LAKH' CAR

Is it possible to profit by marketing a car that sells for less than £1,600? India's Tata Group plans to find out. For several years, the company has been developing an ultra-low-priced compact car with a rear-mounted engine and room for four passengers. When first conceived, the car was to be priced at one lakh, which is 100,000 rupees (equivalent to approximately £1,120 at that time). Although the cost of materials has risen as the car moves through design and testing, Tata still targets a selling price of less than £ 1,600. But is this realistic?

Tata knows how to apply value-based pricing. It markets the Ace, a small lorry, for 1.1 lakh. Not surprisingly, the Ace has proven popular; within a year of its introduction, it had already generated sufficient revenue to cover all development costs. For now, the Ace is sold only in India because it would need substantial (and costly) changes to meet crash and emissions standards in other countries. Moreover, the Ace's profits are being squeezed by the same rising raw-materials costs that will affect the profitability of the 'one lakh' car. Yet through the Ace, Tata has gained design and manufacturing experience that it can use in planning other affordable vehicles. It has also called on Fiat's small-car expertise.

In anticipation of the launch of the 'one lakh' car, Tata is building a new factory and test-driving prototypes of the new design. Despite the start-up expense, Tata believes that demand will be high enough to fuel significant sales, which is why its initial production target is 250,000 per year. Economies of scale will spread the development and production costs over more units, helping the profit picture. Yet Tata could face competition as companies such as Pakistan's Transmission Motor Company and India's Bajaj consider launching their own ultra-low-priced cars. Will the 'one lakh' car be both profitable and popular?[16]

Case questions

1. Why is market-penetration pricing appropriate for the marketing plan to launch Tata's 'one lakh' car?

2. If several competitors introduce ultra-low-priced cars, how would you suggest that Tata's marketers respond?

 APPLY YOUR KNOWLEDGE

Choose a particular business product (such as a tractor or specialized software) and research the marketer's approach to pricing. Then write up your ideas or give an oral presentation to the class.

- What benefits does this product appear to offer to business customers?

- What initial and ongoing costs would business customers perceive in connection with buying and maintaining this product?

- If the product is new, what pricing approach is the company using to launch it? Why is this approach appropriate for the product?

- How does the price reflect the product's positioning and other marketing mix decisions?

- How does the price of one competing or substitute product appear to reflect that product's value (from the customer's perspective)? If you were a customer, would you place a higher value on this competing product than on the product you have been researching? Why?

BUILD YOUR OWN MARKETING PLAN

Continue developing your marketing plan by making pricing decisions about a new or existing product. What pricing objectives will you set for this product? If the product is new, will you use market-skimming pricing or market-penetration pricing – and why? Which external influences are most important to the pricing of this product? How do internal influences affect your pricing decision for this product? What price will you set for this one product and in what situations would you consider adapting the price? Consider how these pricing decisions fit in with earlier marketing decisions and with the objectives you've set, then document them in your marketing plan.

STOP ENDNOTES

1. Bruce Einhorn, 'A Racer Called Acer', *BusinessWeek*, 29 January 2007, p. 48; 'Acer Talks Tough About Future PC Shipments', *PC Magazine Online*, 27 October 2006, www.pcmag.com, n.p.

2. This section draws on concepts in Thomas T. Nagle and John E. Hogan, *The Strategy and Tactics of Pricing*, 4th edn (Upper Saddle River, NJ: Pearson Prentice Hall, 2006).

3. 'Swedish Home Furnisher Finds British Market Its Weakest Link', *Sunday Business (London)*, 3 January 2007, www.thebusinessonline.com; Lisa Margonelli, 'How Ikea Designs Its Sexy Price Tags', *Business 2.0*, October 2002, pp. 106–12.

4. Daniel J. Howard and Roger A. Kerin, 'Broadening the Scope of Reference Price Advertising Research', *Journal of Marketing*, October 2006, pp. 185–204; Wayne D. Hoyer and Deborah J. MacInnis, *Consumer Behaviour*, 3rd edn (Boston: Houghton Mifflin, 2004), p. 262.

5. 'Barbers at the Gate', *The Economist*, 4 November 2006, p. 76; 'Low-Price Barber Operator QB Net to Boots Overseas Operations', *Jiji*, 30 October 2006, n.p.; 'Orix Acquires Low-Price Barbershop Operator QB Net', *Jiji*, 1 August 2006, n.p.; Jim Hawe, 'A New Style', *Wall Street Journal*, 22 September 2003, pp. R3, R7.

6. Leo Magno, 'Nokia Launches Entry-Level Phones for New Growth Markets', *Asia Africa Intelligence Wire*, 1 September 2003, n.p.

7. Michael V. Copeland, 'Hits & Misses: Lemons to "Limited Edition" Lemonade', *Business 2.0*, September 2003, p. 92.

8. 'Colruyt to Enter Luxembourg, Dutch Market, Plans "One or Two Test Stores"', *Forbes.com*, 12 February 2007, www.forbes.com; Dan Bilefsky, 'Making the Cuts', *Wall Street Journal*, 22 September 2003, pp. R3, R7.

9. 'Deep Discount Goes from Drab to Fab', *Grocer*, 11 November 2006, pp. 40ff.

10. 'Call Waiting', *W*, December 2006, p. 96; 'The Origins of Vertu', *The Economist*, 22 February 2003, pp. 62–3.

11. This section draws on concepts in Thomas T. Nagle and John E. Hogan, *The Strategy and Tactics of Pricing*, 4th edn (Upper Saddle River, NJ: Pearson Prentice Hall, 2006).

12. Gina Chon and Stephen Power, 'Can an Itsy-Bitsy Auto Survive in the Land of the SUV?', *Wall Street Journal*, 9 January 2007, p. B1ff.; John Tagliabue, 'A Tale of 2 Carmakers and 2 Countries', *New York Times*, 16 May 2003, pp. W1ff.

13. Daniel Gross, 'What's the Toll? It Depends on the Time of Day', *New York Times*, 11 February 2007, sec. 3, p. 7; 'London Traffic Starts to See Benefits of Toll Levied on Motorists', *Wall Street Journal*, 6 May 2003, p. 1; 'Ken Livingstone's Gamble', *The Economist*, 15 February 2003, pp. 51–3.

14. Luca Ciferri, 'Toyota Ready for European Top League', *Automotive News Europe*, 20 March 2006, p. 5; 'The Asian Invasion Picks Up Speed', *BusinessWeek*, 6 October 2003, pp. 62–4.

15. Gail Edmondson, 'Classy Cars', *BusinessWeek*, 24 March 2003, pp. 62–6.

16. Based on information from Nandini Lakshman and Gail Edmondson, 'Tata and Fiat: Small Is Big in India', *Business Week Online*, 25 January 2007, www.businessweek.com; 'Carmaking in India: A Different Route', *The Economist*, 16 December 2006, p. 64; Peter Wonacott and Jason Singer, 'Ratan Tata Builds Indian Behemoth into Global Player', *Wall Street Journal*, 7 October 2006, pp. B1ff.

8

Planning for channels and logistics

Comprehension outcomes

After studying this chapter, you will be able to:

- Explain the roles of the value chain, marketing channels and logistics
- Describe the various channel levels and intermediaries
- Contrast exclusive, selective and intensive distribution
- Understand the balance between logistics costs and customer service

Application outcomes

After studying this chapter, you will be able to:

- Analyse the value chain for a good or service
- Decide on the number of channel levels and members
- Analyse and plan for logistics

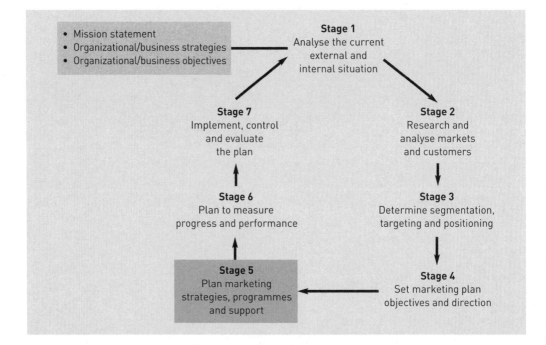

CHAPTER PREVIEW

Zara, based in Spain, is known around the world for 'fast fashion'. Once its designers identify a new trend, they can have new styles manufactured and in company stores within five weeks. Knowing that today's most in-demand style may be unwanted tomorrow, Zara makes much of its clothing in Spain – close to its design centre – and speeds it by lorry to its European stores (by air to stores outside Europe). Yet by controlling supply and transportation costs, Zara has kept its gross profit margin well above 50 per cent.[1] Zara is a good example of the marketing-mix tool of 'place', how a company enables customers to take possession of a product in a convenient place and time, in a convenient form and quantity and at an acceptable price.

As basic as this may sound, planning for this part of the marketing mix is complex because these decisions must fit with your other marketing decisions while simultaneously meeting customers' needs and organizational objectives. Zara, for instance, must get new fashions to stores very quickly – without losing sight of its profit expectations. Focusing on 'place', this chapter opens with an overview of the value chain and its effect on marketing planning. Next, you'll learn about planning for flows and responsibilities within the value chain, followed by a discussion of channel levels and decisions about individual channel members. The closing section examines some important logistics decisions to consider when preparing a marketing plan.

ANALYSING THE VALUE CHAIN

The **value chain**, also known as the **value delivery network** or *supply chain*, is the succession of interrelated, value-added functions undertaken by the marketer with suppliers, wholesalers, retailers and other participants (including customers) to source supplies and ultimately deliver a product that fulfils customers' needs. Figure 8.1 shows a simplified value chain and explains the key areas to be analysed during the marketing planning process. The point is to understand how each participant in the chain adds value to the good or service that your customers buy and use. Then your marketing plan can reflect a 'performance' view of the chain, including activities to enhance the combined efficiency and effectiveness of all partners, where possible.

Imagine Zara as the central link of the value chain. In its role as producer, it's responsible for coordinating the transformation of inputs (fabric, for instance) into outputs (clothing) as well as inbound functions that occur upstream (bringing fabric to factories) and outbound functions that occur downstream (getting clothing to stores). The value added downstream occurs within a **marketing channel** (also known as a **distribution channel)**, the set of functions performed by the producer or intermediaries, such as retailers, to make a particular product available to customers. Zara owns its own stores but other producers sell to wholesalers and/or retailers that resell to consumers.

The profitable flow of products, information and payments inbound and outbound to meet customer requirements is accomplished through **logistics**. One or more parties

Decisions about adding value inbound:
- How to manage suppliers and obtain materials plus other needed inputs (locating suppliers, buying parts, printing product manuals, etc.)
- How to manage logistics (arranging physical, informational and financial flows related to inbound orders, supply availability, deliveries, etc.)

Decisions about adding value through the marketer's functions:
- How to manage flows in marketing (interpreting market data to understand customer needs, developing suitable products and distribution, communicating product differentiation, etc.)
- How to manage flows to transform inputs into outputs (manufacturing tangible items, delivering intangible services)
- How to manage flows through customer service and internal operations (responding to customer enquiries, managing materials, etc.)

Decisions about adding value outbound:
- How to manage product availability for convenient customer interactions (arranging direct or indirect channels, selecting and supervising channel members to handle transactions, etc.)
- How to manage logistics (arranging physical, informational and financial flows related to allocating quantities and assortments to meet demand, expedite transportation, manage inventory, etc.)

Customers

| **FIGURE 8.1** | Areas of focus in a simplified value chain |

must handle inbound transportation of raw materials and components so Zara can produce its apparel; Zara or one of its suppliers must maintain raw materials inventory. Zara has to track production quantities, manage finished goods inventory and despatch finished goods outbound. Moreover, Zara's stores have to manage downstream transactions with buyers.

In planning for channel and logistics decisions, you should take into account the needs and behaviour of targeted customer segments; your SWOT analysis and competitive situation; your product's positioning; and your marketing plan objectives. Then consider which functions in the value chain must be accomplished and which participants should be responsible for each. These decisions lay the groundwork for adding value and meeting customers' needs at an acceptable cost to the customer and an acceptable profit to the organization. Because of the number of alternatives available to you, you should analyse a variety of channel and logistics arrangements before you make a final decision and document it in your marketing plan.

The value chain for services

If your marketing plan is for a service, be aware that your value chain should put particular focus on inbound activities, the service experience itself and outbound activities that involve the customer. Inbound functions cover supplies, information and payments related to providing the service; the service experience occurs in the central link (if delivered by your firm); and outbound functions cover service availability plus associated information and payments. Logistics for services are concerned with having the right supplies (and people) in the right place at the right time. Moreover, because services are perishable – they cannot be stored for future sale or consumption – your plan must carefully manage all flows to balance supply and demand.

The service experience, based on value-chain activities and logistics decisions, influences customer loyalty as well as costs, as the following example illustrates.

MARKETING IN PRACTICE: BRITISH AIRWAYS AND AUSTRIAN AIRLINES

British Airways and Austrian Airlines have made slightly different decisions about how to provide value to air travellers. Both are concerned about costs, especially when the price of fuel is sky high, but they also need to satisfy customers by delivering a comfortable experience. Although some low-fare competitors charge for all food and drink, these two carriers are not taking that route. British Airways recently substituted snacks and drinks for full meals on mid-morning and mid-afternoon flights; this lowered its costs and changed its inbound supply and inflight activities. In contrast, Austrian Airlines increased services for business-class passengers: it hired chefs to prepare gourmet meals on long flights and added several speciality coffees and desserts. This increased its costs and affected suppliers, inbound activities and the service experience itself. Still, the real question is: How will these changes affect long-term customer loyalty and profitability?[2]

Flows and responsibilities in the value chain

Your marketing plan should consider the need for a **reverse channel**, to return goods for service or when worn out and to reclaim products, parts or packaging for recycling. This is particularly important if you're marketing online and want to reassure customers that they can return or exchange what they buy. Amazon.com, for example, has arranged with a specialized company to handle any customer returns, which frees the retailer to concentrate on its retailing business.[3] In addition, look beyond immediate value-chain functions to see whether your suppliers' suppliers are providing the required quality or ecologically safe materials and, if selling to businesses, see how your customers' customers use the final product.

You face difficult trade-offs between value added and cost when making decisions about channels and logistics. Having a wide variety of products immediately available at all times in all locations (or ready to be despatched quickly on demand) is the most desirable situation but often too costly for your organization and for your customer. On the other hand, your customers are likely to be unsatisfied – and may turn to competitors – if you have too few products available; the wrong quantities or models available; and/or slow or expensive transactions.

There is a growing trend toward strengthening long-term relationships with value chain partners for mutual benefit. The Swedish furniture company IKEA forges long-term connections with its suppliers to ensure a steady stream of products designed to its specifications and cost guidelines. The company teaches suppliers to negotiate with their suppliers for the best price, quality materials and delivery schedules. 'When we buy fabric, for example, we have to compare the price from many, many suppliers', says a manager at the Binh Thanh Textile Factory in Vietnam, one of IKEA's suppliers.[4]

PLANNING FOR CHANNELS

Depending on your organization's situation and objectives, you can plan for a value chain that includes direct or indirect channels. With **direct channels**, you make products available directly to customers. For example, Dell uses direct channels, marketing its computers online, by phone and through catalogues. With **indirect channels**, you work through **intermediaries**, outside businesses or individuals that help producers make goods or services available to customers. Figure 8.2 shows how goods or services would reach customers through direct and indirect channels. It also shows the three major types of intermediaries, each of which adds value in a particular way:

- *Wholesalers* buy from producers, sort and store products, create smaller lots for buyer convenience and resell to other intermediaries or to business customers. Some take on duties normally handled elsewhere in the value chain, such as monitoring a customer's inventory.

- *Retailers* are companies such as IKEA and Tesco that resell products, giving consumers easy and convenient access to an array of products. Customers who buy from online retailers must wait for their purchases. Increasingly, however, online retailers such as Dixons in the United Kingdom offer installation and many other services offered by physical stores.[5]

- *Representatives, brokers and agents* (such as insurance agents) bring producers together with customers but generally do not take ownership of the products they market. These intermediaries add value through their knowledge of the market, customers and products.

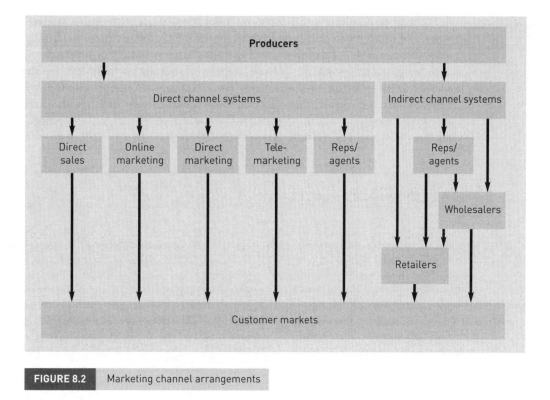

| FIGURE 8.2 | Marketing channel arrangements |

Source: Adapted from Roger J. Best, *Market-Based Management*, 2nd edn (Upper Saddle River, NJ: Prentice Hall, 2000), p. 199.

In your marketing plan, you will have to specify the number of intermediary levels you want to use for each product – in other words, the length of the channel.

Channel length decisions

Longer channels have more intermediary levels separating the producer and its customers; shorter channels have fewer intermediaries. A direct channel is the shortest because there are no intermediaries and the producer deals directly with its customers through any or all of the methods shown at the left in Figure 8.2. This is appropriate when you want as much control as possible over dealings with customers and your organization can handle all outbound functions. If your markets and segments are not well defined or you lack the resources and knowledge to work directly with customers, however, using a direct channel can be inefficient at best and ineffective at worst.

The zero-level channel can work well for both business and consumer marketers, despite differences in products, customers, prices and markets. Nippon Steel, one of the world's largest steel producers, uses direct channels to sell to construction companies, carmakers, shipbuilders and other businesses in its home country of Japan and in other markets.[6]

Some organizations use a direct channel for certain segments (usually business customers) and an indirect channel with one level for other segments (usually consumers). This allows more control over the typically large-volume transactions with businesses and delegates responsibility for the higher number and smaller size of consumer transactions to intermediaries. Carmakers, for instance, use a direct channel when selling to government agencies so they can negotiate specifications, pricing and delivery, but use a separate single-level indirect dealer channel to sell to consumers. Here's a glimpse of Ford's value chain and dealer channel in Russia.

MARKETING IN PRACTICE: FORD IN RUSSIA

Ford is the top-selling car brand in Russia, thanks to a forward-thinking marketing plan. Before any other foreign carmaker invested in local manufacturing, US-based Ford built a factory near St Petersburg and signed dealers to sell its Focus cars and wagons. Today it has 150 dealers in Russia; the southwestern Moscow dealer sells more Fords than any Ford dealer, anywhere. Producing cars locally reduces import duties and transportation costs; it also gets cars to customers more quickly. Although Ford cars are more expensive than those made by local carmakers, customers are willing to pay more for extra features – and they like using Ford's affordable car loans to spread car payments over two or three years.[7]

Longer channels, such as the two- and three-level indirect channels illustrated at the right of Figure 8.2, send products through a series of representatives or agents, wholesalers or retailers before they reach the final customer. Such channel arrangements allow intermediaries to add value when your company is targeting multiple or geographically dispersed markets; you have limited resources or little customer knowledge; your customers have specialized needs; or your products require training, customization or service. Although the price paid by customers reflects a profit for intermediaries at all levels and covers the value they add, you may find that long channels are the best way to make certain products available. Many consumer products, such as packaged cereals and mouthwashes, move through longer channels.

Channel member decisions

If you decide to work with at least one level of intermediary, your marketing plan should indicate how many and what type of channel members you'll need for each level in each market. These decisions depend on the market, the product and its life cycle, customer needs and behaviour, product pricing and product positioning. Figure 8.3 summarizes the three broad choices in number of channel members.

If you use **exclusive distribution**, one intermediary will handle your product in a particular area. If you use **selective distribution**, a fairly small number of intermediaries will sell your product in the area. If you use **intensive distribution**, many

	Exclusive distribution	Selective distribution	Intensive distribution
Value added for customer	• Individual attention • Knowledgeable sales help • Availability of training, other services	• Choice of outlets in each area • Some services available	• Convenient availability in many outlets • Competition among outlets may lower price
Value added for producer	• Positioning of expensive or technical product reinforced • Closer cooperation and exchange of information • More control over service quality, other aspects	• Ability to cover more of the market • Less dependent on a small number of channel members	• Higher unit sales • Ability to cover an area completely • Lower cost per unit
Concerns for producer	• Higher cost per unit • Potentially reach fewer customers	• Medium costs, medium control	• Less control over service quality, other aspects • More difficult to supervise • Possible conflict among channel members

FIGURE 8.3   Exclusive, selective and intensive distribution

intermediaries will handle your product in the area. How do you choose? You can enhance the luxury image of upmarket or specialized goods and services by using exclusive distribution. New products that require extensive customer education may be sold in exclusive or selective distribution. Also, products that require expert sales support or for which customers shop around are often marketed through selective distribution. Finally, consider intensive distribution for inexpensive, everyday products – especially impulse items – because of the opportunity to achieve higher sales volumes.

In addition, you have to choose specific intermediaries for each channel. In a marketing plan for an existing product or a new entry in an existing line, you may want to reassess the value each member is providing; add more channel members to expand market coverage if needed; and replace ineffective or inefficient members as necessary. As coverage increases, however, so does the possibility for conflict among channel members over customers, market coverage, pricing and other issues. When preparing a marketing plan for a new or existing product, allow for educating channel members about the product's benefits; they should be induced to promote it actively. Also look ahead to think about whether a particular intermediary will be a strong partner in marketing the product (and possibly later products) now and in the future.

The following checklist will help you think about channel issues for your marketing plan.

ESSENTIAL MARKETING PLAN CHECKLIST NO.11:
PLANNING FOR MARKETING CHANNELS

☐ How do customers prefer to gain access to the product?

_____

☐ What channels and channel members are best suited to the product, positioning and brand image?

_____

☐ What are the organization's channel costs and will customers pay for access through these channels?

_____

☐ Are the right assortments of products available at the right time and in the right quantities, with appropriate support?

_____

☐ How much control does the organization want over channel functions?

_____

☐ How can channel decisions be used to manage the product life cycle?

_____

☐ What geographical, ecological, legal and regulatory considerations affect channel decisions?

_____

☐ How many channel levels and members are appropriate, given the organization's situation, objectives and targeting decisions?

_____

☐ Do channel members have capable sales and support staff, are they equipped to store and display the product and are they financially sound?

_____

PLANNING FOR LOGISTICS

A good logistics plan can help you compete by serving customers more effectively or by saving money. But details count. For example, Wal-Mart has built a highly profitable retail empire based on driving logistics costs ever lower (*see* the case study). Whatever your plan, you will need clear-cut, non-conflicting objectives. If your objective is to make more products available or get them to customers more quickly, expect your costs to be higher. If your objective is to cut the total cost of logistics, you might maintain lower inventory levels, raising the possibility that you might run out of some products. Your marketing plan must strike a balance between your customers' needs and your organization's financial, marketing and societal objectives.

A growing number of marketers, including Kaufhof's, are testing radio frequency identification (RFID) technology to improve inbound and outbound efficiency.

MARKETING IN PRACTICE: RFID AT KAUFHOF'S

The Kaufhof department store chain in Germany has been testing radio frequency identification (RFID) technology since 2003. Each RFID tag attached to a package or product contains a computer chip, a tiny antenna and a unique identification number. The tags automatically send radio signals to indicate where they (and the items they identify) are located, whether in a warehouse, on a lorry or in the store. In Kaufhof's test, two apparel suppliers have been attaching RFID tags to each box they ship so the retailer can quickly and accurately track shipments in transit and receive the items into inventory at each store. As the chain expands its use of RFID, it will be in a better position to have the right merchandise in stock at the right store at the right time. However, RFID also raises ethical concerns about invasion of privacy. For instance, will the technology be used to track what individual customers buy or how they use certain products?[8]

As Figure 8.4 indicates, logistics decisions about pre- and post-production inventory, storage, transportation, order processing and fulfilment depend on whether your objectives are linked to less service (lower cost) or more service (higher cost).

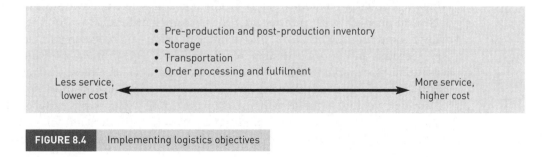

- Pre-production and post-production inventory
- Storage
- Transportation
- Order processing and fulfilment

Less service, lower cost ⟷ More service, higher cost

FIGURE 8.4 Implementing logistics objectives

Inventory decisions

Your decisions about inventory must be made even before the first product moves into the channel. Pre-production, you should identify the inventory level of parts and supplies required for the planned output. Post-production, think about how much inventory of a particular product is needed outbound to meet customer demand, balanced with organizational constraints of budgets, production and storage capacity. Zara, for example, produces limited quantities of each fashion, knowing it can get additional inventory to stores in just a few weeks, if needed. If your inventories are too low, customers will not find products when and where they want and your channel members will lose sales; if your inventories are too high, the organization's investment is tied up and you risk having some products go out of style, spoil or become obsolete.

Increasingly, producers, suppliers and channel members are collaborating to forecast demand and have the right amount of inventory when and were needed. Mistakes can be costly – resulting in empty shelves or, just as bad, warehouses full of obsolete or overpriced products, as Vizio well knows.

MARKETING IN PRACTICE: VIZIO

Vizio, based in southern California, captured 7 per cent of the North American market for LCD televisions in just three years. Its annual turnover exceeds $700 million, thanks to low-cost Asian production, low wholesale prices and fast response to market conditions. How does Vizio do it? In a word, logistics. It carefully monitors every detail, from the quality of the glass in its screens to the merchandise display patterns of its retail channel partners. But the most crucial element is inventory: because intense competition and improved production efficiency are lowering the retail price of LCD sets nearly every month, Vizio tracks stores' stock levels and maintains an on-hand inventory level equal to just two weeks of anticipated sales. This way, the company limits the damage to its profit margins in the event it must cut its wholesale prices unexpectedly.[9]

Storage decisions

Where will you store materials before production and where will you store finished products until needed to fill intermediary or customer orders? How long will you store materials and finished products? Such storage decisions are based, in part, on your inventory decisions and your customers' requirements. If you promise a business customer just-in-time stock replenishment, you might store products in a nearby warehouse or distribution centre for speedy delivery on schedule. Also examine how much space is needed for storing inventory at the site where customers actually gain access to the product.

Also look at the product itself and typical variations in demand when planning for product storage. Is your product perishable? Is it especially large (or small) or fragile?

Does it have other physical characteristics that affect storage? Are large quantities needed quickly during periods of peak demand? Is demand erratic or steady? What are the implications for your marketing plan?

Transportation decisions

In the course of planning inbound and outbound logistics, choose the transportation modes that are appropriate for your product, your budget and your customers' needs and value perceptions. Choices include road transport by lorry (convenient for door-to-door shipments), rail transport (for bulky or heavy items), air transport (when time is a factor and budgets allow), water transport (when time is not a factor but cost is) and pipeline transport (for liquids and natural gases). Often products are despatched by more than one mode of transportation, such as lorry to water, rail or air and back to lorry. Figure 8.5 shows some of the key questions to ask when making transportation decisions for your marketing plan.

Your flexibility in transportation choices depends, in part, on legal and regulatory rules governing competition in pricing and schedules, as well as your balance of cost and customer service. In many areas, transportation companies differentiate themselves through special product handling and convenience. In Canada, CN has invested heavily to increase capacity at its intermodal terminal in Brampton, where containers of merchandise arrive by rail, ready for transfer to lorries. Customers benefit from the CN's use of RFID to pinpoint the location of every container during its journey from point of origin (a railway terminal near a factory or seaport, for example) to Brampton and then on to the recipient's warehouse.[10]

Question	Transportation choices
How quickly must products be at their destination?	Air is speediest; water is slowest
Is steady, predictable receipt of products desirable?	Pipeline allows for fairly steady transport of liquids and gases; water is least predictable
What level of transportation cost is acceptable to customers and organization?	Pipeline and water are least expensive; air is most expensive
Is transportation available from the point of despatch directly to the point of delivery?	Road transport offers the most convenient door-to-door delivery
What capacity is needed to transport this product?	Water and rail easily accommodate large, bulky products

FIGURE 8.5   Questions to ask when planning for transportation

Order processing and fulfilment decisions

Whether you're targeting business or consumer markets, you'll have to include order processing and fulfilment in your marketing plan, with decisions about the method and timing of:

- accepting orders and billing for purchases
- confirmation of order and available inventory
- picking and packing products for despatch
- documenting and tracking the contents of shipments
- handling returns, errors and damaged goods.

A growing number of organizations are planning better customer service through reduced order cycle time. This means your customers (whether consumers or businesses) will have as short a wait as possible between placing an order and receiving delivery. Gruma, Mexico's market-leading flour producer, has reduced cycle time for the tortillas it sells to KFC restaurants in China by building a manufacturing plant in Shanghai. Before the plant opened, Gruma exported frozen tortillas from North America to China for KFC. Now the tortillas are made fresh locally – and Gruma has a base from which to fulfil, quickly and profitably, orders from other Asian customers as well.[11]

You can use the following checklist as a guide to some of the key questions you need to ask when you plan for logistics.

ESSENTIAL MARKETING PLAN CHECKLIST NO.12:
PLANNING FOR LOGISTICS

☐ What logistics arrangements would enable customers to obtain products quickly, conveniently and at an acceptable price?

_____

☐ How can logistics add more value for the customer and the organization by boosting benefits or decreasing costs or both?

_____

☐ What influence are the organization's SWOT and resources likely to have on logistics decisions? Can any aspect of logistics be outsourced if necessary without compromising objectives or service?

_____

☐ How can logistics be used for competitive advantage and to support positioning?

_____

☐ What is the optimal balance of logistics costs and customer service, given the marketing plan objectives?

_____

CHAPTER SUMMARY

The value chain (also called the value delivery network or supply chain) is the succession of interrelated, value-added functions that enable a producer to create and deliver a product that fulfils customers' needs through connections with suppliers, wholesalers, retailers and other participants. The marketing (or distribution) channel refers to the set of functions performed by the producer or by intermediaries in making a product available to customers at a profit. Marketing channels are outbound functions downstream in the value chain, closer to the customer. Logistics refers to the flow of products, information and payments inbound and outbound to meet customer requirements.

Marketers can use direct channels – in which the organization deals directly with customers – and/or indirect channels – in which the organization works through other businesses or individuals (intermediaries). The three major types of intermediaries are wholesalers; retailers; and representatives, brokers and agents. In a channel with one or more levels, marketers can choose exclusive, selective or intensive distribution. The main functions involved in logistics are: pre- and post-production inventory; storage; transportation; order processing and fulfilment. Seeking to raise customer service levels generally raises logistics costs; seeking to reduce logistics costs generally reduces the level of customer service.

CASE STUDY: WAL-MART'S RETAILING EDGE

How did Wal-Mart grow to become the largest retailer on the planet? The chain has several core competencies but perhaps the most important is its mastery of logistics. Think of the complexities of getting merchandise from 4,400 factories worldwide to the right place at the right time to satisfy the 138 million shoppers who visit Wal-Mart's 6,500 European, Asian and American stores every week. Thousands more click to buy on Walmart.com. Behind the scenes, the company maintains more than 150 distribution centres globally and uses RFID and other technology to receive and transfer merchandise quickly, plan inventory and – its hallmark – keep logistics costs down so retail prices are low.

Every new distribution centre represents an opportunity to hone efficiency by reducing the distance that merchandise must be transported inbound and outbound. With replenishment stock so close at hand – and one or more deliveries scheduled every day – Wal-Mart stores can carry lower inventory levels. Moreover, if a product unexpectedly sells out, it can be restocked in one day or even sooner. Inventory turns over so quickly that more than two-thirds of Wal-Mart's products are purchased by customers before the company is scheduled to pay the suppliers.

In fact, supplier collaboration is a critical component of Wal-Mart's logistics superiority. The retailer works directly with its major suppliers to forecast demand months in advance and plan inbound orders that will meet the needed inventory levels and merchandise assortments on a store-by-store basis. Because of this collaboration, suppliers are able to plan their production to meet Wal-Mart's specifications and arrange efficient despatch schedules. Sometimes Wal-Mart has its own fleet of lorries fetch merchandise from suppliers and plans deliveries so precisely that cartons of merchandise move non-stop from inbound lorries to outbound lorries and to the stores without being unloaded in a distribution centre.[12]

Case questions

1. If you were writing Wal-Mart's marketing plan, what would you include when planning for a reverse channel?

2. If you worked for a manufacturer trying to expand its retail distribution, what questions would you ask Wal-Mart before becoming one of its suppliers?

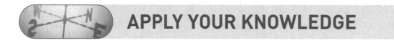

APPLY YOUR KNOWLEDGE

Select a common consumer product, then research and analyse its value chain and its channel arrangements. Prepare a written report or an oral presentation summarizing your analysis.

- Draw a diagram to show a simplified value chain for this product. Is a reverse channel necessary or desirable? Why?

- Is this product available through direct channels such as by mail or from the producer's website? How does this channel arrangement benefit customers and the organization?

- Is the product available through indirect channels such as retailers? Why is this appropriate for the product, the market and the targeted customers?

- Is the product available through exclusive distribution? Through intensive distribution? Do you agree with this decision?

BUILD YOUR OWN MARKETING PLAN

Continue developing your marketing plan by making decisions about channel arrangements and logistics. Should you market this product directly to customers or through indirect channels or a combination? How long should your channel be, and what value will each level add? Will you use intensive, selective or exclusive distribution, and why? What kinds of channel members would be most appropriate? Does your product require any special transportation, storage or post-purchase support? What specific customer needs should you take into account when planning logistics and how will you balance cost with customer service? Record your decisions and explain their implications in your marketing plan.

STOP ENDNOTES

1. Sandy O'Loughlin, 'Is Uniqlo Unique Enough to Crash Fast Fashion Party? Japanese Upstart Aims for H&M/Zara Territory', *Brandweek*, 5 February 2007, p. 15; 'Shining Examples', *The Economist*, 17 June 2006, pp. 4–5; Thomas Mulier and Patrick Donahue, 'Inditex Goes One-Up on H&M', *International Herald Tribune*, 30 March 2006, p. 17.

2. Colin Bake, 'Cost-Cutting Efforts Continue', *Airline Business*, 1 January 2007, n.p.; Avery Johnson, 'Lean Cuisine: European Airlines Cut Perks', *Wall Street Journal*, 8 November 2006, pp. D1ff.

3. Brian Hindo, 'Outsourcing: What Happens to that Scarf You Really Hated', *BusinessWeek*, 15 January 2007, p. 36.

4. Quoted in Margo Cohen, 'IKEA Expects Vietnam Business, with Its Cheap Supplies, to Surge', *Wall Street Journal*, 24 September 2003, p. B13E.

5. Anita Likus, 'Online Retail Traffic Surges in Europe', *Wall Street Journal*, 13 December 2006, p. B3F.

6. 'Nippon Steel Corp. Sales to Auto Makers Help Profit Rise by 33%', *Wall Street Journal*, 31 January 2007, online.wsj.com.

7. Jason Bush, 'They've Driven a Ford Lately', *BusinessWeek*, 26 February 2007, p. 52; Jason Stein, 'Ford Expands in Russia', *Automotive News Europe*, 22 January 2007, p. 3.

8. Jordan K. Speer, 'Kaufhof's Differentiating Factor RFID', *Apparel*, January 2007, pp. 24ff; Mark Roberti, 'RFID Is Fit to Track Clothes', *Chain Store Age*, May 2006, p. 158; Li Yuan, 'New Ways to Tell Where Your Kids Are; Tracking Gadgets, Services Can Pinpoint Exact Location; Weighing the Privacy Issue', *Wall Street Journal*, 27 April 2006, p. D1.

9. Pete Engardio, 'Flat Panels, Thin Margins', *BusinessWeek*, 26 February 2007, pp. 50–1; Tamara Chuang, 'Vizio Sales Strategy Is Highly Defined', *Orange County (Calif.) Register*, 3 October 2006, n.p.

10. 'CN to Invest C$12 million in Major Capacity Improvements at Toronto-area Intermodal Terminal', *Canadian Corporate News*, 2 February 2007, n.p.

11. Geri Smith, 'Wrapping the Globe in Tortillas', *BusinessWeek*, 26 February 2007, p. 54.

12. Based on information from 'Prowess in Logistics Is Big Competitive Edge', *MMR*, 11 December 2006, p. 84; Anthony Bianco and Wendy Zellner, 'Is Wal-Mart Too Powerful?' *Business Week*, 6 October 2003, pp. 102–10; Mike Troy, 'Logistics Still Cornerstone of Competitive Advantage', *DSN Retailing Today*, 9 June 2003, pp. 209ff.; Michael Garry and Sarah Mulholland, 'Master of Its Supply Chain', *Supermarket News*, 2 December 2002, pp. 55ff.; Jerry Useem, 'One Nation Under Wal-Mart', *Fortune*, 3 March 2003, pp. 63–76.

9

Planning for integrated marketing communication

Comprehension outcomes

After studying this chapter, you will be able to:

- Understand the role of integrated marketing communication (IMC)
- Outline the IMC planning process
- Discuss how to use IMC to support marketing plan objectives

Application outcomes

After studying this chapter, you will be able to:

- Set IMC objectives consistent with marketing plan objectives
- Select appropriate IMC tools
- Plan for an IMC campaign

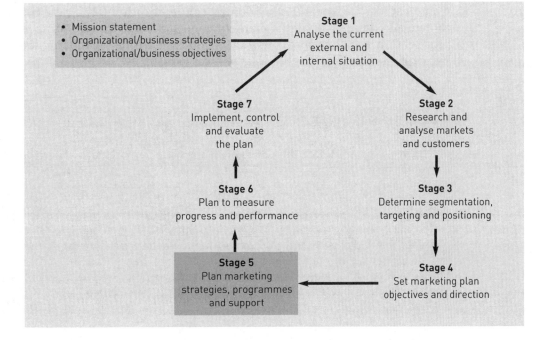

- Mission statement
- Organizational/business strategies
- Organizational/business objectives

Stage 1
Analyse the current external and internal situation

Stage 7
Implement, control and evaluate the plan

Stage 2
Research and analyse markets and customers

Stage 6
Plan to measure progress and performance

Stage 3
Determine segmentation, targeting and positioning

Stage 5
Plan marketing strategies, programmes and support

Stage 4
Set marketing plan objectives and direction

CHAPTER PREVIEW

When the Beeb threw a party with music by Pink, Snow Patrol and other bands, it drew 36,000 people – 30,000 to Dundee, Scotland, and 6,000 to the Second Life website. Why would the British Broadcasting Corp., a UK television network, sponsor a concert in real life and online at the same time? The marketing objective was to engage its audience in new ways and showcase its mastery of digital delivery. In fact, the Second Life concert got Web-savvy opinion leaders talking about the Beeb and its high-tech capabilities, which is exactly what the network wanted.[1]

Even if you don't have the Beeb's money and technical ability to promote your products, you can still plan for effective communication, as this chapter explains. You'll learn the steps in the planning process for a communications campaign: define the target audience; set the objectives and determine the budget; consider legal, regulatory, social and ethical issues; choose tools, messages and media; plan for pre-tests and post-implementation analysis; and evaluate the campaign. The chapter also includes an overview of planning for advertising, sales promotion, personal selling, direct marketing and public relations – the most visible and creative aspects of many marketing plans.

PLANNING FOR INTEGRATED MARKETING COMMUNICATION

No matter what good or service you're marketing, you'll need some kind of communication to inform, influence and interact with customers and prospects. In most cases, you'll choose a combination of communication techniques. That's why your marketing plan must include **integrated marketing communication (IMC)**, the coordination of content and delivery of all the marketing messages in all media for an organization, product or brand to ensure consistency and support the positioning and objectives. Here's an example from the financial services industry.

MARKETING IN PRACTICE: CAPITAL ONE BANK EUROPE

Aggressive direct mail programmes highlighting low rates helped build Capital One's UK consumer credit business. However, facing intense competition and a difficult economy, the company recently repositioned itself on the basis of convenience. Its marketing plan called for coordinated IMC activities under the light-hearted theme 'We make changing easy'. The idea, said the head of the Capital One brand, was 'to make people smile, take notice and tackle those changes they've been putting off'. In addition to television commercials, some direct mail and free 'Lunch and Laugh' comedy events, the campaign included a website with advice about how to make changes in love, life and – of course – finances. Although consumers were the main audience, the company also previewed the new campaign for internal audiences before the public introduction.[2]

Understanding IMC tools

You can plan a communication campaign using one or more of five major IMC tools: advertising (such as Capital One's television commercials), sales promotion, personal selling, direct marketing (such as Capital One's direct mail packages) and public relations (such as its comedy events). These tools are briefly described here (and *see* Figure 9.1) and examined again later in the chapter.

Advertising

Advertising is non-personal promotion paid for by an identified sponsor like Capital One. This is a cost-effective way to inform large numbers of customers or channel members about a brand or product; persuade customers or channel members about a brand's or product's merits; encourage buying; and remind customers or channel members

Advertising (non-personal, marketer controlled and funded)
- Television
- Radio
- Newspaper, magazine
- Cinema
- Posters and billboards
- Transport
- Internet
- CD, DVD

Sales promotion (non-personal, marketer controlled and funded)
- Customer sales promotion
- Channel and sales force promotion

Personal selling (personal, marketer controlled and funded)
- Organization's sales force
- Agency reps, manufacturer's reps, retail sales reps

Direct marketing (either personal or non-personal, marketer controlled and funded)
- Direct mail and catalogues
- Telemarketing
- E-mail and Internet
- Fax
- Direct sales

Public relations (either personal or non-personal, not directly marketer controlled and funded)
- Media relations
- Event sponsorship
- Speeches and publications
- Philanthropy
- Voluntary work
- Lobbying
- Product placement

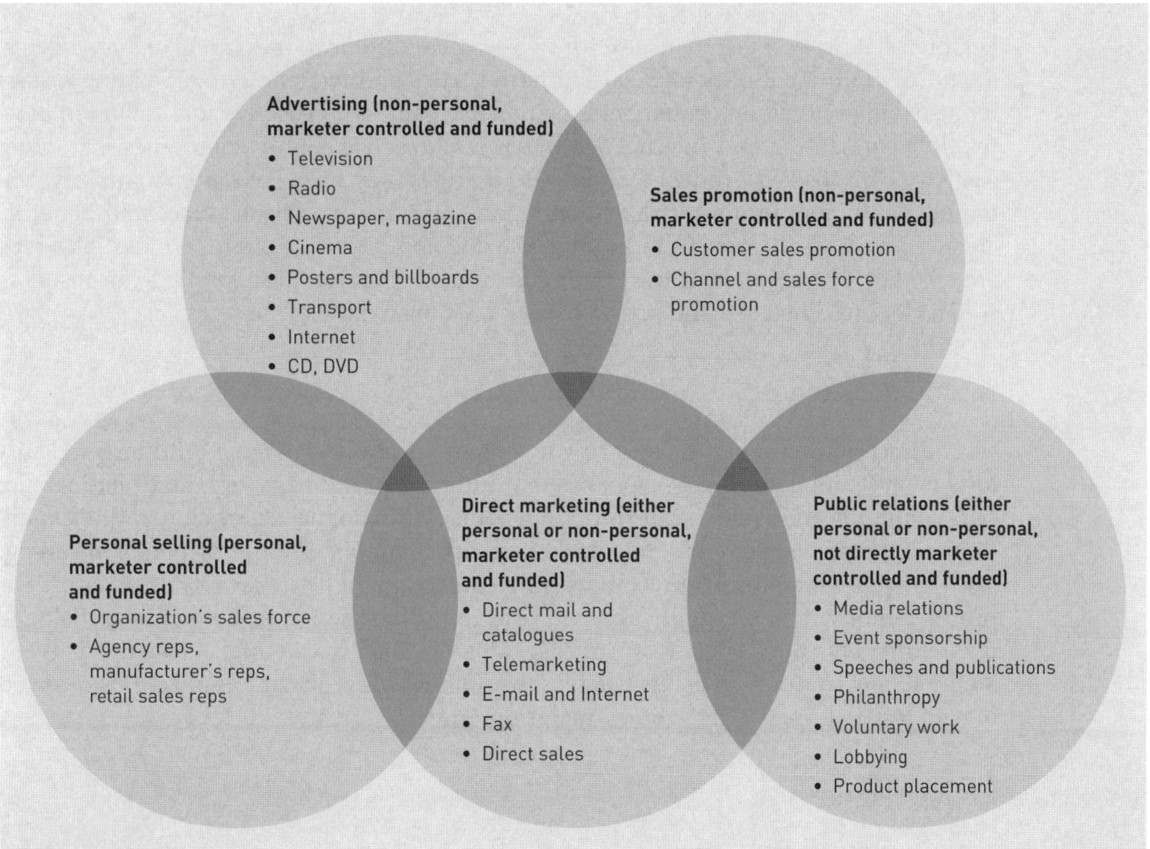

FIGURE 9.1   IMC tools

about the brand to encourage repurchase. Although television advertising remains popular, many companies see online advertising and social networking sites as less costly methods of communicating with more targeted audiences.[3]

Sales promotion

Sales promotion consists of incentives to enhance a product's short-term value and stimulate the target audience to buy soon (or respond in another way). Although advertising is an excellent way to build brand image and awareness and bring the audience to the brink of action, sales promotion provides impetus to take action right away. You can use sales promotion to induce customers to try a new product, for example, or to encourage channel members to stock and sell a new product. You can easily measure the results of most promotions by counting the number of coupons redeemed, the number of people who click on links in e-mail newsletters or on websites, and so on.

Personal selling

Personal selling – especially useful for two-way communication – can take many forms, including traditional in-person sales, Internet sales and telemarketing. Sending a sales representative to call on customers is extremely costly, whereas personal selling in most retail, telemarketing and Internet settings is less expensive. Still, companies marketing costly or complicated products to business markets may need sales reps to qualify customers, learn about their needs, recommend solutions, explain features and benefits, answer questions, demonstrate product use and complete sales transactions. Sales reps are also key players in learning about customers for marketing planning purposes, as well as for building trust and strengthening relationships.[4]

Direct marketing

With **direct marketing**, you use two-way communication to interact with targeted customers and stimulate direct responses that ultimately lead to an ongoing relationship. This communication may occur through letters and catalogues, television, radio, e-mail, Internet ads, newspaper ads, telemarketing, faxes, mobile phones or personal selling. The objective for an initial direct marketing contact might be to have a customer ask for product information or simply agree to receive further messages, launching a dialogue that ultimately culminates in a purchase. One of direct marketing's advantages is the ability to measure actual results (such as the number of credit card applications received in response to Capital One's direct mail programmes).

Public relations

Public relations (PR) activities promote dialogue to build understanding and foster positive attitudes between the organization and its publics. A marketing plan might call for a news conference to launch a new product, for example, or a special event to polish brand image. Because the firm does not directly control or pay for media mentions – and because the communication is not sales-directed – PR is very believable. However, there is no guarantee that the information will reach the intended audience in the preferred form or at the preferred time, if at all.

Defining the target audience

As you can see in Figure 9.2, your first planning decision is to define the audience that you will target. This may be customers in a certain segment; people who influence buyers or users; people who are currently competitors' customers; current or potential channel members; members of the general public; media people; government officials or regulators; or other publics.

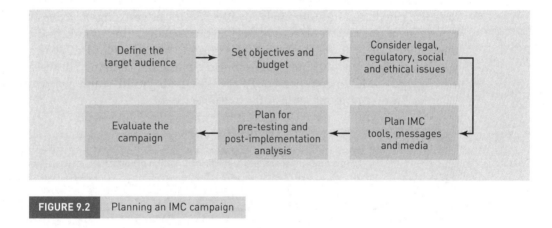

| FIGURE 9.2 | Planning an IMC campaign |

If you target intermediaries in an effort to move or *push* your product through the channel to customers, you're using a **push strategy** to stir channel interest using sales promotion, advertising or other communications techniques. An alternate approach is a **pull strategy**, which targets customers so they will request and buy the product from channel members. This *pulls* the product through the channel from producer to customer.

In your marketing plan, define who each IMC campaign should reach and, through research, indicate what audience members think or feel about the brand, product, organization or idea; their attitudes and behaviour toward competitors; what kind of message, appeal, delivery and timing would be most effective; what the message should contain and how it should be conveyed. For example, Unilever's recent marketing plan for Zhonghua, a toothpaste brand it markets in China, included research about brand perceptions. Zhonghua held a 16 per cent market share, yet wasn't popular with all ages. The brand director explained: 'We found the Zhonghua brand is weak on some attributes [such as] modernity, innovation, appeal to young consumers.' Therefore, Zhonghua planned advertising and sales promotion activities targeting young urban adults who were just entering the workforce and beginning to date.[5]

Setting the objectives and the budget

Your IMC campaign will aim to achieve marketing objectives that move the target audience through a hierarchy of cognitive, affective and behavioural responses. A **cognitive response** refers to a customer's mental reaction, including brand awareness and knowledge of product features and benefits. An **affective response** is a customer's emotional reaction, such as being interested in or liking a product. A **behavioural response** is how the customer acts, such as buying a product or applying for credit. Customers move through these responses in different order, depending on how involved they are in making that type of purchase; product differentiation in that category; and the influence of consumption experience (*see* Figure 9.3).

Usually your IMC objectives will relate to building long-term relationships by attracting customers' attention, communicating about the product or brand, persuading customers to seek out and buy the product once, supporting a positive attitude leading to repeat purchases and ultimately loyalty. Specific advertising objectives may be set to complement or support objectives for personal selling, direct marketing or other IMC tools in your plan. You may also set sales or profit objectives for IMC, particularly when you can measure and attribute the results to a particular campaign or message. Further, you may use IMC to enhance your firm's image or build brand awareness. (Review Chapter 5 for more about setting effective objectives.)

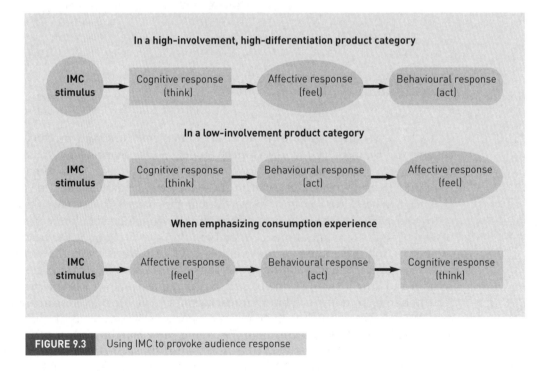

FIGURE 9.3 Using IMC to provoke audience response

Source: After Michael R. Solomon, *Consumer Behavior*, 5th edn (Upper Saddle River, NJ: Prentice Hall, 2002), p. 200–2.

The IMC budget is developed and allocated in the context of your organization's overall marketing budgeting process and budget approval process, which may be driven from the floor up or the top down (or a combination).[6] One floor-up option is to allocate funding according to the IMC objectives and the cost of the tasks needed to achieve those objectives. This directly ties tasks and objectives for better accountability in terms of whether the tasks actually achieve the objectives. However, this method may lead to unrealistic budget requests and may complicate planning if particular tasks can't easily be linked to specific objectives.

Other budgeting methods include the affordability method (a top-down method based on how much the organization can afford to spend); percentage-of-sales method (spending a certain percentage of annual sales revenue or an average industry percentage of sales); competitive parity (budgeting according to what rivals spend). In practice, you may use several methods to construct a preliminary budget, look closely at costs and the market situation, consider both long- and short-term objectives, and then arrive at a reasonable budget. (*See* Chapter 11 for more on budgeting.)

Considering legal, regulatory, social and ethical issues

When planning for IMC, be aware of a wide range of legal, regulatory, social and ethical issues as you think creatively. On the most basic legal and ethical level, your communications should not be deceptive, distort facts or falsify product benefits. Find out whether certain types of messages are illegal; for instance, some nations outlaw comparative advertising while others forbid television commercials promoting tobacco products.

Also take privacy into consideration when planning for IMC. The European Union has strict rules about what personal data companies may collect and under what circumstances they are allowed to exchange such information. Retailers must first obtain permission before gathering customer data, sharing or selling it and using it for store marketing purposes. Companies must delete personal data after a set period, and they are forbidden to send personal data collected in the European Union to countries without equally strong privacy laws.[7] Such concerns about collection, storage, use and disclosure of personal data continue to make privacy a hot issue for marketers.

Planning IMC tools, messages and media

Most marketing plans employ more than one IMC tool to achieve their objectives. Your exact choices depend on your target audience; IMC objectives and budget; other marketing-mix decisions; and legal, regulatory, social and ethical considerations. They also depend on message and media strategy (discussed more fully later in this chapter). For instance, television advertising is generally more expensive than print advertising, so if you have a small budget or want to reach highly targeted audiences you may avoid television or use it sparingly. If your message involves an actual product demonstration, you will probably find radio inappropriate.

An unusually innovative or appealing IMC campaign can start a groundswell of **word of mouth** – people telling other people about the message, the product or another aspect of the marketing. Word of mouth has more credibility because it is not marketer controlled and it reflects what people in the market think, feel and do. Yet as word of mouth spreads, people may not get a complete or accurate message, and many outside the target audience may get the message (while some inside the target audience may not). You can certainly try to initiate positive word of mouth but you cannot control whether your audience picks up on the message and passes it along. In one recent study, the Toyota brand ranked highest on positive word of mouth, based on mentions in blogs, e-mails, phone calls and personal conversations.[8]

A more intense form of word of mouth is **buzz marketing**, in which you target opinion leaders to have them spread information to other people. Buzz marketing can spread product or brand information especially quickly on the Internet. However, buzz can fade quickly, because marketers can't control exactly what's being said, where and when the message spreads or how long it will circulate. Here's how Procter & Gamble has generated buzz through various marketing activities.

MARKETING IN PRACTICE: PROCTER & GAMBLE

Procter & Gamble (P&G), with £35 billion in annual turnover, is a US-based marketer of household products that constantly experiments with buzz. For example, it enlisted 600,000 mothers to converse with friends and family about Dawn dishwashing liquid and other P&G products. The mothers receive free samples and a weekly message asking their opinions about marketing ideas. P&G has also got buzz from mobile marketing for its Max Factor cosmetics. When it invited women to use their mobile phones to register for a prize draw, the contest got people buzzing and drew 250,000 responses. Finally, P&G's humorous campaign for ThermaCare heat wraps, which combined newspaper ads and fake but funny websites, video clips and blog entries, caused enough buzz to bring 11 million consumers into contact with the company's communications.[9]

Planning for pre- and post-implementation analysis and evaluation

To get the information you need for making better IMC decisions, you should plan time and money for research to pre-test messages, creative approaches and use of media. The purpose is to gauge the target audience's response and have the opportunity to make changes, possibly pre-test additional elements and then launch the complete campaign. For example, you can conduct pre-tests to measure recognition (do a sample of the audience recognize what is being promoted?), recall (does the sample remember the message and what it communicated?), affective reaction (do the message, product and brand provoke positive reactions?) and behavioural intentions (are people likely to buy the product or take another action on the basis of the promotion?).

You should also plan for measuring and evaluating the results after full implementation. Specifically, determine whether the message or media failed to reach the target audience at times, and why; how well the audience understood the message; what the audience thought and felt about the product or brand, message and media; which messages and media were especially effective in provoking the desired audience response; and how well the IMC tools, messages and media are supporting the overall positioning and working with other marketing-mix strategies.

PLANNING ADVERTISING

Planning for advertising follows the general IMC planning pattern shown in Figure 9.1. Note that you'll generally wait to make detailed decisions until after your marketing plan is being implemented. Still, you have to plan the general direction of both message and media in order to allocate the overall budget among advertising and other IMC activities.

Planning messages

What will the message actually say? What will it look (and/or sound) like? These are the two main decisions in planning messages. Some messages follow a 'hard-sell' approach to induce the target audience to respond now; others take a more 'soft-sell' approach, persuading without seeming to do so. Capital One, for example, was using a 'soft-sell' approach in its messages.

Message planning is inseparable from media planning because the copy in the advertisement, the design and the creativity of its execution depend on media choice. A creative decision to show the product in action, for instance, can be executed through a visual medium such as television or the Web. Creativity is, in fact, crucial for attracting attention, building awareness and shaping positive attitudes.[10] Although all decision details need not be finalized until the marketing plan is actually implemented, you should have some idea of message and media strategy so you can plan IMC budgets, timing and marketing-mix coordination.

Planning media

Media planning has become more complex due to the multiplicity of media choices and vehicles and the resulting smaller audience sizes for each – **audience fragmentation**. You'll always have budget constraints as you seek to balance reach and frequency. **Reach** refers to the number or percentage of people in the target audience exposed to an advertisement in a particular media vehicle during a certain period. Capital One used television, for instance, to achieve high reach. Higher reach means the message gets to more people, but this usually comes at a cost. **Frequency** is the number of times the target audience is exposed to a message in a particular media vehicle during a certain period. Higher frequency means you expose more people to your message on more occasions, again at a cost.

Should you plan to spend more on reach or more on frequency? Which media and vehicles will get your message to the right people at the right time and in the desired frequency? An alternative to paying for high reach that may include people outside the target audience (which sometimes happens with television commercials, for example) is to use more precisely targeted media. The following checklist summarizes planning considerations for media.

ESSENTIAL MARKETING PLAN CHECKLIST NO. 13: PLANNING FOR MEDIA

Your marketing plan should explain the basic reasoning behind your choices of media and message, although it need not cover every detail of the IMC campaign. Based on the IMC tools you will use, your budget and objectives, the marketing environment and the profile of your target audience, think about each of the following aspects of media planning. Place a tick mark next to each question after you've entered your answers in the space provided.

☐ What media do the audience use and prefer? Are these media available in the geographic region being targeted?

_____

☐ Can the media reach the right people in appropriate numbers to deliver messages during the customers' buying cycle?

_____

☐ Will the audience consider some media excessively intrusive or annoying?

_____

☐ What media are used by competitors and how might competing messages affect audience receptivity, understanding and response?

_____

☐ Should media be used to deliver the message continuously, intermittently or seasonally?

_____

☐ What are the creative possibilities, production requirements and costs for each medium?

_____

☐ Will the IMC budget cover the projected media cost for the desired reach and frequency?

_____

☐ What is the expected payback based on anticipated audience reaction?

_____

PLANNING SALES PROMOTION

Include sales promotion in your marketing plan when you want to stimulate faster response from consumers and business customers, channel members (sometimes called *the trade*) and the sales force. Although such promotions add value for only a limited time, some marketers use them as part of a longer-term strategy to strengthen relationships with the target audience. Sales promotion spending now exceeds advertising spending in a number of industries, reflecting increased competitive pressure and the need to produce immediate results.

However, because sales promotion often adds value by reducing perceived cost – lowering the product's price, in effect – over-use may heighten price sensitivity among customers, diminish brand strength and hurt profitability. Moreover, says promotion specialist Stephen Callender, 'Promotions that go wrong make a brand's strategies appear ill-thought out. That leads to insidious damage to the brand's credibility.'[11] Thus, you should set clear objectives, understand applicable laws and regulations, choose your techniques carefully, monitor implementation and evaluate results to make your sales promotion programmes successful.

Planning for customer sales promotion

Figure 9.4 shows a variety of common sales promotion techniques you can use, depending on your objectives and your IMC strategy. Consider sales promotion to target consumers or business customers when you want to:

- *Encourage product trial*. Potential customers have to try a product at least once before they can form a definite opinion and decide to buy it again (and again). Sales promotion is therefore commonly used to introduce a product and to stimulate higher sales during the maturity stage.

- *Reinforce advertising for a product or brand*. An exciting sales promotion can help customers notice and remember your advertising messages.

- *Attract interest*. Simply getting customers to visit a store or contact a manufacturer about a product can be a challenge. Some marketers use coupons, samples or other techniques in an attempt to get customers to take the first step.

Technique	Description
Sample	Free trial of a good or service
Coupon	Certificate redeemable for money off a product's price
Premium	A free or low-priced item offered to induce purchase of a product
Sweepstake or draw, contest, game	Chance to win cash or prizes through luck, knowledge or skill
Refund, rebate	Returning part or all of a product's price to the customer
Price pack	Special price marked by producer on the package or for multiple products bought together
Loyalty reward	Opportunity to earn gifts or cash for continuing to buy a certain product or from a certain company
Point-of-purchase display or demonstration	In-store materials promoting a product or in-store product demonstration
Branded speciality	Everyday item such as a calendar or T-shirt bearing the product name or brand, for reminder purposes

FIGURE 9.4   Sales promotion techniques targeting customers

- *Encourage purchase of multiple products.* Depending on your product mix, you can use sales promotion to stimulate customer purchases of two, three or even more products.

- *Encourage continued product purchase and usage.* You want to build customer loyalty to increase sales and reduce customer acquisition costs. Airlines do this with their frequent flyer programmes; supermarkets do this with their frequent shopper programmes.

Field marketing is becoming more popular as companies work with outside agencies to engage the target audience by bringing sales promotion to (and sometimes taking orders from) customers 'in the field' – in stores, shopping districts and city centres.[12] It can also be used to build reseller support, as Pernod Ricard has done.

MARKETING IN PRACTICE: PERNOD RICARD

Pernod Ricard, headquartered in Paris, has a €1 billion marketing budget to support its range of liquor products. It recently used field marketing to enlist new UK channel members for its Stolichnaya vodka and Havana Club rum beverages. To start, the company carefully researched the profile of the targeted customer segment for these brands. Then it hired a field marketing agency to visit hundreds of independent convenience stores in the areas where these targeted customers live. This effort added 157 new stores to Pernod Ricard's distribution channel in the first two weeks alone. Within three months, revenue from this expansion had covered all field marketing costs. Thanks to strong marketing support, Havana Club is the number-two rum in Europe.[13]

Planning for channel and sales force sales promotion

Particularly when using a push strategy, you may find sales promotion effective in enlisting the support of channel members and motivating sales representatives. Specifically, you can use channel and sales force promotions to:

- *Build channel commitment to a new product.* So many new products are introduced every year that channel members rarely have the space (or the money) to carry them all. Channel promotions can focus attention on a new product, encourage intermediaries to buy it, motivate the sales force to sell it and provide appropriate rewards.

- *Encourage more immediate results.* Sales promotion aimed at channel members and sales representatives offer inducements to take action during a specific time period.

- *Build relationships with channel members.* Keeping the ongoing support of major retail or wholesale businesses takes time and effort. Channel promotion offers opportunities for interactions that benefit the producer and its channel members.

- *Improve product knowledge.* Support the marketing effort by offering training and information through channel and sales force promotion.

Sales force promotions include contests (with cash or prizes as rewards), sales meetings (for training and motivation) and special promotional material (to supplement personal sales efforts). In planning a channel promotion, you may use monetary allowances (either discounts or payments for stocking or displaying a product); limited-time discounts (for buying early in the selling season or during other specified periods); free merchandise (extra quantities provided for buying a minimum quantity or a certain product); cooperative advertising (sharing costs when a channel member advertises a particular brand or product); or trade shows (setting up a booth or room at a convention centre to demonstrate products and interact with channel members or business buyers).

PLANNING PERSONAL SELLING

One of the most compelling reasons to include personal selling in a marketing plan is to establish solid relationships with new customers and maintain good relationships with the current customer base. Personal attention can make all the difference when your customers have unique problems, require customized solutions or place very large orders. Be sure to coordinate personal selling with all other marketing plan decisions to achieve the desired results. In addition, remind sales people to look beyond individual transactions and build long-term relationships with customers.

When planning for personal selling, consider:

- *Need*. Should your company have its own sales force or sell through retailers, agents or manufacturers' representatives? Some online businesses, such as Overstock.com, offer 'live chats' with reps who can answer questions and check on product specifications.[14]

- *Organization*. Will you organize reps according to geographic market, product, type of customer, size of customer or some other structure?

- *Size*. How many sales reps should you have, based on your objectives and current sales levels?

- *Compensation*. How will you determine sales force compensation?

- *Management*. How will you recruit, train, supervise, motivate and evaluate sales reps? How will sales reps be educated about legal, regulatory and ethical guidelines?

- *Process*. How will you generate sales leads? How will sales personnel access information about prospects and customers? What logistical activities must be coordinated with sales transactions, and who will be responsible?

PLANNING DIRECT MARKETING

Although mail order and telemarketing are hardly new, a growing number of organizations now include these and other direct marketing techniques in their IMC plans. Why? With better technology, marketers can target audiences more precisely, adjust messages and timing according to audience need and form a dialogue to build relationships cost-effectively. Direct marketing costs more than advertising in mass media, yet its interactive quality, selectivity and customization potential may add enough flexibility to make the difference worthwhile. Just as important, you can easily measure customer response and modify the offer or the communication again and again to move customers in the desired direction and achieve your objectives.

In planning direct marketing, first decide what response you want to elicit from the target audience(s), in accordance with your objectives. Many marketers use direct marketing to generate leads for sales representatives; the desired response is to have a potential customer indicate interest in the product by calling, e-mailing or sending a reply by post. Banks and mobile phone companies frequently use direct marketing – especially mailings – to attract new customers, bring former customers back and encourage current customers to buy more.

Now you're ready to select appropriate media and formulate an appropriate offer, based on research into the target audience's media and buying patterns. Different audiences and markets require different media and offers. According to one specialist, Australian consumers are not as accustomed to catalogue shopping as US consumers, for example; another specialist observes that television is just gaining popularity as a direct marketing medium in Japan.[15] Be sure your direct marketing campaign fits with the product's positioning and allow time in the marketing plan schedule for testing the message and the mechanisms for response (such as a freephone number, URL or postage-paid envelope). One of the advantages of direct marketing is that you can quickly see what actually works and use the results to refine your campaign or the overall marketing plan.

PLANNING PUBLIC RELATIONS

At one time or another, nearly every organization has prepared news releases, arranged news conferences and answered questions from reporters. Yet media contact is only one aspect of this flexible and powerful IMC tool. You can use public relations not just to convey the organization's messages but also to build mutual understanding and maintain an ongoing dialogue between your organization and key members of the 'public'. Moreover, your message has more credibility when conveyed by media representatives than when communicated directly by your organization, as noted earlier.

Defining the 'public'

The 'public' in public relations may refer to people in any number of target audiences, such as customers and prospective customers, employees, channel members, suppliers, news reporters, investors and financial analysts, special interest groups, legislators and regulators, and community leaders. Each of these audiences can affect your plan's success and performance, but not all will be addressed in the same way; in fact, not all may be addressed in a single marketing plan.

In general, you can use PR to achieve one or more of the following objectives:

- *Identify and understand stakeholder concerns*. Through PR contacts such as community meetings, surveys and other methods, you can learn what your stakeholders think and feel about important issues such as your products, image, ecological record and so on. Kingfisher, a UK-based home products retailer, seeks out public opinion and government views on social and ecological issues such as buying timber sourced from endangered forests. The idea is to see how public concern is growing so the company can phase in changes over time.[16]

- *Convey the organization's viewpoint or important information.* Knowing your target audience's views, you can adapt your organization's position if appropriate. At the very least, you can use PR to explain your management's viewpoint or educate the public, especially vital in the midst of a crisis.

- *Correct misperceptions.* If one or more target audiences have misperceptions about some aspect of your organization – such as the quality of its products – you can plan to use PR to counteract the inaccuracies by providing more information, answering questions and allowing for periodic updates.

- *Enhance the organization's image.* Many organizations apply PR techniques to enhance their image. If an organization has been embroiled in controversy, PR can show what management is doing to improve and how it has gone beyond minimum requirements to satisfy its publics.

- *Promote products and brands.* You can use PR to communicate the features, benefits and value of your products and promote your brands.

Planning PR techniques

Your marketing plan may include a variety of PR techniques. One of the most commonly used is the news release, written and distributed to media representatives via printed document, e-mail, Web link or **podcasting** (distributing an audio or video file via the Internet). For more significant news, you may want to call a news conference, let media reps hear management speak and hold a question-and-answer session. Also consider whether you should seek publicity by sponsoring an event, the way the BBC sponsored a music festival in Dundee and online in Second Life.

This checklist will help you plan for consistency and a sense of unity in your IMC campaign.

 **ESSENTIAL MARKETING PLAN CHECKLIST NO.14:** INTEGRATING MARKETING COMMUNICATIONS

To achieve your marketing plan objectives and communicate effectively with your target audience, you must integrate the messages and media in each campaign. Consider each of the following questions in turn, placing a tick mark next to each after you've noted your ideas in the space provided.

☐ Are the chosen IMC tools appropriate for the target audience(s), product, company image and IMC objectives?

☐ Is the content of each message consistent with that of other messages, the brand image and the product's differentiating points?

☐ Are the messages and media appropriate in the context of the overall marketing mix?

☐ Is the campaign designed to foster customer receptivity, attention, interest and response?

☐ Does the campaign support the product positioning and the marketing plan objectives?

☐ Is your organization prepared to handle response to the messages?

☐ How can you measure results to determine whether the campaign is effective?

CHAPTER SUMMARY

The purpose of integrated marketing communication (IMC) is to ensure that content and delivery of all the marketing messages in all media are coordinated and consistent, and that they support the positioning and objectives of the product, brand or organization. In IMC planning, first define the target audience and set objectives based on the responses desired from the target audience. Next, determine an appropriate budget and consider any applicable legal, regulatory, social and ethical issues that may affect messages, media or other aspects of IMC planning. Then select and plan for the use of specific IMC tools, messages and media; and plan pre- and post-implementation analysis to evaluate the campaign.

When planning advertising, consider message appeal, creativity and appropriateness for media; balance reach and frequency in the context of the budget. Use sales promotion to stimulate faster response from customers or channel members by adding value (or reducing perceived cost) for a limited time. If personal selling is appropriate, consider in-person sales, Internet sales or telemarketing. For more precise targeting, consider direct marketing to build relationships cost-effectively and have the ability to measure response compared with objectives. Plan for public relations to foster positive attitudes and an ongoing dialogue with key publics.

CASE STUDY: RECKITT BENCKISER REACHES OUT TO CUSTOMERS

Reckitt Benckiser is well known for household brands such as Dettol cleaning products, O'Cedar polishes, Finish dishwashing tabs and Calgon fabric care products. The UK company also offers personal care products in North America under brands such as Boots Healthcare and Clearasil. With annual turnover of £8 billion and a marketing budget exceeding £500,000, Reckitt has such a diverse product mix that its marketing plan calls for using every type of IMC tool.

Not long ago, for example, Reckitt's research found that furniture polish sales were declining because of the increased popularity of furniture that requires no polish and because more people are using household cleaning wipes. In response, the company launched a quirky advertising campaign to communicate how well its O'Cedar liquid polish protects furniture. The campaign reached millions of consumers, reinforced the positive brand image of O'Cedar and set the stage for additional promotions aimed at boosting purchases.

Another example: when Reckitt introduced new Optrex eye-care products, it raised awareness with television commercials and consumer brochures explaining Optrex's features and benefits. In addition, the firm offered training to employees in chemist's shops and provided point-of-purchase displays for store use. The advertising, sales promotion and personal selling worked together to reinforce the products' positioning as a soothing formulation for dry eyes.

Reckitt tailors its sales promotion activities to specific target segments. For instance, it has arranged for young teenagers to receive samples of Clearasil acne control products. And it invites visitors to its websites to subscribe to an e-mail newsletter with household tips, recipes, free samples, coupons and more. Watch for Reckitt's marketing plans to continue putting IMC tools to work as the company reaches out to communicate with consumers in more than 100 nations.[17]

Case questions

1. What kind of response (cognitive, affective or behavioural) do you think Reckitt Benckiser wanted to elicit by giving away Clearasil samples – and why?

2. Why would Reckitt support its Optrex product introductions with consumer brochures as well as point-of-purchase materials and store employee training?

APPLY YOUR KNOWLEDGE

Choose a particular product; find two or more advertisements, promotions or other communications in which it is featured; and analyse the company's IMC activities. Then prepare a brief oral presentation or written report explaining your analysis.

- What target audience do you think these communications are designed to reach?

- What cognitive, affective or behavioural response(s) might these communications provoke?

- What objectives do you think the company has set for these communications and how would you recommend that it measure results?

- What legal, regulatory, social or ethical considerations are likely to influence this firm's IMC planning?

BUILD YOUR OWN MARKETING PLAN

Plan your IMC decisions as you continue developing your marketing plan. What target audience(s) do you want to reach? What are your IMC objectives? What is an appropriate IMC budget, given the available resources, reach and frequency preferences and the chosen tools? Identify any legal, regulatory, social or ethical issues that would affect your IMC decisions. Will you use advertising, sales promotion, personal selling, direct marketing and/or public relations – and why? Outline one IMC campaign, indicating objectives, target audience, general message and media decisions, approximate budget and how results will be measured. Finally, document your ideas in a written marketing plan.

ENDNOTES

1. Kerry Capell, 'BBC: Step Right into the Telly', *BusinessWeek*, 24 July 2006, pp. 51ff.

2. Carrick Mollenkamp and Ian McDonald, 'Outside Audit: Behind the British Debt Magic', *Wall Street Journal*, 31 October 2006, p. C1; 'Mark Ritson on Branding: How a Repositioning Should Be Done', *Marketing*, 13 September 2006, p. 21; 'Capital One Launches New UK Campaign', *Europe Intelligence Wire*, 26 September 2006, n.p.; 'Unloved Capital One Makes £9m Bid to Gain Popularity', *Marketing Week*, 7 September 2006, p. 8.

3. Ellen Sheng, 'Corporate Connections', *Wall Street Journal*, 29 January 2007, p. R8; Louise Story and Eric Pfanner, 'The Future of Web Ads Is in Britain', *New York Times*, 4 December 2006, www.nytimes.com.

4. See Sandy D. Jap and Erin Anderson, 'Testing the Life-Cycle Theory of Inter-Organisational Relations: Do Performance Outcomes Depend on the Path Taken?', *Insead Knowledge*, February 2003, www.insead.edu.

5. Normandy Madden, 'Global Highlight: Unilever's Zhonghua Toothpaste', *Advertising Age*, 19 February 2007, p. 55; 'Unilever Maintains Flexibility by Leasing', *Business Daily Update*, 9 October 2006, n.p.

6. See Nigel F. Piercy, 'The Marketing Budgeting Process: Marketing Management Implications', *Journal of Marketing*, October 1987, pp. 45–59.

7. David Scheer, 'Europe's New High-Tech Role: Playing Privacy Cop to the World', *Wall Street Journal*, 10 October 2003, pp. A1, A16.

8. 'Stats: Keep Your Ear to the Ground', *Marketing News*, 1 September 2006, p. 4.

9. Emily Steel, 'Grabbing Older Consumers via Cellphone', *Wall Street Journal*, 31 January 2007, p. B3; Stuart Elliott, 'Online, P&G Gets a Little Crazy', *New York Times*, 14 December 2006, p. C3; Robert Berner, 'I Sold It Through the Grapevine', *BusinessWeek*, 29 May 2006, pp. 32–4.

10. See John Philip Jones, 'Is Advertising Still Salesmanship?', *Journal of Advertising Research*, May–June 1997, pp. 9ff.

11. Quoted in Belinda Gannaway, 'Hidden Danger of Sales Promotions', *Marketing*, 20 February 2003, pp. 31ff.; other sources: Liz Hamson, 'Measured Approach: There Is a Trade-Off Between Promotions and Profits and, Contrary to UK Marketers' Views, It Can Be Measured', *Grocer*, 19 April 2003, p. 38; Philip Kotler, *A Framework for Marketing Management*, 2nd edn (Upper Saddle River, NJ: Prentice Hall, 2003), pp. 318–19.

12. 'Field Marketing: What Drives Engagement?', *Marketing*, 24 January 2007, p. 31.

13. Doreen Hemlock, 'Cuban Rum Rising', *Hartford Courant*, 24 February 2007, www.courant.com; 'Field Marketing Agency of the Year – Cosine', *Marketing*, 20 December 2006, p. 37.

14. Vauhini Vara, 'That Looks Great on You', *Wall Street Journal*, 3 January 2007, p. D1.

15. Doug McPherson, 'Riding the Wave of Opportunity', *Response*, November 2002, pp. 34ff.

16. Erin White, 'PR Firms Advise Corporations on Social-Responsibility Issues', *Wall Street Journal*, 13 November 2002, p. B10.

17. Based on information from 'The Work: New Campaigns – the World', *Campaign*, 26 January 2007, p. 32; Lisa Sanders, 'JWT Fails to Keep Up with Mr. Jones', *Advertising Age*, 3 July 2006, pp. 1ff; Jack Neff, 'Clearasil Marches into Middle-School Classes', *Advertising Age*, 13 November 2006, p. 8; 'Eye and Ear Care Product News', *Chemist & Druggist*, 5 August 2006, p. 34

10

Supporting the marketing mix

Comprehension outcomes

After studying this chapter, you will be able to:

- Explain why a marketing plan should include customer service and internal marketing strategies

- Understand planning for customer service and internal marketing

Application outcomes

After studying this chapter, you will be able to:

- Plan for customer service to support the marketing plan

- Plan for internal marketing to support the marketing plan

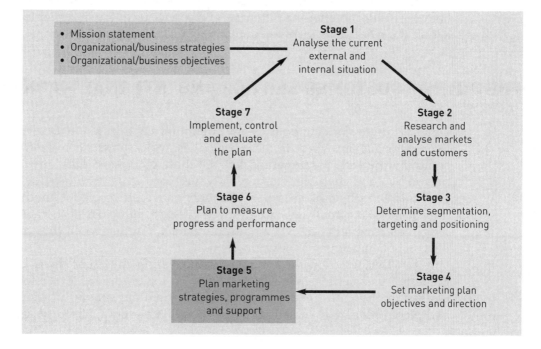

CHAPTER PREVIEW

Dinero Express speaks the language of customer service. A division of Spain's Banco Bilbao Vizcaya Argentaria (BBVA), Dinero Express targets immigrants who need banking services and more. The bright, colourful branches are open 12 hours a day, 364 days a year, offering basic banking services plus fast and affordable international money transfers; bargain-priced Internet access, overseas phone calls and package delivery; and assistance with everyday needs like jobs and housing. Branch employees are immigrants themselves, so they have a good idea of what their customers want and expect. Despite the service extras, Dinero Express branches reach break-even in about 16 months, compared with a break-even period of 24 months for other BBVA branches.[1]

Customers expect good service from any organization, but great service is an especially compelling point of differentiation, as BBVA's marketing personnel know. Great service attracts new customers, encourages repeat business, generates word-of-mouth referrals, draws positive publicity, smoothes the way for bank personnel to suggest additional services and confers a competitive edge. Yet great service does not simply happen – it requires careful planning and skilful marketing to internal audiences, as well.

This is the final chapter about planning for marketing strategies, programmes and support, stage 5 in the marketing planning process. First, you'll learn about the vital role that customer service and internal marketing play in the marketing plan. The next section discusses some of the decisions you must make in planning for customer service, including those about process and outcome; service levels; service before, during and after the purchase; and service recovery. The chapter closes with a look at the decisions involved in planning for internal marketing.

THE ROLE OF CUSTOMER SERVICE AND INTERNAL MARKETING

Dinero Express's pricing policies have definitely contributed to its success, as have its decisions about where to locate branches, which products to offer and how to communicate with the target market. All these marketing decisions must be supported by good customer service, however, for the bank to provide the value it promises. Branch employees aren't the only ones responsible for good service: customer service is actually every employee's responsibility. This is because customers judge service quality at every point of contact, not just when they are making a deposit or complaining about a problem.

In fact, Dell, which markets computers and other high-tech products, prefers to use the term 'customer experience' rather than 'customer service'. Dell's focus is on the quality of the entire experience, from the time customers browse its website and place orders to their satisfaction with delivery, setup, usability, reliability and resolution of any problems.[2] From the customer's perspective, service is an integral part of the experience of dealing with a product or brand. Thus, if a company ignores a request for information, for instance, or a charitable organization fails to acknowledge a monetary contribution, these lapses are perceived as poor customer service.

Unsatisfactory and inconsistent customer service quality can hinder your ability to achieve marketing plan objectives, even if you have meticulously researched targeting and positioning and planned creative marketing activities. Just as bad, dissatisfied customers often tell others about their experiences, generating negative word of mouth that can hurt your product or image.[3] Bad service can cost you customers, often without warning. In one study, 37 per cent of German business customers were so unhappy over telecommunications service problems that they switched providers.[4] Therefore, it's best to view complaints not as annoyances but as opportunities to identify areas for improvement and give the complaining customers tangible reasons to continue the relationship.

As Figure 10.1 indicates, planning for customer service supports the marketing effort outside the organization and is, in turn, implemented with the support of the internal marketing strategy, which focuses on people and processes inside the organization.

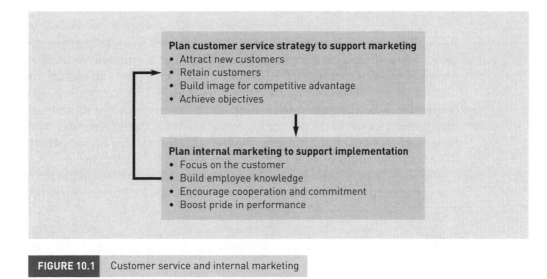

FIGURE 10.1 Customer service and internal marketing

Marketing applications of customer service

Good customer service can make a highly positive contribution to your marketing plan. Specific areas to focus on when planning customer service activities include customer relationships and marketing plan objectives.

Customer relationships

Consider how customer service can add value, helping to attract and retain customers, especially if your service level is competitively superior. For instance, the Czech software company Grisoft, which makes AVG anti-virus software, has dozens of experts available at all times to answer the monthly volume of 24,000 customer phone calls and e-mails requesting help with viruses – a growing problem for computer users.[5] Even manufactured goods such as industrial rubber hoses cannot be marketed without quality service these days. 'Our business is increasingly a service business', observes the president of Summers Rubber Co., a US manufacturer.[6] Company engineers not only match hose design to each customer's particular use, but are available to diagnose any problems that might occur.

If your current customers remain loyal, you'll need fewer or less expensive customer acquisition programmes to meet your marketing objectives. According to the general manager of the Marco Polo Hongkong Hotel, 'Repeat business saves us 10 times the cost and effort of getting new business.' This makes initial customer service contacts even more important: 'Guests judge us immediately. They will not come again if we deliver mediocre service', he says.[7]

Marketing plan objectives

To achieve objectives such as market share, look for ways to leverage good customer service as a competitive strength. Remember that if you deliver good customer service that satisfies customers the first time, you'll save time and money, contributing to the achievement of both financial and marketing objectives. To illustrate, Marten Transport, a family-run freight company, takes great care with deliveries when its refrigerated lorries carry perishable foods such as frozen foods and fresh vegetables. This has helped Marten Transport build a solid foundation for long-term profitability. 'The success of our business is in the details', says the chairman.[8]

France's Saint-Gobain, an industrial materials manufacturer with a worldwide presence, is known for incorporating customer service into its marketing planning.

MARKETING IN PRACTICE: SAINT-GOBAIN ABRASIVES

The UK abrasives division of Saint-Gobain specializes in satisfying the needs of highly demanding business customers. Technical sales representatives and application engineers from the UK manufacturing plant visit customers, learn about their needs, recommend suitable abrasive products such as grinding wheels, plan to customize products as needed and follow up to answer customers' technical questions after the purchase. Thanks to such close customer relationships, Saint-Gobain's marketers gain valuable insight into market trends and can use marketing to amplify the firm's global reputation as a provider of high-quality industrial abrasives.[9]

Marketing applications of internal marketing

Good customer service – and, in fact, effective implementation of the entire marketing plan – depends on **internal marketing**, a carefully coordinated set of policies and activities designed to build internal employee relationships and reinforce and reward internal commitment to the marketing effort and to good customer service. At the very least, internal audiences need advance notice of new promotions, new products and other marketing activities so they're prepared when customers respond. Capital One Bank Europe, for example, recently gave managers and employees a preview of its new marketing campaign prior to the public introduction.[10]

On a larger scale, planning for internal marketing covers decisions about hiring and training managers and employees, motivating and rewarding them for working to satisfy customers and communicating with them about marketing plans and performance. In short, robust internal marketing lays the foundation for implementing your marketing plan and delivering good, consistent customer service.

You can use internal marketing to help in the following areas:

- *Focus on the customer.* Some employees in functions with little customer contact – such as finance or human resources – may get caught up in the daily pressures of work and lose their customer focus. Internal marketing is a good way to refocus on the customer and remind employees that their performance is essential for implementing plans that serve and satisfy customers.

- *Build employee knowledge.* Be sure employees throughout the hierarchy know at least the general outline of the marketing effort, are informed about the needs and expectations of targeted customers and understand what you want to achieve. This knowledge gives them the background they need to serve customers and solve any service problems.

- *Encourage organization-wide cooperation with and commitment to the plan.* Success really is in the details, as the head of Marten Transport observed. If your organization's employees do not understand the plan or resent it, they may not give details the proper attention, let alone implement every tactic to full effect. Remember that marketing is not the only function affected by the marketing plan; manufacturing, finance and all the other departments must cooperate to achieve the objectives and you need senior management's support. Use internal marketing to build relations inside the organization and encourage commitment among those responsible for approving the plan and making it succeed through implementation.

- *Boost pride in performance.* Internal marketing can increase employees' sense of involvement and boost their pride in performing over and above expectations. For example, the Marco Polo Hongkong Hotel gives widespread internal recognition to employees who deliver outstanding service, based on guest comments. Such feedback shows employees that the organization and its customers appreciate good customer service.

The next two sections highlight how you can plan for customer service and for internal marketing as you prepare your marketing plan. Many of the examples in the following pages are from service businesses but the customer service ideas can be adapted for many situations.

PLANNING FOR CUSTOMER SERVICE

Knowing what your customers want and value, you face process decisions about how to make the customer service experience as pleasant as possible. You also face outcome decisions related to whether the customer service is delivered on time, as promised and in a satisfactory manner. Your customers will be dissatisfied if they receive the promised quality of service but find the experience of arranging for it tedious or inconvenient. On the other hand, customers who are satisfied with both the process and the outcomes are likely to become loyal.

The specific process and outcome decisions that you will make depend on your objectives, marketing strategies, resources and capabilities. You must also consider what level of customer service you will promise and be able to deliver; the type of customer service you will offer before, during and after a purchase; and the process you will follow to recover from any customer service lapses (*see* Figure 10.2).

Decisions	Purpose
Process	To create a satisfactory experience for customers who arrange for service delivery
Outcomes	To deliver service on time, as promised and with the expected result for customer satisfaction
Timing	To provide needed service before, during or after a purchase
Service recovery	To handle complaints, fix lapses in customer service delivery and identify areas of improvement

FIGURE 10.2   Key customer service strategy decisions

Levels of service

Few companies can afford the highest level of customer service, with completely personalized attention immediately available on request, but then again, not every customer in every segment can afford (or will expect) such service. Shoppers around the world who buy from London-based Net-A-Porter.com, a luxury fashion retail website, experience customer service pampering such as luxury packaging, style advice, expedited express despatch and free returns. The idea is to provide affluent customers with the same quality of service they would receive in a high-fashion boutique.[11]

In many industries where intense price competition is a consideration, there is a trend toward eliminating extras and cutting costs, often by automating service procedures. Ryanair and easyJet are two no-frills, low-fare airlines that minimize customer service costs by having customers buy tickets online and pay for inflight food and drinks. However, the marketing plan for Bangkok Airways uses the opposite service strategy.

MARKETING IN PRACTICE: BANGKOK AIRWAYS

Going against the trend in the airline business, Bangkok Airways pampers its passengers – travellers to and from Thailand – and charges accordingly. Passengers waiting to board its planes in Thai airports can eat snacks, surf the Net, examine museum-quality ceramics or relax with garden views, all included in the fare; on-board customer service, featuring Thai foods, is also gracious. Bangkok Airways started small but is rapidly expanding as its high level of customer service attracts more passengers and yields profits. Although the airline currently concentrates on Asian destinations, it plans to add destinations in Europe by 2012, using its superior customer service as a point of differentiation to attract new passengers and compete with established carriers on those routes.[12]

The level of customer service you plan should be consistent with the following elements:

- *Customer needs and expectations*. What do targeted customers want, need and expect in terms of customer service? Use marketing research to identify the service levels that would satisfy customers in each targeted segment; uncover trends in customer turnover; and determine whether customers are defecting because of poor customer service. If you segment your market according to service usage and expectations, you may find promising opportunities and steer the organization away from unprofitable segments.[13]

- *Positioning and competitive strategies*. What level of service is consistent with your product's or brand's positioning? What level of service would help the product or brand compete more effectively? Because Commonwealth Bank in Australia understands the value of a positioning based on good customer service, its managers redesigned service processes to produce better service outcomes. As one example, they eliminated redundant bank procedures, rearranged branch layouts and changed staffing (process), aiming to reduce queue times to five minutes or less (outcome). Good service will be even more important in the future because, the bank's head of retail banking services says, 'in terms of what will shape the industry, I can sum it up in a single word – convenience'.[14]

- *Other marketing-mix decisions*. Is the product new or complicated? To provide service for customers who buy its high-end plasma television screens, for example, Philips India has opened a series of Star Service Centres that stock parts and diagnose product problems.[15] How is pricing likely to influence customers' expectations of customer service? Do the product's promotions promise or imply a high level of customer service? What level of customer service can your channel members deliver? How will a certain level of customer service fit in with the strategies and objectives in your marketing plan?

- *Organizational resources and strengths*. What level of customer service fits in with your organization's financial and human resources? Is technology available to support or substitute for customer service delivery? Is good customer service delivery a particular strength? Can or should customer service be outsourced? In deciding about customer service levels, you should carefully analyse the cost–benefit trade-offs for each targeted segment.[16]

Pre-purchase service

Depending on your product and market, customers may have questions and require service assistance before they buy. Business buyers in particular may need help with product specifications or configuration, installation options and warranty or repair information. If you market directly to customers, you must be prepared to provide at least some service before a purchase transaction. If you market through intermediaries, you will be relying on channel members to answer customers' questions and demonstrate features.

Matsushita, the Japanese maker of electronics and appliances, gives its channel members extra support so they can provide good pre- and post-purchase customer service. In the Philippines, for instance, the company holds periodic seminars to introduce dealers and repair technicians to new products and the latest technical features. This attention to customer service has helped Matsushita maintain a strong competitive position in the Philippine market.[17]

Point-of-purchase service

At the time or place of the purchase, your customers may want help in: testing a product; completing the paperwork for a transaction; arranging for delivery or pick-up; arranging payment method or terms; taking advantage of promotions connected with purchasing; or other purchase-related service tasks. If your customer service falls short here, customers may not complete the purchase; conversely, if you deliver good customer service during the purchase transaction, you will build customer satisfaction and encourage repeat purchasing. Here's how W.W. Grainger provides point-of-purchase service.

MARKETING IN PRACTICE: W.W. GRAINGER

W.W. Grainger, the giant US-based distributor of industrial parts and supplies, provides point-of-purchase customer service on behalf of the thousands of manufacturers whose products it sells. When buyers representing any of the firm's 2 million business customers visit a Grainger branch from Seattle to Shanghai, they get prompt and personal attention from staff members. 'You won't find a customer here who waits more than a couple of minutes', says the manager of one branch. 'We stay focused on the customer and make sure they leave here with their problem solved', says another Grainger manager.[18]

Post-purchase service

To encourage repeat business and strengthen customer relations, you will probably have to deliver some sort of customer service after the purchase. This may include: training buyers in product use; explaining maintenance or repair procedures; exchanging defective products; returning products for refunds; installing replacement parts; or other post-purchase services. Some companies are using technology to detect the need for post-purchase service even before customers notice any problems.

Whether your organization has a physical presence or operates only on the Web, post-purchase service should be part of the planning process. Although many retailers allow in-store refunds of merchandise purchased online, recent research shows that the customer service process is sometimes cumbersome and time-consuming; the study also cited as good customer service the ability to return online purchases to stores.[19]

Service recovery

Because customer service may not be delivered perfectly every time, you should plan for **service recovery**, how your organization will recover from a service lapse and satisfy customers. Service recovery offers an excellent opportunity to demonstrate understanding of customers' expectations and needs and – equally important – rebuild ties with customers by implementing a speedy and satisfactory resolution. According to one study, at least 70 per cent of dissatisfied customers will keep buying from a company if their complaints are resolved satisfactorily. If you please these customers you can turn them from potential defectors into advocates for your organization – a good way to stimulate positive word of mouth.[20] For instance, after Lexus recalled one of its models, the automaker presented owners with a free iPod nano to make amends for inconveniencing them.[21]

Internal marketing is vital for service recovery, because employees must have the commitment, skills and authority to clarify the extent and nature of a service lapse, offer a suitable response and see that it is implemented as promised. As you plan for service recovery, focus on both process and outcome (*see* Figure 10.3). Customers will be more dissatisfied if you provide no convenient method for receiving complaints or fail to resolve their complaints satisfactorily. Sometimes customers only want to express their dissatisfaction and receive an apology. The director of customer relations for a regional airline observes: 'Things do go wrong but you have to try to recover. You have to listen and try to find out what the customer needs.'[22]

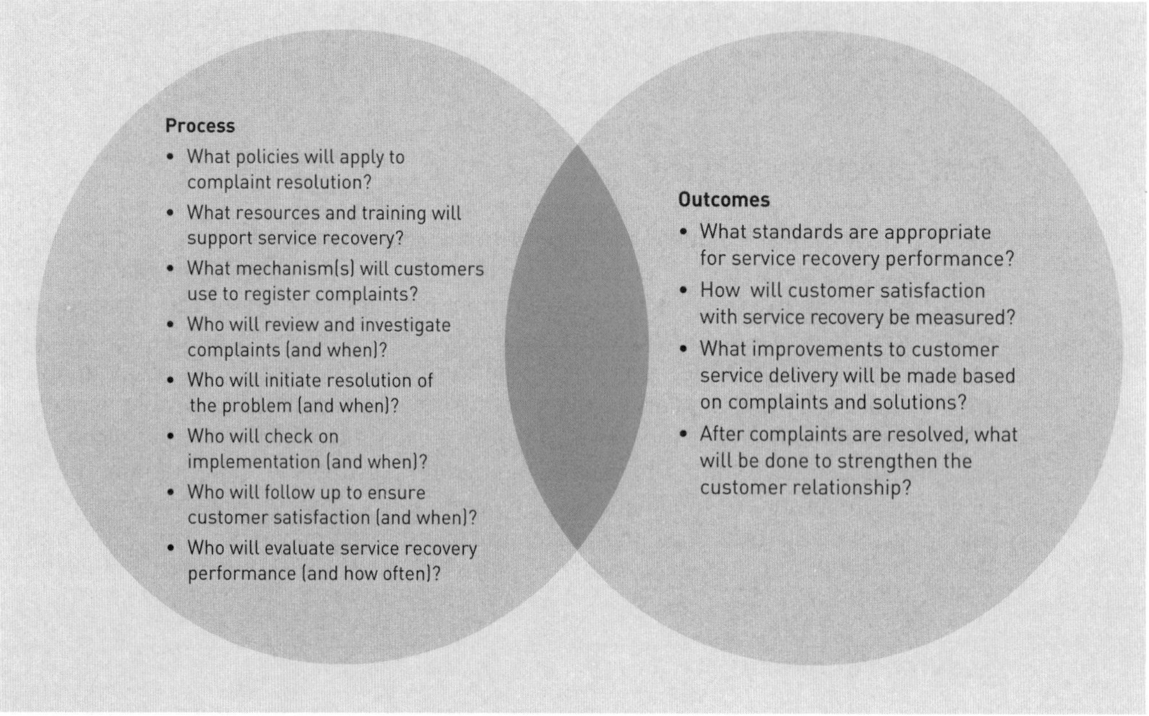

Process

- What policies will apply to complaint resolution?
- What resources and training will support service recovery?
- What mechanism(s) will customers use to register complaints?
- Who will review and investigate complaints (and when)?
- Who will initiate resolution of the problem (and when)?
- Who will check on implementation (and when)?
- Who will follow up to ensure customer satisfaction (and when)?
- Who will evaluate service recovery performance (and how often)?

Outcomes

- What standards are appropriate for service recovery performance?
- How will customer satisfaction with service recovery be measured?
- What improvements to customer service delivery will be made based on complaints and solutions?
- After complaints are resolved, what will be done to strengthen the customer relationship?

FIGURE 10.3   Planning service recovery process and outcomes

Be sure to seek the input of staff members who deal directly with customers when determining what tools and support you need to correct service mistakes. Also solicit suggestions from these employees for practical ways to improve delivery and prevent service lapses.[23] And try to involve top management in service recovery, as doing so will go a long way toward proving your organization's commitment to satisfaction and to keeping the customer relationship alive. The head of Citizens Trust Bank in Atlanta makes a point of listening and responding to service problems. 'Customers are always pleasantly surprised that they can talk directly to me, the president of the bank, when they have a complaint', he says.[24]

As you consider how to incorporate customer service support into your marketing plan, use the following checklist.

ESSENTIAL MARKETING PLAN CHECKLIST NO. 15:
PLANNING CUSTOMER SERVICE SUPPORT

This checklist will guide you through the main issues to research and analyse as you plan for customer service to support your marketing activities. After you write your ideas in the spaces provided, put a tick mark next to the questions you've answered. If your marketing plan is for a hypothetical firm, use this checklist as a guide to the information you'd need to gather to make decisions about customer service.

☐ What level of service do targeted customers need, expect and prefer before, during and after the purchase?

_____

☐ What customer service level is reasonable and practical, based on organizational resources and objectives?

_____

☐ What competitive, industry and market considerations might affect the customer service plan?

_____

☐ What legal, regulatory, ecological, technological, social or ethical issues might affect the customer service plan?

_____

☐ How will you train and reward employees and value chain participants for providing good customer service?

_____

☐ What service recovery plans and policies do you need?

_____

PLANNING FOR INTERNAL MARKETING

Ideally, you want your internal marketing activities to engage the hearts and minds of managers and employees at every organizational level – the internal equivalent of what good external marketing seeks to achieve. First, of course, you will 'market' the marketing plan to gain senior management approval and support. Then, for the approved plan to succeed, you need internal marketing to build enthusiastic commitment among the organization's middle managers, front-line managers and employees.[25] This means going beyond a catchy slogan or one-time special event to develop an ongoing internal marketing strategy that you can adapt as the situation changes.

Although the specifics of internal marketing strategy will differ from organization to organization, most touch on the following:

- *Hiring and training.* Even when you are not directly involved in personnel decisions, you can influence hiring procedures to ensure that new employees have a positive attitude toward customer service. You should also influence or participate in training to build the staff's knowledge of the customer and of the marketing effort.

- *Standards.* What, exactly, constitutes performance in implementing marketing programmes? Your performance standards should be consistent with the marketing plan's (and the organization's) objectives, with other job-related standards, with what customers want and with what you are promising and promoting.

- *Communication.* This is essential for reinforcing objectives and standards; coordinating programmes and implementing responsibilities; keeping employees informed; and keeping them interested and connected. You use any number of communication techniques, from printed newsletters and voice-mail messages to internal websites and teleconferences. For instance, the Marco Polo Hongkong Hotel has condensed its service basics into five succinct messages introduced at a company party, repeated at staff meetings and printed on pocket calendars for employees to check daily. The hotel also circulates the results of customer service studies and compliments submitted by guests.

- *Participation.* Inviting participation in the marketing planning process can encourage stronger support and commitment among those who are charged with implementation. Customer contact personnel, in particular, may be able to suggest how your proposed programmes can be improved. In other words, view internal marketing communication as a two-way, relationship-building dialogue, with information flowing to you and from you.

- *Monitoring and rewards.* Are employees performing up to the standards that have been set and cooperating for smooth implementation of marketing programmes? If not, what needs improvement? If so, how should you reinforce and reward good performance? Your internal marketing reward system must be consistent with the organization's overall system of motivation, performance evaluation and rewards. For instance, at the wireless telecommunications firm T-Mobile, senior managers won't be considered for bonus pay unless they've spent a week working in one of the company's retail outlets and helped out in a store during the busy year-end holiday season. This ensures that managers have first-hand knowledge of what customers expect and appreciate.[26]

See Chapter 12 for more about controlling marketing plan implementation.

CHAPTER SUMMARY

Customer service supports the external marketing effort and, in turn, must be supported by internal marketing focusing on people and processes inside the organization. Customer service can help the organization attract new customers, retain current customers, build image for competitive advantage and achieve its objectives. Internal marketing can help the organization focus on customers, increase employee knowledge, encourage internal cooperation and commitment to marketing and boost pride in performance.

Marketers face decisions about process (the experience customers will have in arranging for customer service) and outcomes (delivering service on time, as promised and to the customer's satisfaction). They also face decisions about the appropriate level of customer service to be promised and delivered; the delivery of customer service before, during and after a purchase; and the process of recovering from any customer service lapses.

CASE STUDY: MERCEDES-BENZ DRIVES CUSTOMER SERVICE SUPPORT

Driving high-quality customer service support throughout the value chain can be a challenge, as the marketers at Mercedes-Benz are well aware. Mercedes brings buyers into showrooms around the world by communicating its vehicles' top-notch engineering, design and performance. Positive experiences with the product and with support services such as routine maintenance generate revenue and encourage brand loyalty. However, if customers have complaints, they expect local dealers to come up with solutions.

Mercedes' service recovery plan is therefore focused on doing what is right for the customer. Consider what happened when 2,000 buyers ordered and paid for E-class Mercedes vehicles with an optional navigation system. Dealers told customers that delays in receiving supplies of the navigation system would result in dealer installation rather than factory installation. But once the navigation system became available, Mercedes decided the retrofit was too complex to be handled by dealers. Instead, it took the unusual step of offering to exchange the original cars for new, factory-outfitted cars (and then sold the original cars as used vehicles).

Many Mercedes dealerships go to great lengths to satisfy customers. For example, one dealer has service vans carrying equipment and parts for on-the-spot maintenance and repair in the customer's home driveway, office car park or even near a golf course. Driving to raise customer satisfaction scores, Mercedes is benchmarking against top European dealerships and providing its employees and dealers with additional service training. Dealers that improve their customer-satisfaction scores will be rewarded with higher margins. Service plays such a key role that Mercedes recently appointed one of its service support managers to be UK marketing director. [27]

Case questions

1. How do Mercedes-Benz's decisions about customer service support fit within the framework shown in Figure 10.2?

2. Do you agree with Mercedes' plan to reward dealers that improve customer service and satisfaction with higher margins? Explain your answer.

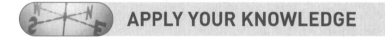

APPLY YOUR KNOWLEDGE

To see how customer service supports a firm's marketing mix, select a retailer with a nearby store location and an online presence. Visit one store, browse the website and then analyse this retailer's approach to customer service. Prepare a brief oral or written report summarizing your analysis.

- Where on the website does the retailer place its customer service policies? Where in the store are such policies displayed? Are the policies practical and easy to understand?

- How would you describe the level of service in the store? Is it consistent with the retailer's positioning and competitive situation, its pricing and its other marketing activities?

- What customer service is offered online? Does the website invite shoppers to interact with service representatives via e-mail, online chat, telephone or some other method?

- Are pre-purchase, point-of-purchase and/or post-purchase services offered in the store? How do these differ (if at all) from the services offered to online customers?

- What changes in customer service would you suggest for this retailer? Why?

BUILD YOUR OWN MARKETING PLAN

Continue your marketing plan by making decisions about customer service and internal marketing. First, what is an appropriate level of customer service to support your positioning and other marketing-mix decisions? Do you know how this level of service fits with customers' needs and expectations? Does your customer service add more value than that offered by competitors? What pre-purchase, point-of-purchase and post-purchase customer service will you plan to offer and what resources will you need? How will you use internal marketing to communicate the marketing plan and build commitment inside the company? Outline a customer service or internal marketing programme, as applicable, indicating the specific audience or market being targeted and what you expect to achieve. Explain how this programme will contribute to meeting your plan's objectives.

STOP ENDNOTES

1. Karina Robinson, 'Banking Matters: Banks Start Targeting the Immigrant Market', *International Herald Tribune*, 18 December 2006, www.iht.com; Karina Robinson, 'Western Europe – Spain: Cost-Effectiveness Scores at Home and Away', *The Banker*, 1 June 2006, n.p.

2. Kemba J. Dunham, 'Beyond Satisfaction: What Is Customer Service, Anyway? And How Do You Measure It?', *Wall Street Journal*, 30 October 2006, p. R4.

3. Jane Spencer, 'Cases of "Customer Rage" Mount as Bad Service Prompts Venting', *Wall Street Journal*, 17 September 2003, pp. D4ff.

4. 'German Firms Value Good Telecoms Customer Service – Survey', *Europe Intelligence Wire*, 11 January 2007, n.p.

5. 'Czech Software Maker Grisoft Expands Global Customer Support Center, Creating 30 New Jobs', *Czech Business News*, 5 April 2006, n.p.

6. Quoted in Clare Ansberry, 'Manufacturers Find Themselves Increasingly in the Service Sector', *Wall Street Journal*, 10 February 2003, p. A2.

7. Quoted in Wendy Ng, 'Guests Help Hotel to Raise Levels of Service Excellence', *Asia Africa Intelligence Wire*, 29 March 2003, n.p.

8. 'Trucker Rewards Customers for Good Behavior', *Wall Street Journal*, September 9, 2003, p. B4.

9. 'Grinding: Speciality Coated Abrasives', *Metalworking Production*, 30 November 2006, p. 83; 'Delivering Manufacturing Excellence', *Foundry Trade Journal*, April 2003, pp. 26ff.

10. 'Mark Ritson on Branding: How a Repositioning Should Be Done', *Marketing*, 13 September 2006, p. 21.

11. Christina Passariello, 'Style – Retailing: Luxury Brands Spin a New Web', *Wall Street Journal*, 4 November 2006, p. P3; Cathy Horyn, 'Point, Click and Strut', *New York Times*, 15 December 2005, p. G1; www.net-a-porter.com.

12. 'Thailand: Bangkok Airways to Add Routes to Neighboring Countries', *Thai Press Reports*, 22 February 2007, n.p.; 'Rolling Out the Red Carpet', *The Economist*, 7 September 2002, p. 58; 'Bangkok

Airways Orders A350s For Thailand-Europe Service', *Wall Street Journal,* 3 January 2006, p. 1.

13. See Russell G. Bundschuh and Theodore M. Dezvane, 'How to Make After-Sales Services Pay Off', *McKinsey Quarterly*, no. 4, 2003, www.mckinseyquarterly.com.

14. 'Impudent Newcomers Take on Incumbents in Retail Banking', *Australian Banking & Finance*, 30 September 2006, pp. 6ff; 'Harley Focuses on the Service Experience', *Australian Banking & Finance*, 15 July 2003, p. 11.

15. 'Philips Now for Star Service at Premium End', *Asia Africa Intelligence Wire*, 28 July 2003, n.p.

16. See Simon Glynn and Ewan Jones, 'The Satisfaction Payoff', *Marketing Management*, September–October 2003, pp. 26ff.

17. 'Matsushita Electric Corp. Strengthens Customer Service', *Asia Africa Intelligence Wire*, 1 August 2003, n.p.

18. Quoted in Nancy Syverson, 'Inside Grainger', *Industrial Maintenance & Plant Operation*, November 2002, pp. 20ff. Also: Victoria Fraza Kickham, 'Go Global, But Stay Local', *Industrial Distribution*, 1 January 2007, pp. 20ff.

19. Valerie Seckler, 'Shopping Woes Deter Retailers from Web', *WWD*, 29 August 2003, p. 13.

20. Rod Stiefbold, 'Dissatisfied Customers Require Recovery Plans', *Marketing News*, 27 October 2003, pp. 44–6.

21. Jena McGregor, 'Customer Service Champs', *BusinessWeek*, 5 March 2007, pp. 52ff.

22. Don Oldenburg, 'Seller Beware', *Washington Post*, 9 September 2003, p. C10.

23. Ron Zemke, 'The Customer Revolution', *Training*, July 2002, pp. 44–8.

24. Quoted in Charles Haddad, 'Eyes on the $1 Billion Prize', *Business Week*, 7 April 2003, p. 72.

25. See 'Internal Comms Failing to Capture Hearts and Minds', *PR Week* (UK), 11 July 2003, p. 2.

26. See note 21 – McGregor, 'Customer Service Champs'.

27. Kim Scherer, 'Mercedes Store Offers Service on the Go', *Automotive News*, 1 January 2007, p. 23; 'Mercedes Offers New Cars to 2,000 Customers', *Wall Street Journal*, 22 July 2003, p. D4; Jason Stein and Diana T. Kurylko, 'Mercedes Begins Push to Bolster CSI Scores', *Automotive News*, 16 October 2006, p. 8; Harald Hamprecht, 'Mercedes Wants Friendly, Profitable Dealers', *Automotive News Europe*, 6 February 2006, p. 22; 'Mercedes Car Group Picks Marketing Director for UK', *Marketing Week*, 2 November 2006, p. 6.

11

Planning to measure performance

Comprehension outcomes

After studying this chapter, you will be able to:

- Understand how to use forecasts, budgets and schedules in marketing planning
- Explain the role of metrics in tracking progress toward marketing performance

Application outcomes

After studying this chapter, you will be able to:

- Prepare for forecasting, budgeting and scheduling
- Select metrics to measure progress toward marketing plan objectives

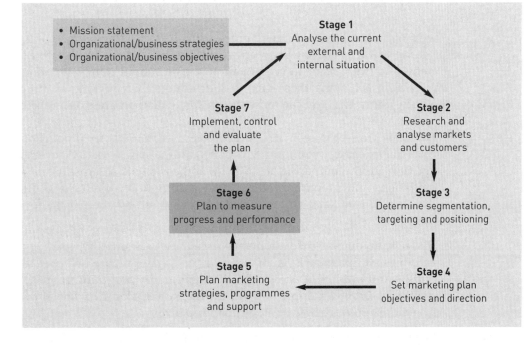

- Mission statement
- Organizational/business strategies
- Organizational/business objectives

Stage 1
Analyse the current external and internal situation

Stage 7
Implement, control and evaluate the plan

Stage 2
Research and analyse markets and customers

Stage 6
Plan to measure progress and performance

Stage 3
Determine segmentation, targeting and positioning

Stage 5
Plan marketing strategies, programmes and support

Stage 4
Set marketing plan objectives and direction

CHAPTER PREVIEW

Even Mickey Mouse needs to measure marketing performance. Consider the marketing plan for the opening of the Hong Kong Disneyland theme park. The park's marketers expected first-year attendance to be 5.6 million people. They targeted travel agents and consumers, especially vacationers from China, with marketing activities to build interest and attract visitors. Although attendance surged during peak periods such as the Lunar New Year holiday, it was much lower than anticipated during some months. Just before the park's first anniversary, park officials hinted that the 12-month attendance target wouldn't be reached on time, without discussing progress toward financial targets. Looking ahead in a brief preview of the second-year plan, the park announced new programmes to sell thousands of annual passes.[1]

Hong Kong Disneyland must measure marketing performance to determine whether its plans are having the intended effect. The time to plan for measuring progress is before implementation, so measurement standards and checkpoints can be established in advance. Then, after implementation, you can see when and where performance is not meeting expectations and prepare to improve results by applying marketing control (*see* Chapter 12). In this chapter, you'll learn how to use four tools for measuring marketing progress: forecasts, budgets, schedules and metrics.

TOOLS FOR MEASURING MARKETING PROGRESS

Stage 6 of the marketing planning process involves deciding on measures to track performance toward meeting marketing, financial and societal objectives. Every programme and every tactic in your marketing plan should contribute, if only in a small way, toward achieving these targets and, ultimately, your organization's goals. As shown in Figure 11.1, you can measure marketing plan progress using these four tools:

- **Forecasts** project the estimated level of sales (for example, by product or market) and costs (for example, by product or channel) for the specific period covered by the marketing plan. By comparing actual sales and costs with forecast levels, you can spot deviations and prepare to adjust your assumptions or your activities as trends develop. This is what Hong Kong Disneyland did by comparing actual first-year attendance with forecast attendance.

- **Budgets** are time-defined allotments of financial resources for specific programmes, activities and products. As an example, you may prepare one overall advertising budget and allocate it across specific campaigns, programmes, products or geographic areas. After implementing the marketing plan, you check whether actual spending is above, below or at the budgeted level.

- **Schedules** are time-defined plans for coordinating and accomplishing tasks related to a specific programme or activity, such as new product development. You will prepare

Tool	Description	Use	Example
Forecast	Forward-looking estimate expressed in unit or monetary terms	Projected level of sales or costs against which to measure actual results	Forecast of product sales
Budget	Funding allotment for specific programme or activity	Guideline for spending against which to measure actual expenditures	Budget for advertising
Schedule	Series of target dates for tasks related to a particular programme or activity	Guideline for anticipated timing against which to measure actual timing	Schedule for launching new product
Metric	Specific numerical standard measuring an outcome that contributes to performance	Target for interim achievement against which to measure actual outcome	Metric for customer retention

FIGURE 11.1   Measuring marketing plan progress

individual schedules showing starting and ending dates as well as responsibilities for the major tasks within a programme, plus an overall schedule reflecting the key tasks and target dates for implementing marketing plan programmes.

- **Metrics** are specific numerical standards used on a regular basis to measure selected performance-related activities and outcomes. The point is to examine interim results by applying metrics measurements at set intervals and analyse progress toward meeting marketing plan objectives. British academic Tim Ambler stresses that the metrics used by top management should be vital to the business, precise, consistent and comprehensive.[2]

If you achieve the expected results day after day, you will move ever closer to accomplishing both short-term objectives and long-term goals. However, avoid over-emphasizing short-term measurements because of the risk that you might lose sight of what your customers really want and what your organization is striving to achieve. At the same time, don't wait too long to act if you identify significant shifts in competition or other elements that begin to affect the progress you expected to make toward your objectives.[3] In short, try for a balanced perspective as you apply the forecasting, budgeting, scheduling and metrics discussed in the remainder of this chapter.

FORECASTING AND THE PLANNING PROCESS

The purpose of forecasting is to project future sales and costs so you can make marketing decisions and coordinate internal decisions about manufacturing, finance, human resources and other functions. (Depending on the coming year's forecasts, your organization may need to expand or reduce manufacturing capacity; change inventory levels; reallocate budgets; and increase or reduce the workforce.) Forecasting is challenging because of the dynamic business environment, unpredictable competitive moves, changeable demand and other uncertainties that can affect marketing performance.

Moreover, your product forecasts must take into account the interrelationships between products in the marketplace. For business markets, apply the principle of **derived demand**: the demand you forecast for a business product is based on (derived from) the demand forecast for a related consumer product. When industry analysts forecast higher consumer sales of digital cameras, for example, personal computer manufacturers raise their own forecasts knowing that many camera buyers will use computers to view, store and alter images. In turn, higher forecasts for computer sales prompt manufacturers of semiconductors, disk drives and other computer components to raise their sales forecasts, and so on through the supply chain.[4]

Forecasts are, at best, only informed estimates, even when based on statistical data and carefully adjusted for the effect of external influences such as market growth, economic conditions, technological developments and industry trends. Still, aim to make your forecasts as accurate as possible to improve the quality of information supporting the decision-making process.

You may want to develop forecasts for the most optimistic situation, the most pessimistic situation and the most likely situation you will face, then – if possible – statistically estimate the probability of each. This helps you think about the diverse ways in which your product, industry, competition and market may develop. *Harvard Business Review* magazine creates multiple sales forecasts: 'We prepare three sets of numbers and then we try to come up with what we think is going to be the consensus', explains the vice president of consumer marketing.[5] Once the marketing plan is implemented, the magazine uses software to analyse actual monthly subscription and retail sales. On the basis of these results, marketing personnel fine-tune the sales forecasts for the remainder of the year. More companies are, in fact, reforecasting future sales and costs using actual results throughout the planning and implementation period.[6]

Types of forecasts

What forecasts do you need for your marketing plan? Most organizations start at the macro level by forecasting industry sales by market and segment, then move to the micro level by forecasting sales for their company; sales by product; sales costs by product; and sales and costs by channel. With these forecasts in hand, you can estimate future changes in sales and costs to examine trends by product and by channel. Such analyses will show the magnitude of projected sales increases or decreases for your market, segment and individual products as well as the expected rate of change over time for sales and costs.

Market and segment sales forecasts

The first step is to project the level of overall industry sales in each market and segment for the coming months and years, using the external audit and the market analysis completed earlier in the planning process. Here you will forecast sales in the qualified available market and in your targeted segment of this market, adjusted for external influences such as expected legal restrictions and the economic outlook. Car manufacturers such as Germany's BMW project industry and company sales five years or longer in advance because of the lead time needed to design new vehicles, build or retrofit assembly facilities and plan for other operational activities. They regularly adjust their forecasts in accordance with the latest economic indicators and other external influences.

MARKETING IN PRACTICE: BMW LOOKS AT THE ROAD AHEAD

BMW forecasts worldwide vehicle sales and prepares model-by-model unit and revenue forecasts for each of its products in each market. These forecasts include projections for vehicles under the BMW, Mini-Cooper and Rolls-Royce brands as well as for BMW motorcycles. BMW's marketers check progress by comparing actual with forecast sales during each month and quarter as well as at the end of the fiscal year. When they notice deviations, they investigate and, if necessary, reforecast for the remainder of the period and adjust the following year's forecast accordingly. Foreign exchange rates, new vehicle introductions, economic conditions and competitive actions are just some of the elements that can affect BMW's forecasting and its actual results.[7]

Once you've forecast the size of the market, you can forecast the share you aim to achieve with your marketing plan, as well as estimating the future share for each competitor. Then bring industry sales forecasts down to the segment level to support your targeting and strategy decisions. The next step is to project sales for your company and for each product.

Company and product sales forecasts

Use your market and segment forecasts, your market and customer analyses and your knowledge of the current situation to develop sales forecasts at the company and product levels. Also factor in earlier decisions about direction, strategy and objectives when thinking about future company sales.

Most marketers prepare month-by-month sales forecasts for the coming year, although some firms prefer week-by-week forecasting and some project sales 15–18 months ahead. Manufacturers of industrial equipment and cars typically prepare monthly sales forecasts for at least two years ahead, on the basis of top-down and floor-up input, so they can plan supply acquisition and production capacity. Involving value chain partners can improve accuracy and give suppliers the data they need for better forecasting to meet your organization's needs.

If your marketing plan covers at least one new product introduction, forecast those sales separately so you can measure results and track progress toward product-specific objectives. Also consider the effect that other value-chain participants could have on your product forecasts.

Cost of sales forecasts

Now you're ready to forecast the total costs you can expect to incur for the forecast sales levels and project when these costs will occur. This gives you an opportunity to consider the financial impact of your forecasts and revise them if necessary. Your forecasts will be more realistic if you discuss cost figures with line managers or others who are knowledgeable about the products and markets. Be aware that you may need to adjust your overall cost forecasts after the marketing plan is implemented. Nonetheless, estimating these costs during the planning process helps you allocate funding to individual programmes and products.

Channel forecasts

Companies that work with multiple channels and channel members often forecast sales and costs for each, including the cost of logistics. In addition to providing benchmarks against which to measure actual channel results and costs, these forecasts give you an opportunity to reconsider your channel and logistics decisions if the costs seem too high (or surprisingly low). Even companies that own their own stores can use channel forecasts to project sales on a store-by-store basis. Ideally, you should forecast unit sales and revenue results by product and by channel (perhaps down to the store or wholesale level) so you can track progress after implementation and make changes if actual performance varies significantly from forecasts.

Forecasting approaches and data sources

There are a number of approaches to forecasting sales and costs, as shown in Figure 11.2. Some rely on statistical analysis or modelling, whereas others rely on expert judgement. Note that for a forecast developed with a time series or causal analysis to be at all accurate, you must have sufficient historical sales data. Also note that judgemental forecasting approaches such as the jury of executive opinion can be very valuable if applied in a systematic way.[8] Incorporate external information and expertise to avoid too narrow an internal focus. You may arrive at better forecasts by using both statistical and judgemental approaches. For a final 'reality check', compare your forecasts with the actual outcome of recent periods to identify major anomalies.

In preparing forecasts, review the background information you've gathered about your markets, customers, channels and costs. Also consult industry associations, government information and financial analysts' reports when estimating future sales and

Technique	Description	Benefits/limitations
Sales force composite estimate	Judgemental approach in which sales personnel are asked to estimate future sales	Can provide valuable insights from customer-contact personnel but may introduce bias
Jury of executive opinion	Judgemental approach in which managers (and sometimes channel members or suppliers) are asked to estimate future sales	Combines informed judgement of many but may give too much weight to some individuals' estimates
Delphi method	Judgemental approach, in which outside experts participate in successive rounds of input, that leads to a consensus forecast	Minimizes possibility of bias or over-weighting one individual's estimates but is time-consuming and accuracy depends on choice of experts
Survey of buyer intentions	Research-based approach in which buyers in a given market are asked about their purchasing intentions	Solicits market input but the resulting forecast may not be indicative of customers' actual behaviour
New product test marketing	Research-based approach in which a new product's sales performance in limited markets is tested and the results used to forecast future sales	Reflects actual customer behaviour but may be affected by competition or other factors
Time series analyses	Statistical approaches in which the patterns of historical data are analysed to predict future sales; examples: moving averages, exponential smoothing	Uses actual purchase data to produce forecast estimates quickly but assumes that similar buying trends will continue in future
Causal analyses	Methods that statistically determine the relationship between demand and the factors that affect it; examples: regression analysis, neural networks	Provides insights into relationships between factors that affect long-term demand but requires sufficient data for analysis

FIGURE 11.2   Selected approaches to forecasting

costs, especially at the macro level. Finally, before relying on any secondary data for forecasting purposes, carefully check the source, collection method, credibility, completeness and timeliness.

PREPARING BUDGETS AND SCHEDULES

With sales and cost forecasts complete, you can develop an overall marketing budget and, within that budget, estimate spending for specific programmes and activities in line with your marketing plan objectives. Every marketer must make hard choices because marketing budgets (and other resources) are never unlimited. As with forecasts, some marketers budget for the most optimistic, most pessimistic and most likely scenarios so they are prepared to tackle threats and opportunities.

Your organization may set budget requirements for return on investment; limit the amount or percentage of funding that can be allocated to certain activities or products; set specific assumptions; cap cost increases; or prefer a particular budget method or format. Porsche, for instance, has traditionally attracted affluent buyers through print advertising, which accounts for the majority of its marketing budget. The company tested online advertising one year but waited three years before again including this technique in its marketing budget. That second online campaign accounted for 20 per cent of Porsche's total marketing budget. If the campaign achieved its objectives, Porsche was ready to allocate even more of its marketing budget to online advertisements.[9]

Budgeting methods

Budgets may originate in the marketing department and move upward for review (floor up); at the top management level and move downward for specific allocations (top down); or be constructed through a combination of floor-up and top-down methods (*see* Figure 11.3). The **objective and task budget method**, a floor-up option common in large organizations, allocates marketing funding according to the cost of the tasks to be accomplished in achieving marketing plan objectives. If you can relate specific tasks to specific objectives, this method offers good accountability; however, the combined cost may result in too high a budget, given your organization's resources. For this reason, a growing number of corporations are using the **econometric modelling method** to calculate programme or activity budgets using formulas that take into account anticipated customer response, budget constraints, product profitability, competitive spending and other relevant variables.[10]

On the other hand, your organization may use one of the top-down budgeting methods. With the **affordability budget method**, senior managers set the amount of the marketing budget on the basis of how much the organization can afford (or will be able

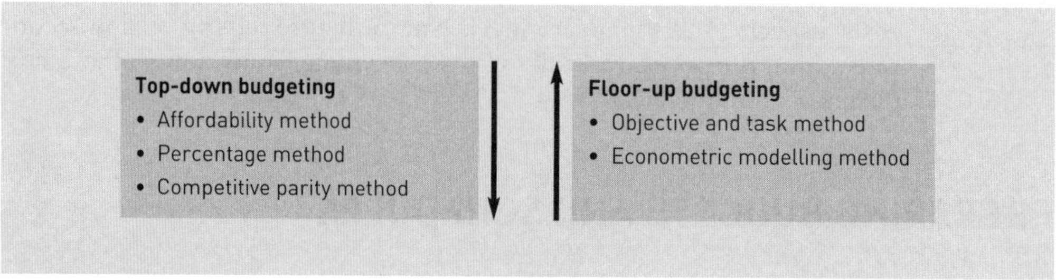

Top-down budgeting
- Affordability method
- Percentage method
- Competitive parity method

Floor-up budgeting
- Objective and task method
- Econometric modelling method

FIGURE 11.3 Top-down and floor-up budgeting methods

to afford during the period covered by the plan). Although simple, this method has no connection with market conditions, opportunities, potential profits or other factors. With the **percentage budget method**, the overall marketing budget is based on a percentage of the previous year's annual turnover; next year's expected turnover; the product's price; or an average industry percentage. Note that this method has no connection to market conditions. With the **competitive parity budget method**, managers set a total marketing budget at least equal to that of competitors. But because no two organizations are exactly alike, mimicking another organization's budget may be disastrous for yours.

The top-down budgeting methods are relatively easy to apply, but they fail to relate costs to objectives. Compared with the affordability method, the objective and task budgeting is more sophisticated; results in larger marketing budgets; and is related to better profitability.[11] In practice, most marketing budgets combine top-down and floor-up methods, guided by higher-level strategic planning and product or brand-level input relative to objectives and costs.

Budgets within budgets

At this point, you can create separate budgets for specific marketing activities and programmes, schedule planned expenditures and fix responsibilities for spending. This allows you to compare the actual outlays with the budgeted outlays after the marketing plan has been implemented. You will want to prepare budgets (for annual, monthly and perhaps weekly costs) covering individual marketing-mix programmes matched with appropriate objectives (such as projected profit or return on investment).

In addition, you can establish budgets within your overall budget reflecting planned expenditures by market, segment, region, business unit, product or line/category, brand, activity or responsibility. The UK-based Barclays Bank establishes budgets for each market, for each product, and for specific marketing activities such as direct mail, online ads, television ads, branch signs and more.[12] This allows examination of performance market by market and activity by activity so management can change budget priorities as appropriate.

Planning schedules for implementation

When planning schedules for implementation, you will estimate the timing and deadlines for each programme or task to coordinate concurrent activities, prevent conflicts, obtain needed resources and track progress toward completion. Each individual activity will require careful scheduling, as the marketers at Texas Instruments are well aware.

MARKETING IN PRACTICE: TEXAS INSTRUMENTS SCHEDULES CUSTOMER CONTACT

US-based Texas Instruments (TI) makes chips used in mobile phones and other electronic devices, ringing up $14.3 billion in annual turnover. One of its target markets consists of engineers in companies around the world who design products that incorporate chips. Although the company wants to remain in close contact with these engineers, it doesn't want to overwhelm or confuse them with too many messages. Therefore, it has a specific schedule for communicating with the 300,000 engineers on its e-mail list. The manufacturer sends more than four million marketing e-mails yearly, yet, through careful scheduling, it ensures that no recipient receives more than one per week.[13]

Although you may not have to include detailed programme schedules when documenting your marketing plan for management review, you need a schedule to summarize the timing and responsibilities for major programmes. Then, if tasks do not start or finish on schedule, you can determine the effect on other tasks, work to regain the expected timing and get back on track toward results. Also review the new timing (and cost changes, if any) with management and communicate with the major customers and suppliers who would be affected.

As with budgeting and forecasting, you may want to develop schedules for the most optimistic, most pessimistic and most likely situations – and be ready to make changes in response to emerging opportunities, threats or other factors. When the UK travel company TUI Thompson was planning a new online division, its marketers originally scheduled advertising and other promotions to support a springtime launch. However, because holiday travel sales were dropping off, they postponed some of the activities, continued monitoring the environment and then rescheduled a number of promotions for summer months.[14]

MEASURING PROGRESS WITH METRICS

After implementation, how will you (and your management) know whether progress is being made toward achieving the marketing plan's objectives? Metrics allow you to measure the outcomes and activities that really contribute to performance. Organizations are concerned about holding marketing accountable for achieving the expected results, which is why the use of metrics is an important part of marketing planning. But you will need clear objectives and baseline measures against which to compare interim results and ultimate performance. Here's how the UK charity Global Ethics used metrics to measure the results of an important promotion.

MARKETING IN PRACTICE: GLOBAL ETHICS AND ONE WATER

The mission of the UK charity Global Ethics is to give one billion people worldwide access to clean drinking water. To accomplish this mission, it markets bottled water under the One brand. Global Ethics recently implemented a promotion to increase awareness of its cause, add supporters to its e-mail list and raise more money through higher sales of One water. The promotion included special labelling on 1 million bottles of One water sold in Waitrose and other grocery chains, plus outdoor posters and online advertising. Global Ethics used several metrics to assess the results, including the size of the e-mail list and the percentage change in sales. Metrics show that 'promotions work for us – delivering up to 200 per cent sales increases', according to the managing director.[15]

Yet just because you *can* measure something does not mean you *should* measure it – nor should you measure everything. The key is to identify the specific metrics that apply to the most significant activities and results affecting marketing performance. Best suggests four categories of metrics to measure progress toward objectives: internal in-process, external in-process, internal performance (end-result) and external performance (end-result) metrics (*see* Figure 11.4 for examples).[16]

Achieving in-process market metrics paves the way for achieving marketing and financial objectives. For example, the metric of product awareness measures progress

Measurement perspective	Time of measurement	
	In-process metrics	End-result metrics
Internal (in-company)	Product defects Late deliveries Billing errors Accounts receivable Inventory turnover	Net profit/earnings Return on sales Profit margin per unit Return on assets Asset turnover
External (in-market)	Customer satisfaction Relative product quality Relative service quality Intentions to purchase Product awareness	Market share Customer retention Relative new product sales Revenue per customer Market growth rate

FIGURE 11.4   Categories of process and performance metrics

Source: Adapted from Roger J. Best, *Market-Based Management*, 2nd edn (Upper Saddle River, NJ: Prentice Hall, 2000), p. 32.

toward the marketing objective of strengthening and expanding customer relationships: the higher the awareness, the higher the probability that prospects will become customers. In contrast, internal and external performance metrics measure results that more directly contribute to specific financial and marketing objectives. Be sure to measure before, during and after programme implementation so you can make changes if necessary to improve performance.

Hilton Hotels is one of many companies using a marketing dashboard to track actual performance. A **marketing dashboard** is a computerized, easy-to-read depiction of marketing outcomes, as measured by key metrics, used to monitor progress and identify deviations from expected results. Hilton's dashboard monitors customer loyalty, revenues and other metrics chosen by management. The company says that being able to track performance and determine where improvement is needed has helped it increase profit margins at its 2,300 hotels and resorts.[17]

Selecting metrics

Hilton's metrics cover not only short-term results (measuring current revenues) but also longer-term objectives (measuring customer loyalty). When you select metrics, look for measures that will help you evaluate progress throughout the course of each programme and into a new marketing plan period, so you can follow progress and assess results. *See* Figure 11.5 for sample metrics.

Thus, when selecting metrics:

- *Match metrics to programme and marketing plan objectives*. Be sure your metrics are relevant to your objectives. A company seeking 10 per cent higher sales in the coming year would check performance by regularly measuring unit or monetary sales and market share. However, if it measures the number of sales leads generated but has no metric for conversion rates, it will not know the ultimate outcome of lead generation, which directly influences sales objectives.

- *Measure activities or outcomes that show progress toward fulfilling the organization's mission and moving in the desired direction*. Your metrics should track results that are consistent with your mission and direction. Andersen Corp., which makes timber windows, uses metrics to monitor relationships with dealers and the construction trade, two channels that directly affect the company's turnover and connections with consumers. Among the metrics measured are the channel members' willingness to recommend Andersen windows; willingness to carry more Andersen products; and willingness to make Andersen their sole window supplier.[18]

- *Measure the non-financial and financial outcomes that can be quantified and that matter to customers*. Supported by marketing research, you can select and measure metrics for changes in customers' perceptions of company image, product quality and value, all of which affect customers' attitudes and behaviour. You might use metrics to track the number of defectors, percentage change and reason for defections. To follow the

Type of objective	Sample metrics
Financial objectives	• To increase sales: performance metrics measuring results by product, region, channel, customer segment or company • To increase profitability: performance metrics measuring annual gross or net margin by product, region, channel, customer segment or company • To achieve return on investment levels: performance metrics measuring the return by programme, product or activity • To improve cash flow by reducing the time between billing and receiving payment: in-process metrics constantly measuring the age and status of accounts receivable by customer segment, product, region or manager
Marketing objectives	• To acquire new customers: performance metrics measuring the annual number or percentage of new customers added; in-process metrics measuring customer awareness, attitudes and buying intentions at designated intervals • To retain existing customers: performance metrics measuring the number or percentage of customers who continue purchasing; performance metrics measuring the number or percentage of customers who defect during the period; performance metrics measuring size and frequency of repeat purchases by existing customers • To increase speed of new product development: in-process metrics measuring the time for each step from idea generation to product launch and the total time needed to introduce a product
Societal objectives	• To improve public image: in-process metrics measuring stakeholders' attitudes at certain intervals • To reduce waste: performance metrics measuring amount of waste generated by or resulting from products and processes at certain intervals; performance metrics measuring level of recycling at certain intervals

FIGURE 11.5   Sample metrics for marketing plan objectives

Source: After Marian Burk Wood, *The Marketing Plan: A Handbook* (Upper Saddle River, NJ: Prentice Hall, 2003), p. 115–16.

development of customer relationships, track your progress in acquiring customers, selling additional products to current customers, retaining customers, reactivating dormant relationships and re-establishing relations with defectors. Consider metrics to track profit per customer and acquisition costs in line with your objectives so you have data for future marketing decisions.[19]

- *Measure appropriate internal metrics.* By tracking internal performance using metrics such as measuring order fulfilment accuracy and on-time shipping, you can quickly identify areas for improvement in processes and procedures that affect customer satisfaction and loyalty.

- *Use metrics to reinforce ongoing priorities.* You can use metrics to track the proportion of sales made to more profitable customers compared with those made to less profitable customers as a way to reinforce marketing priorities for long-term success. As another example, using metrics to track the ratio of new product sales to existing product sales can show the extent to which new product innovation is fuelling growth.[20]

The specific metrics selected depend on your organization, its mission and objectives, your marketing plan objectives and the programmes you will implement. Most companies select metrics to measure profitability and profit margins, sales, product awareness and number of new products, among others – with profitability and sales metrics seen as the most valuable in assessing progress.[21] Other vital areas to monitor through metrics are channel and sales force performance; product portfolio performance; new product pricing, price changes and effect on profitability; and the value of individual customers and relationships.[22] Rather than simply replicate the metrics common to your industry, select metrics that pertain to your organization's particular situation. You can also select narrowly defined metrics to track progress toward particularly crucial outcomes or activities, such as the number of new products in development.

Applying metrics

You will need pre-implementation numbers for every metric so you can track progress from that point forward. If possible, obtain benchmark metrics (from your industry or best-in-class organizations) against which to compare your progress. E-commerce companies, for instance, strive to beat the typical 1–2 per cent conversion rates measuring the percentage of website visitors who actually buy, in addition to measuring progress toward programme objectives.[23]

Depending on your organization, objectives and technology, you may apply selected metrics weekly, monthly, quarterly or yearly. In especially volatile markets, you may check metrics daily or even hourly. Be sure to analyse the direction and rate of change in measurements taken at different intervals as well as the total progress from pre-implementation levels. This will show how quickly you are moving toward your objectives (and reveal problem areas for attention). Check your previous results to see the progress measured in comparable pre-implementation periods as a way of identifying unusual trends. By documenting your measurements, you will have historical data for comparison with future results. Also analyse your metrics in the context of competitive results whenever possible – an especially important point with measures such as market share, profitability and quality perceptions.

Remember that the metrics you apply today may not be as useful tomorrow because of environmental shifts; new competition; changes in organizational strategy; or evolving customer attitudes and behaviour. Finally, keep the use of metrics in perspective. Marketing judgement is vital for interpreting what metrics measure. Quantifiable measures are necessary but so are innovation and insight.[24] In fact, metrics are only one input in decisions about adjusting marketing programmes if interim results fail to meet expected results, as discussed in Chapter 12.

Use this checklist as you consider suitable metrics for your marketing plan.

ESSENTIAL MARKETING PLAN CHECKLIST NO. 16: PLANNING METRICS

☐ What metrics will help you and your management track the marketing results that contribute to achieving long-term objectives and fulfilling the mission?

_____

☐ What metrics will help you track marketing results that relate to managing the life cycle of a customer relationship, including satisfaction, loyalty and retention?

_____

☐ What metrics will help you measure progress toward achieving the plan's financial, marketing and societal objectives?

_____

☐ What metrics will help you determine whether specific marketing programmes have achieved their objectives?

_____

☐ What metrics will help you track how each marketing-mix element contributes to interim performance?

_____

☐ How often should you measure interim progress using each metric?

_____

CHAPTER SUMMARY

Marketers use forecasts to project the estimated level of sales and costs for the marketing plan period so they can compare actual results and identify deviations. Some prepare forecasts for the most optimistic, most pessimistic and most likely situation.

Budgets are used to allot financial resources to specific programmes, activities and products and then compare actual spending to budgeted spending to pinpoint deviations. Budgets may be developed using floor-up methods (objective and task, econometric modelling), top-down methods (affordability, percentage budget, competitive parity) or a combination of methods. Marketers use schedules to define the timing of tasks to plan and implement specific programmes and activities.

Marketers use metrics to measure selected performance-related activities and outcomes numerically and on a regular basis. The point is to examine interim results at set intervals and track progress toward meeting marketing plan objectives, long-term objectives and the organization's mission. These include internal in-process metrics, external in-process metrics, internal performance (end-result) metrics and external performance (end-result) metrics. A marketing dashboard is a computerized, easy-to-read depiction of marketing outcomes, as measured by key metrics, used to confirm progress and identify deviations from expected marketing results.

CASE STUDY: AIR DECCAN FLIES ON METRICS

According to the Centre for Asia Pacific Aviation, the combined market share of India's low-fare airlines is currently 44 per cent but is forecast to rise to 70 per cent by 2010. One of the fastest-growing of these no-frills airlines is Air Deccan, which enjoys a 20 per cent market share. It began operating in 2003 with a single airplane and three flights per day. Today the airline has 300 daily flights and is expanding so rapidly that it has ordered 90 new airplanes, to be delivered at a rate of one per month as Air Deccan builds its customer base and adds new destinations.

For long-term success, the airline must keep profits high, keep costs low and continue attracting passengers in an increasingly competitive market. Its metrics reflect these priorities. Air Deccan tracks the number of passengers per flight, a metric that allows management to determine whether that flight achieves break-even (balancing revenues against costs such as staff salaries, fuel and so on). The airline also tracks the number and type of passengers it serves every year. Its research indicates that more than half of its passengers have never flown before – a metric that shows how effectively the company has communicated the value of its offering to a very large market segment.

Using metrics to measure profit margins and revenues enables Air Deccan to evaluate short-term progress toward financial objectives. One key objective since its founding has been to achieve profitability, which it did at the end of 2006. Air Deccan also monitors the profitability of each route. Ordinarily, a route becomes profitable after about a year. When the airline began to serve Kandla, Kullu and Pathankot, however, it achieved profitability on those routes within three months, in part by timing its departures and arrivals to maximize aircraft productivity.

Finally, Air Deccan tracks ticket purchasing in each channel. Although customers can buy through travel agents and airport booking desks, the company's marketing encourages online or mobile phone purchasing because of the low cost of serving customers directly.[25]

Case questions

1. Some of Air Deccan's destinations had no previous air service. How would you have prepared sales forecasts for those markets?

2. What types of in-process metrics would you recommend that Air Deccan's marketers use internally and externally, and why?

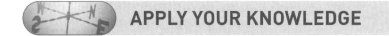

APPLY YOUR KNOWLEDGE

Review your work researching a company's marketing, financial and societal objectives in the 'Apply your knowledge' exercise in Chapter 5. In a brief oral or written report, answer the following questions about measuring progress toward those objectives.

- Has the company revealed any of its forecasts or budgets? If so, what are they based on and how do they relate to its objectives?

- What secondary data sources would you consult if you were preparing a forecast for one of this company's products? Be specific.

- Has the company discussed any schedules for marketing activities, such as launching a new product or starting a new advertising campaign? If so, what connection do you see between the schedules and forecasts or budgets?

- Does the company explain any metrics used to measure interim progress? What metrics would you recommend, given your knowledge of this company and its objectives?

BUILD YOUR OWN MARKETING PLAN

Move ahead with your marketing plan by researching and estimating sales and costs, plus forecasts for industry, company and product sales; cost of sales; and sales and costs by channel. What sources will you use? Do your forecasts represent the most optimistic, most pessimistic or most likely situation? Are they appropriate for the current marketing situation? Next, develop a month-by-month marketing budget using the objective and task method and a budget for a specific programme or activity such as advertising. List any factors that would affect your budgets for the most optimistic, most pessimistic and most likely situations. Now identify appropriate metrics, explaining how, when and why you will use them to measure progress in achieving your objectives. Document your decisions in a written marketing plan.

STOP ENDNOTES

1. Wendy Leung, 'Magic Back as Disney Sells 50,000 Passes', *The Standard (Hong Kong)*, 2 March 2007, n.p.; Vicki Rothrock, 'H.K. Disney Park Short of Visitor Goals', *Daily Variety*, 6 September 2006, p. 15; Geoffrey A. Fowler, 'Hong Kong Disney Misses Target', *Wall Street Journal*, 5 September 2006, p. D2.

2 Tim Ambler, *Marketing and the Bottom Line* (London: Financial Times Prentice Hall, 2000), p. 5.

3. Don E. Schultz, 'Use Atypical Tools for Today's Marketing Plan', *Marketing News*, 15 February 2007, pp. 7, 10.

4. Jim Kerstetter, 'PCs: The Elves Are Working Overtime', *Business Week*, 10 November 2003, p. 50.

5. Quoted in Leslie Brokaw, 'Eraser Heads', *Folio*, 1 March 2003, n.p.

6. See Richard Barrett, 'From Fast Close to Fast Forward', *Strategic Finance*, January 2003, pp. 24ff.

7. David Rising, 'BMW Profit Rises in 2006', *Associated Press*, 8 March 2007, www.forbes.com/feeds/ap/2007/03/08ap3498522.html; Christoph Rauwald, 'BMW Posts 28% Gain in 2006 Net Profit', *Wall Street Journal*, 8 March 2007, www.wsj.com.

8. Gary L. Lilien and Arvind Rangaswamy, *Marketing Engineering*, 2nd edn (Upper Saddle River, NJ: Prentice Hall, 2003), pp. 174–5.

9. 'Porsche Allocates One-fifth of Marketing Spend to Online Ads', *New Media Age*, 15 February 2007, p. 4.

10. See note 8 – Lilien and Rangaswamy, *Marketing Engineering*, 2nd edn, pp. 312–15.

11. Nigel Piercy, 'The Marketing Budgeting Process: Marketing Management Implications', *Journal of Marketing*, October 1987, pp. 45–59.

12. 'Barclays Hikes TV Spend in Refocus on Products', *Marketing*, 25 October 2006, p. 3.

13. Mary E. Morrison, 'Digging Deeper into Metrics: E-Mail Marketing Is Not Exempt from the Pressure to Perform, Leading to Increased ROI', *B to B*, 25 September 2006, p. 18; Bob Sechler, 'Texas Instruments Records Slight Net, Revenue Gains', *Wall Street Journal*, 23 January 2007, p. C9.

14. 'TUI Launches "Modern" Budget Holiday Brand', *Marketing*, 6 March 2003, p. 3; 'TUI Backs Online Budget Holidays with Pounds 2M Activity', *Marketing*, 3 July 2003, p. 4.

15. 'On-pack: "Life-changing" Activity for One', *Promotions & Incentives*, 23 October 2006, p. 5; www.we-are-one.org.uk/.

16. Roger J. Best, *Market-Based Management*, 2nd edn (Upper Saddle River, NJ: Prentice Hall, 2000), pp. 30–2.

17. Christopher Hosford, 'Hilton's Dashboards Graphically Depict Five "Value Drivers" at Hotel Properties', *B to B*, 11 December 2006, p. 18.

18. Lawrence A. Crosby and Sheree L. Johnson, 'Do Your Metrics Reflect Your Market Strategy?', *Marketing Management*, September–October 2003, pp. 10–11.

19. See Werner Reinartz, Manfred Krafft and Wayne D. Hoyer, 'Measuring the Customer Relationship Management Construct and Linking It to Performance Outcomes', *Insead*, January 2003, www.insead.edu.

20. See June Lee Risser, 'Customers Come First', *Marketing Management*, November–December 2003, pp. 22ff.

21. See note 2 – Ambler, *Marketing and the Bottom Line*, p. 163.

22. See Paul W. Farris, Neil T. Bendle, Phillip E. Pfeifer and David J. Reibstein, *Marketing Metrics:*

50+ Metrics Every Executive Should Master (Upper Saddle River, NJ: Wharton School Publishing, 2006), pp. 2–5.

23. Nick Evans, 'How Palm, Coca-Cola and Crutchfield Excel at Online Customer Relationship Management', *InternetWeek*, 29 September 2003, n.p.

24. John Nardone and Ed See, 'Free Yourself from the Tyranny of Metrics', *Advertising Age*, 20 November 2006, p. 12.

25. Based on information from Sam Wollaston, 'Scared About What Flying Is Doing to the Planet?', *Guardian (London)*, 25 January 2007, p. 31; 'Air Deccan Flies into Black on Firm Margins', *Economic Times (New Delhi)*, 27 January 2007, n.p.; 'New Entrants Corner 44% of Aviation Mart' *India Business Insight*, 24 February 2007, n.p.; 'Deccan Lures India's New Jet Set with Executive Charters', *Flight International*, 17 October 2006, n.p.; Rasheed Kappan, 'Air Deccan to Link "Unconnected" Towns in South', *The Hindu*, 13 August 2003, www.thehindu.com; airdeccan.net.

12 Controlling marketing and implementation

Comprehension outcomes

After studying this chapter, you will be able to:

- Explain the role of marketing control
- Understand how marketing control works at various levels
- Discuss planning for annual, financial, productivity and strategic control

Application outcomes

After studying this chapter, you will be able to:

- Diagnose interim marketing results and plan corrective action
- Use marketing control to evaluate plan performance
- Prepare for contingency and scenario planning

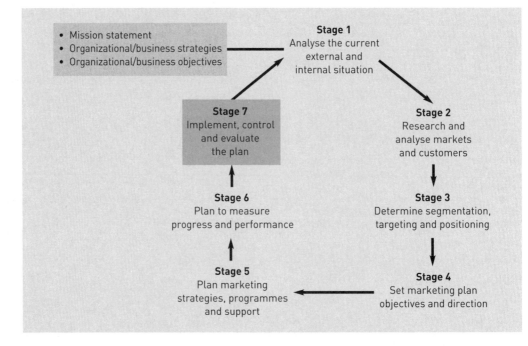

CHAPTER PREVIEW

Marketing control has improved profit margins in Brazil for Syngenta, which manufactures fungicides, seeds and other products for agricultural use. Using software to evaluate the financial performance of each product, market and channel, Switzerland-based Syngenta discovered that its salespeople in Brazil were selling some products at unprofitable prices. Why? Their sales targets focused on volume, not profitability, and they were unaware of how factors such as currency fluctuations and delivery costs affected profits. Once Syngenta clarified its targets and gave its sales team the tools and training to estimate each transaction's profitability, its margin in Brazil increased by four percentage points within a year. To achieve its financial objectives, Syngenta's marketing plan also called for withdrawing low-margin products from high-cost markets.[1]

Syngenta's experience with profit performance illustrates the importance of the final stage in the marketing planning process, when the plan is implemented, controlled and evaluated. Remember that even the best plan will be ineffective without proper implementation – and a poor plan will not be improved by superb implementation. This chapter opens with a look at the importance of marketing control. The next sections describe the levels of marketing control and the use of annual, financial, productivity and strategic control. The final section discusses contingency and scenario planning for marketing.

PLANNING FOR MARKETING CONTROL

Marketing control is the process of setting standards and measurement intervals to gauge marketing progress, measuring interim results after implementation, diagnosing any deviations from standards and making adjustments if needed to achieve the planned performance. Without marketing control, you can't determine whether your marketing plan is leading to the performance you and your organization expect. With marketing control, you can see exactly where and when results fall short of or exceed expectations – and come to a decision about the action you will take, the way Syngenta did by withdrawing low-margin products from high-cost markets. Figure 12.1 shows how the marketing control process works.

The use of marketing control assumes that the organization is willing and able to make changes after implementing the marketing plan. Syngenta's profit margin in Brazil might not have improved without the changes it made. Marketing control is intended to help you identify the warning signs of an emerging problem early enough to take corrective action. This may entail a small change or a major decision such as discontinuing a product or increasing marketing spending. Here's how Hershey, the US sweets marketer, recently took corrective action.

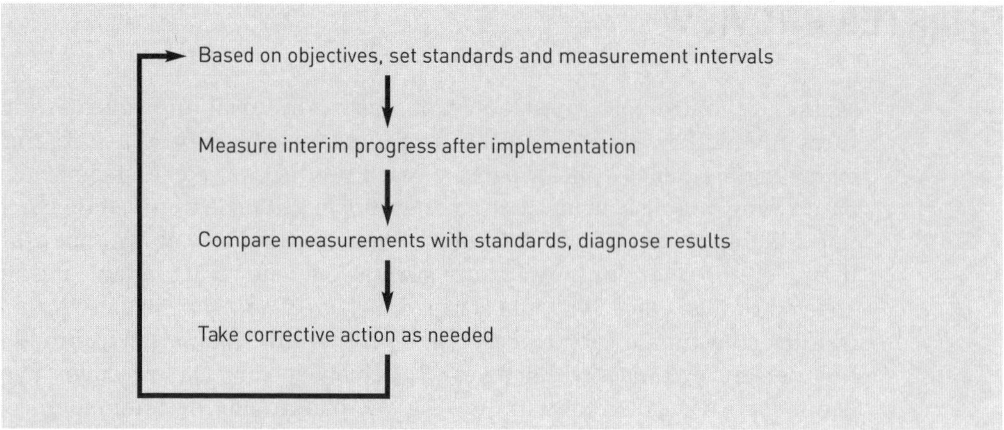

Based on objectives, set standards and measurement intervals

↓

Measure interim progress after implementation

↓

Compare measurements with standards, diagnose results

↓

Take corrective action as needed

FIGURE 12.1 Applying marketing control

MARKETING IN PRACTICE: HERSHEY SWEETENS ITS AD BUDGET

The company famous for Hershey's Kisses and other chocolate treats faces fierce competition from Mars (which makes M&Ms) and other rivals. Not long ago, Hershey's marketing plan included lower spending on media advertising and higher spending on retailer support. The CEO said that in-store marketing yielded a higher return on investment than advertising to consumers. Then Hershey's financial results fell short of expectations, key products lost market share, the company recalled some products because of possible contamination and competitors unleashed aggressive consumer campaigns. Just four months after implementing the marketing plan that cut consumer advertising, Hershey's took corrective action. To improve performance, it doubled ad spending on Reese's and other major products and increased advertising for new product introductions.[2]

Note that the use of marketing control can raise ethical questions. Will marketers set less stringent standards or lower short-term sales forecasts in order to qualify for bonuses or promotions? Will they honestly and adequately explain deviations from expectations and amend or reverse their earlier decisions if necessary? Will marketers apply marketing control laxly or inconsistently if they feel pressured by senior managers to produce ever-higher quarterly results? This can lead to myopic concentration on short-term progress to the detriment of long-term objectives and, as in several highly publicized instances, decisions to make current sales or profits look better than they actually are.

The marketing control process

The marketing control process starts with the objectives you have already set and the detailed forecasts, budgets, schedules and metrics you have developed to track post-implementation progress toward objectives. Next, determine exactly which standards must be met to show progress at each interval of measurement. Suppose your forecast calls for selling 500 units of a product in June; your financial metrics specify an average gross profit margin of 30 per cent; and your advertising budget for June totals £3,000. During June you can get early indicators of progress by measuring actual results weekly; at the end of June you can measure full-month results and see if you are meeting your forecast, metrics and budget standards.

The standards and measurement intervals used for marketing control will vary from organization to organization. Supermarket chains such as Tesco can measure store, product category, brand and individual item sales by day, week, month, quarter and year; some track store sales by the hour for staffing purposes as much as for marketing purposes. Fashion retailers like Zara measure product sales daily or at even shorter intervals so they can identify fast-selling merchandise for immediate reorder and see the effect of pricing and other decisions.

Whatever standards and intervals you choose should provide sufficient information and time to recognize an emerging problem and be able to diagnose it. You do this by comparing actual interim results with pre-set standards, examining the magnitude and direction of variations and calculating the rate of change from the previous period's results. Assume that your non-profit organization actually receives £2,000 in contributions during November, although your monthly forecast standard is £2,500. Your results are 20 per cent lower than the standard, which is a sizeable variation. However, sharply lower November results would signal an even more problematic trend if your October contributions were 10 per cent lower than the standard and your September contributions were 5 per cent lower.

How can you diagnose the cause and significance of any deviations from standards? Examine your actual results and recent trends in the context of your marketing activities, previous results and overall industry results. Use internal and external audits to identify and analyse changes that may have affected your progress. Internally, you might find staffing shortages, budget cuts or operational difficulties contributed to worse-than-expected results. Externally, you might find that better-than-expected results were due, in part, to a competitor's troubles or reduced unemployment in targeted markets. Look upstream and downstream in the value chain: on the supply side, production may depend on just-in-time deliveries; on the demand side, sales may depend on demand for certain consumer products. Also look for answers by researching customer behaviour, perceptions, attitudes and relationships.

If measurements show no deviations, you can continue implementation as planned. You may do this even if you find deviations, to allow more time for a definite trend to develop and avoid acting prematurely. If you decide to respond to a deviation, you can take one of three corrective actions: (1) adjust marketing programmes, schedules or budgets; (2) adjust the standards or measurement intervals; or (3) change the assumptions factored into your marketing plan, such as the prevailing economic climate or increased price competition. In turn, changing a key assumption may cause you to change your objectives or other aspects of the marketing plan. Finally, if interim results are much better than expected, you can use your diagnosis to maintain these outstanding results and enhance the implementation of other programmes (*see* Figure 12.2).

Action	Description
Continue with implementation	Leave programmes, timing, expenditures, responsibilities, standards and measurement intervals as planned
Adjust implementation to solve a problem	Change marketing programmes, timing, expenditures, responsibilities as suggested by diagnosis of deviation
Adjust standards or measurement intervals	Make changes that will allow more accurate or timely identification of emerging problems
Adjust marketing plan assumptions	Change relevant assumptions on which strategies and programmes are based to fine-tune planning and implementation
Act to maintain outstanding results and enhance implementation	Use the diagnosis to find ways of sustaining superior results and enhancing the implementation of other programmes

FIGURE 12.2   Responding to the diagnosis of interim results

Levels of marketing control

During plan implementation, you can apply marketing control at a number of different levels, as your organization chooses. These levels include:

- *Business unit*. Is the marketing plan of a particular business unit achieving interim results as expected? How do these results compare with the results of the company's other units and with the industry in general?

- *Marketing-mix activities*. Are the planned product, channel, pricing and IMC activities achieving the desired results? Is each product meeting sales targets and other interim standards? Are sales through each channel (and channel member) up to expectations?

Are advertising campaigns achieving their awareness and response objectives? Are price changes stimulating sales to the desired degree?

- *Programme.* How is each programme performing relative to the standards for interim results? Which programmes are yielding better results and which are yielding disappointing results?

- *Product or line.* Are individual products (or the entire line) meeting standards for interim progress toward objectives? Are the products or line moving toward market share targets?

- *Segment.* What are the interim results for each customer segment being targeted?

- *Geography.* What do interim results look like for each branch or region? What area-specific elements could cause deviations in certain branches or regions?

- *Manager.* For accountability, what is the status of each manager's results compared with agreed-upon standards?

- *Brand.* Is each brand performing up to the pre-set standards, in financial and marketing terms? How do interim results compare with those of other brands in the portfolio and with those of competing brands?

Organizations usually apply marketing control at multiple levels, both macro and micro. Zara and other fashion retailers give special emphasis to marketing control at the product and store level; consumer packaged-goods marketers such as Unilever look closely at the business unit, region, product line and brand levels. Here's how Toyota has used marketing control by brand, segment and geography in its marketing plan for Scion.

MARKETING IN PRACTICE: TOYOTA AIMS TO SELL FEWER SCIONS

When Toyota's marketers found that US sales of its Scion small cars exceeded forecast sales by 10 per cent, they changed the brand's marketing plan. Even though Toyota is always aiming to increase global turnover and market share, marketers worried that selling more Scions would dilute the brand's appeal to the target segment of young adults. An estimated eight out of ten Scion buyers have never owned a Toyota before – and most choose a Scion or another Toyota brand for their next car. Scion is therefore an important entry point for building relationships with potentially high lifetime-value customers. To limit sales and keep the brand trendy, Toyota cut production, cut the brand's ad budget, planned special events and enlarged Scion's online presence in Second Life and other sites that draw young adults.[3]

Don't depend only on one or two levels of control; if you do, you'll get an incomplete or distorted picture of interim results and might therefore take action inappropriately.

Remember, forecasts and schedules are targets; your actual results may be slightly higher or lower at each measurement interval as you move toward achieving full-year performance. When applying marketing control, you want to act soon enough to make a difference in the final outcome of your marketing plan without overreacting.

Types of marketing control

To determine the overall effectiveness of your marketing plan at its conclusion and to gauge progress while it is being implemented, you will use annual, financial, productivity and strategic control, applied at the various levels you have chosen. Figure 12.3 summarizes these four types of marketing control, which are discussed in more detail in the following sections.

Annual control
- Evaluate full-year and interim marketing plan performance
- Identify ineffective or unsuitable programmes and activities
- Identify ineffective or mishandled implementation

Financial control
- Use financial measures to assess performance
- Compare actual financial results with budgets, forecasts, metrics
- Analyse profit and cost results at multiple control levels

Productivity control
- Evaluate the efficiency of marketing planning, processes, activities
- Assess productivity due to higher output or lower costs
- Gauge ability to transfer marketing learning and tactics

Strategic control
- Evaluate performance in managing the marketing function
- Evaluate performance in managing key relationships
- Evaluate marketing performance with regard to social responsibility and ethics

FIGURE 12.3   Annual, financial, productivity and strategic control

Annual control

Annual control allows you to evaluate the current marketing plan's performance in preparation for developing next year's marketing plan. This annual control process provides an important check of what your plan has achieved and where improvements can be made, feeding back to the environmental scanning and analysis for next year. Start with a broad overview of the plan's performance. How do the full-year results match up with the primary marketing, financial and societal objectives such as increasing sales and profits, strengthening customer loyalty or improving corporate image? Volkswagen, for example, has used annual control to confirm achievement of profit targets and identify opportunities for boosting sales and market share through additional marketing attention.[4]

Looking at performance measured by a few vital objectives can suggest strengths and weaknesses to be further investigated through internal analysis. Now look at whether other marketing plan objectives were achieved, and by what margin. Using these targets, was full-year performance below expectations, at the expected level or above expectations? At the micro level, how did each programme and marketing activity perform relative to its objectives? What can you learn from the pattern of interim progress measurements throughout the year that will help in next year's forecasting and implementation? Can line managers and others responsible for implementation and customer contact offer constructive feedback about the programmes, objectives, activities or anything else connected with the marketing plan?

A particular challenge is distinguishing ineffective or unsuitable programmes and activities from ineffective or mishandled implementation so you can make changes during the next planning cycle. Did a programme fail to meet objectives because its planning was flawed or because its implementation was flawed? How do the current conditions differ from those previous situations, and what conclusions can you draw? At worst, annual control will reveal poor marketing performance and the need to address bad planning or bad implementation. At best, it will indicate superior marketing performance and confirm the soundness of the plan or the implementation – or identify an unintended result brought about by the organization's marketing.

Financial control

Businesses and non-profit organizations alike apply **financial control** to evaluate the marketing plan's interim and overall performance according to key financial measures such as sales (or contributions), profits, gross and net margin, costs and return on investment. Interim measurements show progress toward full-year objectives; full-year financial results clarify the big picture of marketing performance. You can compare actual expenditures with planned budgets; actual sales and costs with forecasts; and profit objectives with profit results at multiple levels (by product, market, segment, channel and so forth).

Tokyo-based Canon, which makes cameras, scanners, printers and other imaging-related equipment, has used financial control quite effectively.

MARKETING IN PRACTICE: CANON LOOKS AT THE PROFIT PICTURE

Canon analyses financial performance by product, product line and product category, as well as by market and channel. When marketers found that film-based cameras accounted for only 17 per cent of Canon's sales and they forecast diminishing lower revenue and profits from such products, they cut nearly all film-based cameras from the product mix. Top management recognized that developing new film-based cameras would be costly and time-consuming, so the marketing plan for cameras was refocused on digital models, where demand has grown steadily. Months later, Canon announced record profits and pointed to higher digital camera sales as one reason – confirming that the decision to eliminate film-based cameras made financial sense.[5]

Productivity control

The purpose of **productivity control** is to evaluate the marketing plan's performance relative to the efficiency of key marketing processes and activities. Whereas financial control is concerned with financial measures of performance, productivity control focuses on improvements to processes and activities that either decrease costs or increase output. Different organizations apply productivity control in different ways (and at different intervals); some common business examples include:

- *Overall plan productivity*. Has the current plan yielded better results with smaller-than-usual marketing budgets? Has the current plan maintained expected results without budget increases? Have implementation costs increased without corresponding increases in marketing results?

- *Advertising and sales promotion productivity*. Without higher budgets, are reach and brand/product awareness increasing over time? With lower budgets, are reach and brand/product awareness levels sustained? Which sales promotions yield the best response for the investment? ING Direct, a financial services firm, has found online advertising to be particularly productive. The company spends 10 per cent of its marketing budget on Web advertisements – and brings in 40 per cent of its customers that way. The deciding factor in promotion productivity is the company's cost of acquiring a new customer. The company has also invested in interactive promotions as a cost-efficient way to engage customers online.[6]

- *Sales force productivity*. Is the sales force contacting more prospects and making more sales without higher budgets? With lower budgets, is the sales force maintaining productivity on the same measures? Which salespeople and territories are the most productive?

- *Product and development productivity*. Are more new products being generated on a stable development budget? Are more new products moving from the concept stage to commercialization, resulting in higher sales and profit potential? Are some products more productive (yielding higher profitability relative to their costs) than others? Should some products be dropped because they are less productive?

- *Channel productivity*. Are some channels more important for long-term sales and profit productivity? Do some channels require disproportionately high investment for the level of return? Can results be maintained with lower channel costs?

- *Price productivity*. Did a price promotion stimulate revenues to offset the lower profit margin? Did a reduced price stimulate sufficient sales to bring a product to the break-even point earlier than planned? Did a price increase yield higher total profit despite lower unit sales?

- *Segment and customer productivity*. Are the marketing costs for some segments or customers too high relative to the payback? Which yield the best returns on investment? Should some be dropped because they are relatively unproductive in generating returns?

Strategic control

Strategic control is used to evaluate marketing's performance in managing strategic areas such as the marketing function itself, key relationships, social responsibility and ethics. Applied annually or semi-annually – generally by marketing management and top executives – strategic control shows whether marketing is doing its job; whether the organization is forging relationships with publics that are important; and whether social responsibility and ethics objectives are being achieved. The purpose is to assess strengths and weaknesses in these areas, identify where improvement is needed and build on success when developing future marketing plans.

To assess the marketing function's performance, your organization can conduct a **marketing audit** – a formal, detailed study of the planning process, plan implementation, personnel skills, use of resources and responsiveness. This chapter's practical marketer checklist offers questions to ask when assessing marketing planning and implementation. As part of the marketing audit, management should look at the skills and motivation of marketing personnel.

Customer relationships are at the heart of any company's success, which is why strategic control should evaluate marketing performance in acquiring and retaining new customers, building loyalty, increasing satisfaction and supporting positive perceptions. Moreover, it is important to examine performance in managing relationships with shareholders, suppliers, channel partners and other groups that can significantly affect the organization's ability to achieve objectives.

Finally, use strategic control to assess marketing's performance with regard to social responsibility and ethics. Is marketing effectively conveying the organization's involvement in socially responsible causes? Are societal objectives being set and achieved? Are marketing decisions being made and implemented in an ethical manner? What else can marketing do to demonstrate that the firm is socially responsible and committed to strict ethical standards?

Contingency and scenario planning

To supplement your implementation plan, you may need a **contingency plan** to be implemented in response to or anticipation of significant changes in the marketing situation that could disrupt important marketing activities. Look at your forecasts, schedules and budgets representing the most pessimistic and the most optimistic scenarios that could occur during the planning period; identify the worst-case scenarios that could be most damaging to your ability to achieve marketing plan objectives; then create plans for coping with those scenarios. Figure 12.4 presents the main components of contingency planning for marketing. Note that top management may incorporate marketing contingency plans into a comprehensive organization-wide contingency plan.

Contingency plans may also be the outcome of a sophisticated scenario-planning process in which managers develop detailed descriptions of future situations to anticipate and plan for major shifts in external forces, industry trends, technological

Planning action	Purpose
Identify emergency situations and analyse their potential consequences for marketing	To understand the marketing activities, people and operations most likely to be disrupted by each possible emergency
List advance preparations that can be made to minimize disruptions and restore normalcy	To have materials and procedures ready in the event an emergency erupts
Establish warning signs of impending crises	To help recognize when an emergency is developing and provide triggers for contingency plan implementation
Assign specific actions, responsibilities and priorities for containment and customer service	To prevent the crisis from becoming more severe by organizing and coordinating an effective initial response to contain the problem and continue serving customers
Create a contingency communication plan	To keep internal and external stakeholders informed about the situation, the response and future steps
Resolve the crisis and analyse how well the contingency plan worked	To improve the contingency planning process by eliminating ineffective actions and using lessons learned for better advance preparation

FIGURE 12.4 Contingency planning for marketing

developments and organizational resources.[7] With **scenario planning,** marketers look beyond historical trends and short-term projections to envision broad, long-term changes in the marketing environment that could affect future performance, then prepare contingency plans with the most likely scenarios in mind.[8]

Contingency plans are valuable for coping with large-scale emergencies brought on by uncontrollable external factors such as: natural disasters, an outbreak of a disease, terrorism, sabotage, computer system failures or transport cuts, unusual competitive pressures or the sudden withdrawal of a key supplier or customer. A severe, prolonged crisis may physically threaten employees, customers or suppliers; damage facilities or equipment; destroy products and supplies; and shut down channels. The London-based HSBC Group, for example, has contingency plans for operating with only half of its staff if bird flu should cause widespread absences.[9] Less severe emergencies may disrupt (but not cripple) internal or external marketing activities.

Use the following checklist as a guide to assessing performance after marketing planning is complete and the plan has been implemented.

ESSENTIAL MARKETING PLAN CHECKLIST NO. 17:
AFTER IMPLEMENTATION

☐ Were the appropriate personnel (internal and external) involved in planning and implementation?

_____

☐ Were suitable metrics and measurement intervals selected for measuring progress toward achieving the plan's financial, marketing and societal objectives?

_____

☐ Were marketing plan decisions made after investigating multiple options and selecting the most likely scenario? Were contingency plans ready for extreme situations?

_____

☐ Were marketing forecasts, schedules, budgets, metrics and implementation responsibilities clearly delineated, realistic, coordinated properly and communicated effectively?

_____

☐ Were marketing resources, internal activities and value chain activities properly coordinated and managed during implementation?

_____

☐ How did marketing personnel deal with interim results that deviated from standards?

_____

☐ How can marketing planning and implementation be improved in the future?

_____

_____

CHAPTER SUMMARY

The process of marketing control consists of: (1) setting standards and measurement intervals to gauge progress toward marketing objectives; (2) measuring interim results after implementation; (3) comparing measured results with standards and diagnosing any deviations; and (4) taking action as needed. The purpose is to pinpoint where results are below or above expectations, understand why and decide to leave the programmes and implementation unchanged; make changes to solve problems; or apply lessons learned to improve progress toward standards and, ultimately, objectives. The decisions made at the end of the process feed back to the beginning, providing feedback for changing standards, measurement intervals or even objectives.

Annual plan control is used to evaluate the current marketing plan's performance in preparation for developing next year's marketing plan. Financial control is used to evaluate the marketing plan's performance according to key financial measures such as sales and profits. Productivity control is used to evaluate the marketing plan's performance relative to the efficiency of key marketing processes and activities. Strategic control evaluates effectiveness in managing strategic areas such as the marketing function and social responsibility/ethics. Marketers formulate contingency plans to be implemented in response to or anticipation of significant, potentially disruptive changes in the organization's situation.

CASE STUDY: BLUE NILE NEEDS TO CONTROL ALL THE DETAILS

Blue Nile, an online retailer of diamonds and jewellery, knows that careful implementation and tight control are as important as effective marketing planning. In fact, the US company, which maintains separate Web-based stores for the United Kingdom, the United States and Canada, needs to control every marketing detail with the same precision it applies to handling its precious products. Details count when a specially designed diamond necklace or ring can sell for more than £26,000.

Using productivity control, Blue Nile recently shortened the time needed to create and despatch custom-designed jewellery by one day. Improving fulfilment productivity is important because buyers tend to be more satisfied and loyal when their orders arrive quickly. The company monitors channel productivity by examining turnover in each online store and comparing the results to forecasts and to historical sales trends.

During one recent quarter, Blue Nile recognized that the external environment (particularly competition) was so challenging that corrective action would be needed to achieve the expected results. After the company decided to price more aggressively, market response was so strong that the company was able to attract many new customers and increase its share of the diamond engagement-ring market. Applying marketing control allowed Blue Nile to generate higher revenue and market share while generating profits as well. Looking ahead, strategic control will be vital because the

CEO aims 'to perfect the Blue Nile experience for our customers so they become Blue Nile customers for life, and a great source of referral'.[10]

Case questions

1. Is annual control appropriate for a Web-based business such as Blue Nile? Why?

2. What worst-case scenario(s) and contingency plan(s) would you recommend that Blue Nile consider and why?

APPLY YOUR KNOWLEDGE

Build on your research and responses for the 'Apply your knowledge' exercises in Chapters 5 and 11 to answer the following questions about your chosen company's marketing control. Prepare a brief written or oral report summarizing your ideas.

• What revenue and profit results has this company announced in recent months? How does this performance compare with the company's forecasts and/or budgets?

• If the company's actual financial performance is different from the planned results, what corrective actions have been taken?

• Did this company recently report changes related to marketing relationships, such as market share? How do these compare with the expected performance? What marketing control steps, if any, do you think this company should take right now – and why?

• Based on what you know of this company, identify one issue that could interfere with achieving marketing plan objectives and explain how you would address this in a contingency plan.

BUILD YOUR OWN MARKETING PLAN

Finalize your marketing plan by selecting the levels at which you will apply marketing control and the types of marketing control you will need to prepare for. How often will you measure results and what standards are most important for monitoring interim progress? How would you diagnose a situation in which actual expenditures exceeded budgeted costs? What corrective action might you take if actual unit sales for an important channel fell below your forecast? Should you reconsider your measurement intervals or standards if actual performance deviates significantly from your plan? Is it important to apply marketing control by segment, geography, manager and/or brand? What areas will require strategic and productivity control? What worst-case scenario might require contingency planning? Document your thoughts in a written marketing plan.

(STOP) ENDNOTES

1. Jaclyne Badal, 'Theory & Practice: A Reality Check for the Sales Staff', *Wall Street Journal*, 16 October 2006, p. B3; Karen Richardson, 'New Seeds May Sow Stock Gains for Syngenta,' *Wall Street Journal*, 20 November 2006, p. C1.

2. Stephanie Thompson, 'Hershey CEO Abandons Plan to Curb Ad Spending', *Advertising Age*, 12 February 2007, p. 8; 'Hershey Earnings Decline as Mars Cuts into US Market Share', *New York Times*, 25 January 2007, p. C13; 'Hershey Lowers Profit Forecast, Blaming a Recall', *New York Times*, 7 December 2006, p. C6.

3. Steve Miller, 'Let's Get Small: Kia Latest to Face Scion', *Brandweek*, 5 March 2007, p. 4; Gina Chon, 'A Way Cool Strategy: Toyota's Scion Plans to Sell Fewer Cars', *Wall Street Journal*, 10 November 2006, p. B1.

4. Christoph Rauwald, 'Volkswagen Sees Sharp Rise in Profit on Strong Vehicle Sales', *Wall Street Journal*, 9 March 2007, www.wsj.com.

5. 'Canon Inc.: Digital-Camera, Printer Sales Lift 2006 Earnings to Record', *Wall Street Journal*, 30 January 2007, n.p.; Reiji Yoshida, 'Canon Exits Film Cameras amid Digital Dominance', *Japan Times*, 26 May 2006, n.p.

6. Todd Davenport, 'ING Direct Recasts the Internet Model', *American Banker*, 1 December 2006, pp. 17Aff; Matthew De Paula, 'Forget Click Rates, Now View-Throughs Matter', *Banking Wire*, 19 August 2003, p. 24.

7. See Craig S. Fleisher and Babette E. Bensoussan, *Strategic and Competitive Analysis* (Upper Saddle River, NJ: Prentice Hall, 2003), pp. 284–97.

8. Don E. Schultz, 'Use Atypical Tools for Today's Marketing Plan', *Marketing News*, 15 February 2007, pp. 7, 10; 'Planning Ahead Is Necessary – But How Far Ahead?', *MMR*, 30 October 2006, p. 17.

9. 'HSBC Plans for Up to 50% Absences During Pandemic', *America's Intelligence Wire*, 10 January 2006, n.p.

10. 'Q4 2006 Blue Nile Inc. Earnings Conference Call, Part 1', *America's Intelligence Wire*, 12 February 2007, n.p.; Gary Rivlin, 'When Buying a Diamond Starts With a Mouse', *New York Times*, 7 January 2007, sec. 3, p. 1.

The fictitious company Lost Legends Luxury Chocolatier is planning to market premium gourmet chocolates to adults in the United Kingdom and, later, in Western Europe. Although many confectionery companies target the children's chocolate sweets market, fewer are active in the adult segment and fewer still in upmarket chocolates. The United Kingdom has the highest per capita consumption of and spending on chocolates, compared with other European nations, making it a very attractive market for our gourmet products. Also, our gourmet products will tap rising demand for dark chocolate products, which is forecast to grow much faster than overall chocolate demand.

This sample marketing plan illustrates how the marketing director for Lost Legends Luxury Chocolatier is preparing to enter the market. Notice how the contents, order of topics and section headings are tailored to fit the company's situation. Also notice that details (such as product-by-product pricing, programme schedules and budgets) are not in the main body of this plan but would be available in the appendix of an actual plan for readers who want more specifics.

EXECUTIVE SUMMARY

Lost Legends Luxury Chocolatier is a new company planning to market premium gourmet chocolates to adults in the United Kingdom and, later, in Western Europe. In monetary terms, this market is smaller than the children's chocolate sweets market; however, confectioners offering gourmet, premium-priced chocolates under well-regarded brands can potentially earn higher profit margins by targeting specific segments of the consumer and business markets. We will target three consumer segments and three business segments at the high end of the gift, holiday and affordable personal luxury market. Our Belgian Legends product line will be introduced in September to allow time for building brand awareness and product trial prior to the Christmas season, when our seasonal Limited Edition Legends line will be featured.

Our financial objectives relate to first-year turnover in the UK market, a minimum level of sales for each retail outlet, achieving break-even within 15 months and aiming for 10 per cent gross profit margin by the end of our second year. Our marketing objectives relate to first-year brand awareness among consumers and businesses, arranging for retail distribution, launching the e-commerce website and planning for new products to be introduced in the second year. Our societal objectives relate to buying only Fairtrade Marked cocoa and using recycled materials in product packaging.

Key strengths are our family recipes, patented roasting process, cost-effective hand production and glamorous history. Weaknesses include lack of brand awareness and image, limited resources and lack of channel relationships. Our marketing plan will address three major opportunities: higher demand for premium chocolates; growing interest in treats with mystique; and growing interest in socially responsible products. The main threats we must counter are intense competition, market fragmentation and uncertain supply prices.

CURRENT MARKETING SITUATION

The company was founded by the British descendants of a nineteenth-century Bruges chocolate maker who was famous for his unusually dark and intensely flavoured chocolates. In this pre-automation era, he mixed small batches using the finest ingredients; kneaded and tempered the chocolate to achieve a smooth, refined texture; and poured his confections into hand-made moulds one at a time. Dozens of his recipes were handed down from generation to generation as the family moved from Bruges to the London area, but the chocolates were never produced commercially – until now. After experimenting with roasting cocoa beans and updating the recipes as they prepared for a St Valentine's Day party, two entrepreneurial family members were inspired to patent the roasting process and launch a new business. The name 'Lost Legends Luxury Chocolatier' was chosen because it captured the romance of dark, rich Belgian chocolates made in the old-fashioned way from treasured recipes.

Europe has a long tradition of chocolate making, from leading brands such as Lindt, Suchard-Tobler, Nestlé, Cadbury, Godiva, Perugina and Lenôtre to locally owned and operated gourmet chocolatiers. The top brands enjoy high awareness and high customer loyalty. Upmarket stores such as Harrods and Fortnum and Mason also sell private-label branded chocolates as well as domestic and imported upmarket brands, which adds to the competitive pressure. Nonetheless, a number of smaller companies are successfully targeting specific niches within the adult chocolate market by offering hand-made chocolates; exotically-flavoured chocolates; Fairtrade chocolates; all-natural chocolates; lower-fat chocolates; holiday chocolates; and gift chocolates.

In this environment, Lost Legends Luxury Chocolatier will compete at the higher end of the gift, holiday and affordable personal luxury market. Our positioning is based on the hand-made, top-quality nature of our premium chocolates made from the finest, freshest ingredients; our distinctive product and package differentiation; our exclusive brand image; carefully controlled production output; and highly selective distribution. Some of our marketing focus will be our use of Fairtrade Marked cocoa, a programme ensuring that growers receive a fair price for their cocoa. By actively promoting socially responsible sourcing of top-quality cocoa (and other ingredients), we can encourage positive associations with our brand and products.

MARKET SUMMARY

Although North and South America are the largest global markets in terms of chocolate sales, chocolate sales in Europe have been growing steadily. UK sales of chocolate exceed £4.3 billion annually and annual per capita UK consumption is estimated at 10 kg. Looking at other EU nations, estimated annual per capita consumption of chocolate in Germany is 8.1 kg per year; in France, 6.8 kg per year; in Spain, 3.9 kg per year; and in Italy, 2.2 kg per year. UK sales of all chocolates are forecast to grow by 6 per cent by 2010 but the niche of dark chocolates is forecast to grow by 48 per cent during the same period. Eastern Europe is expected to experience rapid growth in chocolate consumption, so we will explore opportunities there after establishing our brand and building sales in our home market of the United Kingdom and then in Western Europe.

Looking at customer buying patterns, chocolate sales are subject to seasonality. Sales increase markedly before holiday periods such as Easter, Christmas and St Valentine's Day. On the other hand, sales can drop in extremely hot weather because (1) stores must keep chocolate products chilled, which reduces the opportunity for impulse purchases; and (2) customers tend to buy sweets that are less perishable and retain their quality. We plan to introduce our first products in September, building awareness and word of mouth so we can attract buyers during the critical year-end holiday period.

Consumer market

The three consumer market segments targeted by Lost Legends Luxury Chocolatier are middle- to high-income adults who: (1) like (or want) to reward themselves or their families with the affordable luxury of gourmet chocolates; (2) view upmarket chocolates as a suitable gift; (3) buy fine chocolates as a tradition on St Valentine's Day, at Christmas or another holiday.

According to research, women account for the majority of purchases in this segment, and they are increasingly interested in product and packaging as expressions of pampering and personality. Not surprisingly, the affluent adults in our targeted segments have sophisticated tastes, high expectations and demanding standards. But we will give buyers of premium chocolate another reason to feel good about Lost Legends Luxury Chocolatier: they will be buying a brand that is socially responsible as well as top quality, an uncommon benefit combination among upmarket brands. Thus, as shown in Figure A1.1, we can plan to provide features that deliver valued benefits for the different needs of these targeted consumer segments.

Business market

The business market segments targeted by Lost Legends Luxury Chocolatier consist of professionals and businesspeople who select or give gifts: (1) to clients and other

Targeted segment	Characteristics and needs	Feature/benefit
Adults with middle to high income levels who buy fine chocolates for themselves or their families	• Appreciate premium chocolates • Prefer the cachet of luxury brands • Like small indulgences • Willing to splurge for themselves or loved ones	• Customers can select type and quantity of chocolates to accommodate tastes and budget • Premium brand image enhances perception of chocolates as special treat for individual or family • Fairtrade Marked cocoa balances self-indulgence with social responsibility
Adults, primarily women, with middle to high income levels who buy fine chocolates for gifts	• Seek a gift that reflects personality of giver or recipient • Seek a gift with high perceived value • Seek a gift to delight the senses • Seek a gift that is unique yet not excessively extravagant • Seek a gift with emotional overtones • Seek a gift that is socially responsible	• Lavish/distinctive gift packaging adds to visual appeal, personality, perceived value • Top-quality, limited-edition chocolates make our products unique and uncommon • Fairtrade Marked cocoa balances gift status with a sense of social responsibility
Adults with middle to high income levels who buy fine chocolates for holidays	• View holidays as occasions to enjoy special treats • Have or want to create a regular custom of enjoying special treats on certain holidays	• Seasonal/holiday packaging adds to our product's appeal for special occasions • Limited-edition line reinforces exclusivity • Fairtrade Marked cocoa combines holiday custom with social responsibility

FIGURE A1.1 Targeted consumer segments

business contacts; (2) to colleagues or managers on holiday occasions; (3) customized by product, packaging or business logo. These segments represent a significant opportunity to build repeat purchasing and loyalty among businesses that require unique corporate gifts with wide appeal for various occasions. Many small chocolate shops accept or invite customized orders but Lost Legends Luxury Chocolatier will aggressively target this segment and seek to build longer-term customer relationships spanning gift-giving occasions.

Figure A1.2 summarizes the features and benefits we can deliver to satisfy the needs of these targeted segments of the business market.

Targeted segment	Characteristics and needs	Feature/benefit
Professionals and executives who give gifts to clients and other business contacts, or who are responsible for selecting such gifts	• Want a gift with high perceived status and value • May influence selection but not actually purchase gifts • May give gifts but not actually make the purchase • May make the purchase but not actually give the gift	• Purchasers can select type and quantity of chocolates to accommodate budget and occasion • Premium brand image enhances perception of chocolates as gift • Fairtrade Marked cocoa balances luxury with social responsibility
Professionals and businesspeople who give gifts to colleagues or managers at holiday times	• Seek a gift with high perceived status and value • Seek a gift that is recognized as unique and exclusive • Seek a gift that is socially responsible	• Lavish gift packaging adds to the visual appeal and perceived value • Top-quality, limited-edition chocolates make our products unique and unusual • Fairtrade Marked cocoa balances gift status with a sense of social responsibility
Professionals and businesspeople who give customized gifts	• Want to reinforce corporate name in a tangible and memorable way • Want to give a gift that is not available to the general public • Want recipients to anticipate high-quality customized gifts • Want recipients to feel good about the social responsibility aspect of the gift	• Chocolates and packaging can carry business logo as a visual reinforcement of corporate name • Special packaging customized for particular businesses reinforces the uniqueness and exclusivity of the gift • Fairtrade Marked cocoa combines gift-giving custom with social responsibility

FIGURE A1.2   Targeted business segments

Market trends and growth

The overall European chocolate confectionery market is projected to grow at an annual compound rate of 3.5 per cent during this decade, a positive trend that indicates strong demand for our type of product. Although annual per capita UK chocolate consumption is not expected to increase by 2010, overall UK sales of chocolate is expected to reach £4.6 billion during the same period. Moreover, UK chocolate sales represent 25 per cent of the total European market for chocolates, which supports our decision to launch first in the United Kingdom.

Gourmet chocolate brands clearly have higher wholesale and retail value than mass market chocolates, although per capita consumption does not match that of mass market chocolates. A growing number of Fairtrade chocolates have gained distribution in national chains such as Waitrose as well as in independent shops. National advertising and sales promotions support sales of Cadbury, Nestlé, Mars and other mainstream chocolate marketers, especially prior to Easter and other holidays. Lindt has captured a share from premium chocolate marketers with a wide range of dark, organic chocolate treats.

Further, product proliferation in the European chocolate market is adding to competitive pressure. In fact, chocolate products represent a significant fraction of all new food products introduced during any given year. Both for-profit and not-for-profit companies are introducing chocolate bars, truffles and novelties made from Fairtrade ingredients. Smaller companies are making speciality chocolate products for niche markets, such as chocolates for people who want to avoid dairy products, chocolates for people who are diabetic and chocolates for people who prefer natural or organic flavourings and ingredients. Established companies constantly introduce variations of truffles, bars, bonbons, pralines and other favourites to satisfy customers' variety-seeking behaviour and encourage loyalty. In many cases, companies are offering their products directly to customers through online and printed catalogues.

Marketing research

To stay in touch with our targeted segments and track emerging market trends, we are commissioning qualitative research that will investigate perceptions, attitudes and behaviour related to premium chocolate products in general and Lost Legends Luxury Chocolatier in particular. We will use both secondary and primary research to support new product development, plan public relations activities, understand our competitive situation and monitor progress toward awareness objectives. In addition, we will commission marketing research to examine customer and channel satisfaction and identify opportunities and threats to which we must respond. Finally, we will solicit feedback through our website and through manufacturer's representatives as part of our ongoing research.

CURRENT PRODUCT OFFERINGS

Initially we will offer two main product lines, both based on modern adaptations of family recipes and a proprietary cocoa bean-roasting process we recently developed. The first, Belgian Legends, features 12 dark chocolates named for Belgian cities, such as: Antwerp (dark, fruity flavour) and Bruges (extra dark, sprinkled with *fleur de sel*). This product line will be available all year and both the chocolates and packaging can be customized for corporate gift giving. In subsequent years, we will add between two and four new varieties in this line and retain the best-selling eight to ten chocolates from the previous year, as measured by volume. We will also offer special packaging for three important holiday seasons: Easter, Christmas and St Valentine's Day.

Our product plan has the following advantages: (1) the product line and packaging are freshened and updated on a regular basis; (2) customers can find their favourites year after year, holiday after holiday; (3) the product line and the names of individual chocolate varieties reflect our family's background and tradition. The plan supports steady year-round purchasing and encourages impulse and gift purchases during peak selling periods.

The second product line, Limited Edition Legends, features chocolates in one of two seasonal shapes and matching packaging: seashells for summer and snowflakes for winter. Each season we will bring back the seashell or snowflake favourites in new packaging. By restricting production and distribution of these limited-edition chocolates – and planning each seasonal announcement as a media event, similar to those for new wine vintages – we will build customer anticipation and demand. Premium chocolates have been offered in limited editions for some time, but mainstream manufacturers such as Nestlé and Mars have brought the practice to a wider audience by offering limited editions of well-known chocolate treats.

The use of limited editions has the following advantages: (1) the temporary introduction of seasonal varieties will give sales a strong, relatively predictable boost during specific periods; (2) loyal customers will be able to buy some favourite chocolates in every season; (3) the perceived value as a gift will be higher because these varieties are not available throughout the year. As a result, we can capture customer interest in between the peak holiday periods and fulfil consumer and corporate needs for unique, value-added gifts.

BUSINESS ENVIRONMENT

Lost Legends Luxury Chocolatier will begin operations in an environment shaped by national and regional political–legal forces; economic uncertainty; growing concerns about social responsibility and ecology; powerful social–cultural forces; and strong competition. This section discusses how the business environment is likely to affect our marketing and performance and this is followed by a SWOT analysis of our strengths, weaknesses, opportunities and threats.

- *Political–legal forces*. As chocolate makers, we must comply with prevailing local, national and (when we export) regional laws and regulations governing product quality, labelling, ingredients and many other aspects of the business. For example, if we decide to introduce an 'organic' chocolate product, we must abide by EU rules for organic certification.

- *Economic uncertainty*. Economic conditions are not uniform throughout the European market, which will affect our ability to forecast sales and profits during the first year. Industry records show that demand falls slightly during economic downturns, because buying premium chocolate allows consumers to indulge themselves in a small way. We must also monitor the economic climate in Ghana, where we source our Fairtrade Marked cocoa beans.

- *Social responsibility and ecology*. The Fairtrade Marked system, designed to ensure that growers are equitably compensated for their cocoa beans, is emblematic of a larger movement toward socially responsible business operations, with which we will be associated. We will also take steps to keep production and packaging ecologically friendly. As consumers and business customers become more knowledgeable about the social issues connected with chocolate production, our offerings are likely to be perceived favourably.

- *Social–cultural trends*. Our products take advantage of the trend toward supporting small, local brands in a world dominated by giant multinational corporations. We also recognize that attitudes toward sweets are influenced by concern about nutrition and unhealthy foods. Yet some research suggests that the flavanol in chocolate can have health benefits. Lost Legends Luxury Chocolatier is deliberately using the best ingredients to create fine chocolate products intended as special treats, not as a steady diet.

- *Competition*. We must confront serious competition from Lindt, Neuhaus, Perugina, Nestlé, Cadbury and Godiva, among other rivals. These companies have established brands and sizeable advertising budgets yet they are not immune to industry competition and the effect of economic conditions on product sales. Duc d'O and other speciality chocolate makers are promoting their products through new packaging, increased advertising and new point-of-purchase displays. Divine Chocolate sells online and through stores such as Boots and Starbucks. Lost Legends Luxury Chocolatier will preserve our upmarket status by restricting distribution to selected shops, using our heritage and sense of social responsibility to differentiate our products, promoting our patented roasting method and our commitment to hand-made quality.

SWOT analysis

Lost Legends Luxury Chocolatier can leverage several core competencies and key strengths in addressing potentially lucrative opportunities in both consumer and business market segments. As a new and unknown company, however, we must counter a few critical weaknesses that could threaten our ability to build profitability by serving the targeted segments. Figure A1.3 summarizes our SWOT analysis.

Strengths	Weaknesses
• Unique, time-tested recipes • Patented roasting process • Cost-effective hand production • Glamorous history	• Lack of brand awareness, image • Limited resources • Lack of channel relationships

Opportunities	Threats
• Higher demand for premium chocolates • Growing interest in treats with mystique • Growing interest in socially responsible products	• Intense competition • Market fragmentation • Uncertain supply prices

FIGURE A1.3   SWOT analysis

Strengths

Among the internal capabilities that support our ability to achieve long-term and short-term objectives are:

- *Unique, time-tested recipes*. No other chocolatier sells the unusually rich, flavourful chocolates we can offer, updated from dozens of original recipes developed in the Steenstraat section of Bruges – a city renowned for delicious hand-made chocolates.

- *Patented roasting process*. Our legally protected, proprietary process for roasting cocoa beans results in a distinctively rich flavour and complex aroma that add sensory appeal to the finished product.

- *Cost-effective production*. Drawing on family records and supplier connections, we have perfected a cost-effective method for producing consistently high-quality chocolates by hand.

- *Glamorous history*. Publicizing the legend of our family's original recipes and generations of chocolate making will evoke vivid images of old-fashioned quality and enhance the brand's glamour.

Weaknesses

Some of the internal factors that might prevent Lost Legends Luxury Chocolatier from achieving our objectives include:

- *Lack of brand awareness and image.* Lost Legends Luxury Chocolatier is a new company and therefore has no brand awareness in its targeted segments. We must effectively position our brand, create a premium image and communicate product benefits in order to build positive perceptions and attract customers.

- *Limited resources.* Much of our first-year budget is committed to funding production and internal operations, leaving limited funds for paid marketing messages. We will therefore put more emphasis on special packaging, public relations and special events to generate buzz, boost sales promotion and our Internet presence.

- *Lack of channel relationships.* Most of our competitors own their own shops or have long-established relationships with leading retailers serving affluent customers. We are in the process of convincing exclusive speciality shops, leading department stores and other select retailers that our products are compatible with their merchandise assortments and will be profitable to carry.

Opportunities

We plan to exploit the following key opportunities:

- *Higher demand for premium chocolates.* More people see premium gourmet chocolates as an affordable luxury and therefore buy such products for themselves and for gifts. UK customers are familiar with premium chocolates and accustomed to paying more for ultra-high-quality products. Also, corporate demand for premium chocolates is rising more quickly than consumer demand due to interest in status products that can be given as gifts to almost any business contact (unless restricted by religious or cultural custom).

- *Growing interest in treats with mystique.* Research suggests that customers (both consumers and business buyers) want more than a chocolate treat – they want to know the story behind the product and share in the product's mystique. Our company's connection with the family's legendary Bruges chocolates is an intriguing story to be publicized; the unique recipes, limited-edition products and special packaging add to the mystique.

- *Growing interest in socially responsible products.* The use of Fairtrade Marked cocoa (and coffee) will appeal to consumers who like the idea of supporting socially responsible products. It will also differentiate our products from those of companies using cocoa beans not grown by Fairtrade Marked farmers. We estimate that two dozen companies currently produce Fairtrade chocolate products for the UK market, which shows how interest has grown and also shows how competitive the environment has become.

Threats

We recognize the need to counter the following threats as we begin marketing our chocolates:

- *Intense competition and market fragmentation.* In addition to the major luxury chocolate makers with established brands, national advertising campaigns and sizeable market share, many smaller, local chocolate makers are attracting loyal customers. Among the two dozen companies that feature Fairtrade chocolates in the UK market are Divine Chocolate, Green & Black's, Chocaid and Traidcraft. The resulting market fragmentation threatens our ability to build a solid customer base effectively and efficiently.

- *Uncertain supply prices.* Initially, we will be buying supplies in limited quantities and will not qualify for the most favourable volume discounts. Also, the price of ingredients can vary widely according to crop conditions, weather and other factors. Thus, we must allow for an extra margin when we set retail prices and recalculate break-even and profit levels as we come to know our supply prices.

Key issues

Because weather is an uncontrollable environmental factor, it has a major effect on chocolate sales and cocoa bean production. Heatwaves generally hurt sales and can affect chocolate production; cool weather allows both channel members and consumers more flexibility in storing chocolates. Lost Legends Luxury Chocolatier will forecast modest sales for the hottest summer months and be ready to increase production output if the weather is not extremely warm. Dry or unusually cold weather conditions in Ghana will hurt cocoa bean production, making this key ingredient scarce and expensive. We must be prepared to buy from alternative Fairtrade sources if our primary growers cannot fulfil their contracts, in order to meet our first-year sales objectives.

Product and package design are becoming increasingly important drivers of gift chocolate purchasing. Some companies are targeting niche markets such as golf-ball-shaped chocolates for men who play golf. Others are packaging premium gift chocolates in keepsake boxes that communicate status and elegance. Companies that emphasize Fairtrade connections generally explain their positioning on labels and packaging. We will monitor these trends and research opportunities in both niches during the coming year.

MISSION, DIRECTION AND OBJECTIVES

The mission of Lost Legends Luxury Chocolatier is to bring the family's expertise and tradition of making top-quality, premium chocolates to adult consumers and business buyers who buy luxury sweets for themselves or as gifts. All of our chocolate products will be updates or variations of cherished family recipes and produced by hand from the finest, freshest ingredients. We are committed to contracting for Fairtrade Marked cocoa, coffee and other ingredients from socially responsible sources. Our priority is to build our brand first in the UK market and then gradually expand our focus to other European markets.

Our initial year's direction is controlled growth through the establishment of the brand, development of two main product lines and targeting adults in consumer and business segments. In the second year, we will pursue growth through both market penetration and market development. Because of ongoing plans for limited-edition chocolate products, our growth will depend on product development as well. Based on this mission and direction, we have formulated the following primary objectives for our marketing plan:

- *Financial objectives*. The main financial objectives for Lost Legends Luxury Chocolatier are to (1) achieve first-year turnover of £500,000 in the UK market, (2) achieve full-year retail sales of at least £10,000 per outlet in the retail channel, (3) reach the break-even point for UK operations within 15 months and (4) achieve 10 per cent gross profit margin in our second year of operation.

- *Marketing objectives*. The main marketing objectives are to (1) generate first-year brand awareness of 35 per cent within consumer segments and 40 per cent within business segments, (2) place our products in 50 exclusive shops and high-end department stores located in affluent areas of the United Kingdom, (3) have our UK direct-sales website fully operational when the first products launch and (4) research and develop between two and four new Belgian Legends variations, based on family recipes and traditions, for introduction in the second year.

- *Societal objectives*. The main societal objectives are to (1) support socially responsible trade by buying all cocoa and coffee from Fairtrade Marked sources and (2) increase the proportion of recycled materials used in product packaging from 25 per cent at start-up to 35 per cent by the end of the first full year.

TARGETING AND POSITIONING DECISIONS

As shown in Figures A1.1 and A1.2, we are targeting specific segments of the consumer and business markets. In demographic terms, these are adults with middle to high income levels; professionals; and business people. In behavioural terms, the targeted consumer segments consist of adults who buy fine chocolates for themselves, for the holidays or as gifts. The targeted business segments consist of business people who buy fine chocolates as gifts, customized or not. Because the corporate gift market is growing faster than the consumer chocolate market – and because of the potential for higher customer lifetime value and better return on investment – we will put more emphasis on the targeted business segments.

We will use differentiated marketing to reinforce the positioning of Lost Legends Luxury Chocolatier as a marketer of gourmet chocolates hand-made from 'legendary' family recipes using strictly fresh, high-quality ingredients drawn from socially responsible sources. This positioning sets us apart competitively and helps establish a positive, upscale image in the minds of the consumers and business customers we are targeting.

PRODUCT AND BRAND DECISIONS

Both of our initial product lines are based on updates of traditional family recipes and use our proprietary, patented cocoa bean-roasting process. The 12 chocolates in the Belgian Legends line are named for Belgian cities: Antwerp, Bruges . . . The chocolates in the Limited Edition Legends line will be shaped like seashells (for the summer season) and snowflakes (for the winter season).

Packaging for both product lines will carry through the Belgian theme with stylized nineteenth-century artwork of the major cities on the boxes and foil wrappings; velvet and satin ribbons; and choice of ornate holiday or seasonal ornaments to top each box. Our Lost Legends Luxury Chocolatier packaging will be instantly recognizable because of the distinctive colours and graphics. Customized orders will allow for corporate logos on each chocolate and on the packaging (foil wrapping, ribbon and/or box). Limited-edition chocolates will also be individually wrapped in foil that is changed from season to season, adding to the feeling of luxury and exclusivity. Although some packaging will be retained year to year, we will build customer anticipation by introducing elaborate new packaging for each holiday (Christmas, St Valentine's Day and Easter) and each new limited-edition line. Figure A1.4 summarizes the main marketing decisions for our product.

The coming year's product development efforts will focus on researching and creating new chocolates to replace the slowest sellers in the Belgian Legends line. All new products must fit the high-quality tradition of our family recipes yet incorporate new flavours or other product elements that will trigger repeat purchasing from current customers and attract new customers. Also, every new product should take advantage of our proprietary bean-roasting process and our commitment to socially responsible sourcing of ingredients.

The competitively distinctive 'legends' concept is central to our brand image. For identity purposes, the Lost Legends Luxury Chocolatier name will appear on every package, along with the name of the product line (Belgian Legends or Limited Edition Legends). Packaging, public relations and other aspects of our marketing will emphasize the 'legends' concept. We want customers to associate our brand with a decades-old family history of making top-quality chocolates by hand in the Bruges tradition, using the finest, freshest ingredients. And we want them to respond to our brand's association with social responsibility, as demonstrated through purchases of Fairtrade Marked cocoa and coffee.

(In an actual marketing plan, more information about individual products, design, packaging and new product development would be shown here, with additional detail being shown in an appendix.)

Product mix	(1) Offer Belgian Legends line year round
	(2) Offer Limited Edition Legends line seasonally (one for summer, one for winter)
Product life cycle	(1) Retain the top-selling 8–10 chocolates in Belgian Legends line each year
	(2) Replace the slowest-selling chocolates yearly with new flavours/variations
	(3) Bring back Limited Edition Legends in summer and winter to extend growth part of the life cycle
New product development	(1) Develop at least two new Belgian Legends flavours or variations each year by updating family recipes
	(2) Track customer preferences and market trends as input for new product decisions
Quality and performance	(1) Use only the finest and freshest ingredients
	(2) Hand-produce chocolates that meet highest customer standards for competitively superior taste and texture
Features and benefits	(1) Offer a range of flavours and variations to satisfy different customers' tastes
	(2) Offer year-round, holiday and customized packaging to satisfy needs for gift status
Brand	(1) Emphasize the 'legends' concept to communicate the long family heritage of gourmet chocolate
	(2) Link the Lost Legends Luxury Chocolatier brand to attributes such as: exclusivity; superior taste and quality; freshest ingredients; socially responsible sourcing
Design and packaging	(1) Offer chocolate in distinctive shapes and combinations that convey a sense of luxury and tradition
	(2) Create packaging that communicates the Bruges background and tradition of our chocolates
	(3) Offer special seasonal packaging for Limited Edition line
	(4) Offer special holiday packaging for Belgian Legends line
	(5) For corporate orders, design custom chocolates, foil wrapping and packaging with company logos

FIGURE A1.4 Summary of product marketing decisions

PRICING DECISIONS

We will price our two product lines differently. On the basis of our research, we will make Belgian Legends available in 200g, 300g and 500g packages with introductory retail prices of £14, £18 and £29. Our wholesale prices will be 50 per cent lower than the retail prices, not including quantity pricing for retailers who sell a higher volume of our products. The Limited Edition Legends line will be priced at £1 higher per package, reflecting the limited period of availability and allowing Lost Legends Luxury Chocolatier to recoup higher costs related to these seasonal products. Holiday packaging will add between £1 and £2 to retail prices, depending on the package and ornaments selected. These prices support our premium positioning and the high value that our products represent.

For comparison, the following is a sample of competitive prices:

- Large UK chocolate maker offers a satin gift box with 1,800g of assorted fine chocolates for £65 and a smaller, star-shaped satin gift box with 280g of chocolates for £14. The company provides a special Web page for corporate orders.

- Family-owned chocolate retailer sells 12 hand-made truffles for £11; a gift box of 36 chocolates for £18; and charges varying prices for gift and Christmas packaging options.

- Speciality gift company sells a 150g box of gourmet chocolates for £7 and a 400g box for £14. Chocolates in more deluxe packaging are priced at £19 for 300g and £33 for 550g.

- Mid-sized UK chocolate maker that uses organic Fairtrade ingredients sells three 150g gourmet bars for £10 and a 500g gift box of gourmet chocolates for £24.

Corporate orders will be priced higher depending on the amount of customization required, the size of the order and the delivery instructions. We will charge more if chocolates, foil wrapping and packaging are all customized with corporate logos. For customers' convenience, we will pack and address all corporate orders; include a business card or a seasonal greeting; and despatch all gifts for a nominal delivery fee. Once a corporate customer has provided names and addresses of gift recipients, we will keep the information on file and automatically provide it for updating when the customer places another order.

By aggressively pursuing these more profitable corporate orders, we expect to attain our objective of breaking even on UK operations within 15 months. However, the timing is subject to change if the cost of cocoa (or other ingredients) rises dramatically. As shown in the financial details section, our pricing is planned to support the objective of attaining 10 per cent gross profit margin on our second-year turnover.

(In an actual marketing plan, more information about pricing, costs and break-even would be shown here, with additional detail included in the appendix.)

CHANNEL AND LOGISTICS DECISIONS

One of our major first-year objectives is to establish strong relationships with 50 upmarket shops that cater to affluent UK customers and have temperature-controlled storage for our chocolates. By restricting distribution to only one retail store in a given area of the country, we can strengthen our luxury image and more effectively reach higher-income customers. We will also use exclusive distribution to our advantage by educating store personnel about our patented roasting process, our Fairtrade Marked ingredients, our recipes and our family 'legends'. During the initial product introduction period, we will provide channel members with sample chocolates and display packaging; posters publicizing the 'legends' concept; product nutrition information; and literature about Fairtrade Marked sourcing.

To reinforce exclusivity, we will phase in Limited Edition Legends during each season. In the first week, only the top 20 per cent of our retail outlets (measured by volume) will receive the snowflake or seashell chocolates. During the second week, the next 20 per cent of the outlets will receive these seasonal chocolates. By the third week, all of our outlets will carry the product line. This approach rewards retailers that do the best job of selling our chocolates and gives their customers access to seasonal chocolates before anyone else. We will be using a push strategy to educate retail sales staff about our company and products.

We will also have our own UK direct-to-consumer website operational by the time we launch the Belgian Legends line. The site will follow the 'legends' theme in describing our company background, recipes and hand-production methods. We will allow visitors to view each product and package in a larger format and check ingredients, nutrition information and other details before buying. The site will have separate ordering pages for consumer and business buyers and allow pre-orders for seasonal and holiday offerings (to be fulfilled through retail partners). Although non-UK buyers will be able to order online for direct delivery, we will open a separate European website during our second-year expansion, when we work with retailers outside the United Kingdom.

Our logistics plan includes: obtaining quality ingredients (including cocoa and coffee from Fairtrade Marked sources) and packaging components on schedule and in sufficient quantities; maintaining constant, optimal product temperature and protective packaging when delivering to retail outlets; checking that retailers store and display chocolates under proper conditions; and using shipping containers that preserve product quality when fulfilling orders placed online or by corporate customers.

(In an actual marketing plan, more information about channel relationships and logistics would be shown here, with additional detail included in the plan's appendix.)

MARKETING COMMUNICATION DECISIONS

Given the company's start-up costs, our marketing communication activities will rely less on paid advertising than on public relations and special events, sales promotion, personal selling and direct marketing. Our marketing messages will use the emotional appeal of status, incorporate the 'legends' concept and be consistent with our product's

Technique	Activities
Advertising	• Targeted magazine advertising to build brand awareness and acceptance among channel members and corporate customers • Channel-only campaign to announce seasonal products as part of push strategy • No advertising specifically targeting consumer segments
Public relations	• Media interviews, special events and news releases to build brand awareness and positive word of mouth among consumers, businesses, channel members • Communicate 'legends' concept and link it with the image of Lost Legends Luxury Chocolatier products • Communicate use of Fairtrade Marked cocoa to enhance public perception of company as socially responsible • Gather information about each public's attitudes and perceptions to shape messages and policies
Sales promotion	• Channel sales promotion to pave the way for personal selling by manufacturer's representatives, as part of push strategy • Selective consumer sales promotion in the form of product samples distributed through luxury hotels and restaurants • Participate in industry trade shows • Sales force promotion to reward manufacturer's reps for placing Lost Legends Luxury Chocolatier in upscale shops, part of push strategy
Personal selling	• Contract with manufacturer's sales reps to visit targeted retail stores and place Lost Legends Luxury Chocolatier products, part of push strategy • Arrange for periodic personal or telephone follow-up to gather feedback from channel, business customers
Direct marketing	• Encourage corporate customers, in particular, to visit the website and order customized products • Encourage consumers to visit the website to learn more about the 'legends' concept, see the two product lines, locate nearby stores and send queries or comments to management • To build relationships, invite website visitors to sign up for a quarterly e-mail newsletter and receive announcements about seasonal product availability

FIGURE A1.5 Summary of marketing communication activities

upscale, superior-quality positioning. We are choosing media that will bring our messages to the attention of prospective channel members and executives who buy or influence the purchase of corporate gifts. Consumer advertising in upmarket magazines will be considered in our second year of operation.

We are designing public relations programmes to support our financial and societal objectives and to achieve our marketing objectives of (1) generating first-year brand awareness of 35 per cent within consumer segments (and 40 per cent within business segments) and (2) placing our products in 50 exclusive shops and department stores. As shown in Figure A1.5, we will use a combination of public relations activities to communicate with the key stakeholders of channel members, business customers and consumers.

Our sales promotion programmes will encourage channel participation and reward the outside manufacturer's representatives handling our products for arranging distribution through appropriate upmarket shops and department stores. The only consumer sales promotion we will use during the first year is arranging for luxury hotels and restaurants around the country to give away product samples. Our direct marketing effort will centre on the website, with separate sections devoted to product and company information, the 'legends' behind our family recipes, corporate ordering, store locations and social responsibility activities. We will also invite visitors to e-mail feedback and subscribe to our free monthly newsletter.

(In an actual marketing plan, more information about programmes, messages and schedules would be shown here, with additional detail included in the plan's appendix.)

CUSTOMER SERVICE AND INTERNAL MARKETING

To support our marketing plan, we need good customer service to build positive relationships with channel members, corporate customers and consumers. We recognize that customers who buy premium chocolates expect perfection, as do our retailers. Therefore the manufacturer's reps who call on our retailers will be allowed to replace chocolates and settle channel complaints as necessary. We are holding monthly briefing sessions to keep our reps and our employees fully informed about our products, marketing programmes, product line performance and future plans. Further, we will keep reps and employees updated about the latest products and promotions by sending them the company's monthly e-mail newsletter one week before customers receive it.

We have a separate plan for delivering pre-purchase service, post-purchase service and service recovery to our business buyers. Two employees will be responsible for answering business customers' questions before orders are placed; monitoring order fulfilment; communicating with customers about delivery schedules; tracking deliveries; contacting customers after the sale to check on satisfaction; and handling any questions or complaints as quickly as possible. On the basis of our interaction with business customers, we will adjust offerings, policies and procedures to improve our service over time and build our share of this potentially profitable market.

(In an actual marketing plan, additional information about service support and implementation would be included here and in the plan's appendix.)

MARKETING PROGRAMMES

Given below are summaries of our main integrated marketing programmes leading up to our product line introductions in September and mid-November and continuing during the year-end holiday period. Associated schedules, budgets and responsibilities are included in the appendix.

- *August*. Our push strategy will be strongest one month before the Belgian Legends line is introduced, to prepare channel members for the new product. Employees and manufacturer's reps will visit each participating retailer to provide product training, samples and display materials. Full-page colour advertisements in major confectionery and chocolate industry magazines will introduce the brand and the 'legends' concept. Simultaneously we will start our public relations efforts with media interviews and news releases focusing on the 'legends' concept and the family's Bruges-style chocolate recipes. One special media event planned for August is the arrival of a shipment of Fairtrade Marked cocoa. Family members will post blog entries and the company will offer podcasts and video segments for downloading and sharing.

- *September*. To launch the new product line, Lost Legends Luxury Chocolatier's founders and family members will travel to each retail outlet in an elegant horse-drawn coach and present the manager or owner with an ornate package containing all Belgian Legends varieties. This public relations event will focus attention on the legendary family heritage of chocolate making and the old-fashioned gourmet quality of our products. During this month participating upmarket hotels and restaurants will receive their first deliveries of Belgian Legends samples, also delivered by family members arriving by coach. Manufacturer's reps will follow up to ensure that every channel member has sufficient inventory and marketing material for the launch.

- *October*. We will place colour advertisements in business magazines to generate response from professionals and executives who buy premium chocolate as gifts for clients, colleagues and other business contacts. All advertisements will include the Fairtrade Marked logo and a brief description of this trade programme. Our website will also be prominently featured, along with the store location function. Our public relations programme for the month will focus on Fairtrade Marked sourcing. Our manufacturer's reps will participate in a sales contest to pre-sell the Limited Edition Legends line, which is launched in mid-November. The first issue of our e-mail newsletter will be sent out this month.

- *November*. Our website home page will promote Christmas gifts, especially the seasonal Limited Edition Legends chocolates and special holiday packaging. Our channel promotions will highlight the Limited Edition Legends line for gift giving and encourage retailers to order early. Public relations activities will draw media attention to the original family recipes on which our products are based. We will also send samples to opinion leaders to stimulate positive word of mouth and generate buzz.

- *December.* Our website will offer suggestions for last-minute chocolate gifts for consumers and business contacts. Manufacturer's reps will visit every participating retailer to check on inventory, provide sales assistance, deliver additional display materials and provide other support as needed. Publicity and special events will showcase the 'legends' concept and our family's tradition of gourmet chocolate making. Marketing research will gauge interim awareness levels and attitudes among the targeted consumer and business segments. Our monthly e-mail newsletter will offer chocolate gift ideas. Internally, we will be preparing for the summer line of Limited Edition Legends and for other new products.

(In an actual marketing plan, additional programme details would be shown in the appendix.)

FORECASTS AND FINANCIAL DETAILS

We are forecasting £500,000 in annual company turnover during our first full year of operation, with a minimum of £10,000 in sales per participating retail outlet. Our forecasts call for annual turnover increases of 20 per cent to 30 per cent during the next three years. We expect to reach the break-even point on UK operations within 15 months and then achieve 12 per cent gross profit margin by the end of our second year.

Owing to constant variations in the price of ingredients, we can only estimate our cost of goods and then only for two or three months in advance. As our volume increases and we buy supplies in larger quantities, we will be able to stabilize variable costs for up to six months. Therefore, our financial projections are subject to revision during the year.

(In an actual marketing plan, additional details would be shown in the appendix.)

IMPLEMENTATION AND CONTROL

To ensure that our two product lines are launched on time, we will adhere to weekly schedules and assign management responsibilities for: supervising manufacturer's reps; coordinating sales promotion activities; and briefing the public relations, advertising, research and website experts.

Among the metrics we have selected to monitor progress toward our objectives are:

- unit and monetary sales (analysed weekly by product, product line, channel, outlet)

- customer perceptions of and attitudes toward brand (twice-yearly research)

- business customer retention and profitability (monthly analysis)

- competitive standing (annual research)

- channel member participation and satisfaction (quarterly analysis)

- image as socially responsible company (twice-yearly research)

- use of recycled materials in packaging (quarterly analysis)

- order fulfilment speed, accuracy (monthly analysis).

We will review interim progress weekly during the first year of operation, comparing actual results with forecasts, schedules and budgets and adjusting activities if needed. We have also developed a comprehensive contingency plan to ensure a continuous supply of Fairtrade ingredients if unfavourable weather conditions threaten cocoa production.

(In an actual marketing plan, additional details about implementation and control would be included in the appendix.)

SOURCES FOR SAMPLE PLAN

Based on information in: 'Lindt Nibbles Away at Rivals with Dark-Chocolate Play', *Evening Standard (London)*, 23 January 2007, n.p.; Allen Salkin, 'No Golden Ticket, But More than Candy', *New York Times,* 7 January 2007, sec. 9, p. 12; 'Brits Take the Choc Award', *International Food Ingredients,* August–September 2006, p. 21; Katy McLaughlin, 'Food: Chocolate (User's Manual Enclosed)', *Wall Street Journal*, 10 February 2007, p. 1; Lauren Young, 'Pure Chocolate Indulgence', *BusinessWeek,* 12 February 2007, p. 88; 'Dark, Sour and Skinny Candy Trends for 2006-2007', *The Food Institute Report,* 19 June 2006, p. 1; Adrienne Carter, 'Chocolate: Belly Up to the Bar', *BusinessWeek,* 8 May 2006, pp. 106–7; 'Cocoa Market: 2005–2006 World Cocoa Supply and Outlook', *World Cocoa Foundation,* www.worldcocoafoundation.org; Ed Levine, 'Chocolate for the Inner Child', *Business Week*, 8 December 2003, pp. 104–5; Renee M. Kruger, 'Premium Gourmet: Premium Chocolate Reigns as the Supreme Affordable Luxury', *Confectioner,* January–February 2003, p. 48; Association of the Chocolate, Biscuit and Confectionery Industries of the EU, www.caobisco.com; Biscuit, Cake, Chocolate and Confectionery Alliance, www.bccca.org.uk; Fairtrade Foundation, www.fairtrade.org.uk.

Glossary

advertising Non-personal promotion paid for by an identified sponsor

affective response Customer's emotional reaction, such as being interested in or liking a product

affordability budget method Method in which senior managers set the total marketing budget on the basis of how much the organization can afford or will be able to afford during the period covered by the plan

annual control Type of marketing control used to evaluate the current marketing plan's full-year performance as a foundation for creating next year's marketing plan

attitudes Consumer's assessment of and emotions about a product, brand or something else

audience fragmentation Trend toward smaller audience sizes due to the multiplicity of media choices and vehicles

available market All the customers within the potential market who are interested, have adequate income to buy and adequate access to the product

Balanced Scorecard Broad performance measures that help organizations align strategy and objectives to manage customer relationships, achieve financial targets, improve internal capabilities and attain sustainability

behavioural response Customer's action in response to a marketing communication, such as buying a product

benefits Need-satisfaction outcomes that a customer expects or wants from a product

blog Short for *web log*, an informal online journal where people can exchange ideas and opinions

brand equity Extra value that customers perceive in a brand, which builds long-term loyalty

brand extension Widening the product mix by introducing new products under an existing brand

brand promise Marketer's vision of what the brand must be and do for consumers

branding Giving a product a distinct identity and supporting its competitive differentiation to stimulate customer response

break-even point Point at which a product's revenues and costs are equal and beyond which the product earns more profit as more units are sold

budget Time-defined allotment of financial resources for a specific programme, activity or product

business (organizational) market Companies, institutions, non-profit organizations and government agencies that buy goods and services for organizational use

business strategy Strategy determining the scope of each unit and how it will compete, what market(s) it will serve and how unit resources will be allocated and coordinated to create customer value

buying centre Group of managers or employees that is responsible for an organization's purchases

buzz marketing More intense form of word of mouth in which the organization targets opinion leaders, with the aim of having them spread information to other people

cannibalization Situation in which one product takes sales from another marketed by the same organization

category extension Widening the mix by introducing product lines in new categories

cause-related marketing Marketing a brand or product through a connection to benefit a social cause or non-profit organization

cognitive response Customer's mental reaction, such as awareness of a brand or knowledge of a product's features and benefits

competitive parity budget method Method in which senior managers establish a total marketing budget at least equal to that of competitors

concentrated marketing Targeting one segment with one market mix

consumer market People and families who buy goods and services for personal use

contingency plan A plan to be implemented in response to or anticipation of a significant change in the marketing situation that could disrupt important marketing activities

core competencies Organizational capabilities that are not easily duplicated and that serve to differentiate the organization from competitors

customer lifetime value Total net long-term revenue (or profit) an organization estimates it will reap from a particular customer relationship

data mining Sophisticated analyses of database information used to uncover customer buying and behaviour patterns

demand How many units of a particular product will be sold at certain prices

derived demand Principle that the demand forecast for a business product ultimately derives from the demand forecast for a consumer product

differentiated marketing Targeting different segments with different marketing mixes

direct channel Marketing channel used by an organization to make its products available directly to customers

direct marketing The use of two-way communication to engage targeted customers and stimulate a direct response that leads to a sale and an ongoing relationship

diversification strategy Growth strategy in which new products are offered in new markets or segments

econometric modelling method Use of sophisticated econometric models incorporating anticipated customer response and other variables to determine marketing budgets

elastic demand Relationship between change in quantity demanded and change in price, in which a small percentage change in price produces a large percentage change in demand

elasticity of demand How demand changes when a product's price changes

environmental scanning and analysis The systematic and ongoing collection and interpretation of data about internal and external factors that may affect marketing and performance

ethnographic research Observing customer behaviour in real-world situations

exclusive distribution Channel arrangement where one intermediary distributes the product in an area

external audit Examination of the situation outside the organization, including political–legal factors, economic factors, social–cultural factors, technological factors, ecological factors and competitive factors

features Specific attributes that contribute to a product's functionality

field marketing Working with outside agencies on sales promotions that take place in stores, shopping districts and office locations

financial control Type of marketing control used to evaluate the current marketing plan's performance according to specific financial measures such as sales and profits

financial objectives Targets for achieving financial results such as revenues and profits

fixed costs Business costs such as rent and insurance that do not vary with production and sales

forecast Projection of the estimated level of sales and costs during the months or years covered by a marketing plan

frequency The number of times people in the target audience are exposed to an advertisement in a particular media vehicle during a certain period

goals Longer-term targets that help a business unit (or the organization as a whole) achieve performance

indirect channel Marketing channel in which intermediaries help producers make their products available to customers

individualized (customized) marketing Tailoring marketing mixes to individual customers within targeted segments

inelastic demand Relationship between change in quantity demanded and change in price, in which a small percentage change in price produces a small percentage change in demand

integrated marketing communication (IMC) Coordinating content and delivery of all marketing messages in all media to ensure consistency and to support the chosen positioning and objectives

intensive distribution Channel arrangement in which as many intermediaries as possible distribute the product in an area

intermediaries Businesses or individuals that specialize in distribution functions

internal audit Examination of the situation inside the organization, including resources, offerings, previous performance, important business relationships and key issues

internal marketing Coordinated set of activities and policies designed to build employee relationships within the organization and reinforce internal commitment to the marketing plan and to good customer service

lifestyle The pattern of living reflecting how consumers spend their time or want to spend their time

line extension Lengthening a product line by introducing new products

logistics Flow of products, associated information and payments through the value chain to meet customer requirements at a profit

market The group of potential buyers for a specific product

market development strategy Growth strategy in which existing products are offered in new markets and segments

market leader Firm that holds the largest market share and leads others in new product introductions and other activities

market-penetration pricing New product pricing that aims for rapid acquisition of market share

market penetration strategy Growth strategy in which existing products are offered to customers in existing markets

market segmentation Process of grouping consumers or businesses within a market into segments based on similarities in needs, attitudes or behaviour that marketing can address

market share The percentage of unit or monetary sales in a particular market accounted for by one company, brand or product

market-skimming pricing New product pricing in which a high price is set to skim maximum revenues from the market, layer by layer

marketing audit Formal, detailed study of the marketing planning process and the marketing function to assess strengths, weaknesses and areas needing improvement

marketing control Process of setting standards and measurement intervals to track progress toward objectives, measure post-implementation interim results, diagnose any deviations and make adjustments if needed

marketing dashboard A computerized, easy-to-read depiction of marketing outcomes, as measured by key metrics, used to confirm progress and identify deviations from expected results

marketing (distribution) channel Set of functions performed by the producer or participating intermediaries in making a particular product available to customers

marketing objectives Targets for achieving results in marketing relationships and activities

marketing plan Internal document outlining the marketplace situation, marketing strategies and programmes that will help the organization achieve its goals and objectives during a set period, usually a year

marketing planning Structured process that leads to a coordinated set of marketing decisions and actions, for a specific period, through analysis of the current marketing situation; clear marketing direction, objectives, strategies and programmes; customer service and internal marketing support; and management of marketing activities

marketing strategy Strategy used to determine how the marketing-mix tools of product, place, price and promotion – supported by service and internal marketing strategies – will be used to meet objectives

mass customization Developing products tailored to individual customers' needs on a large scale

metric Numerical standard used to measure a performance-related marketing activity or outcome

mission statement Statement of the organization's fundamental purpose, pointing the way toward a future vision of what it aspires to become

motivation Internal force driving a consumer's behaviour and purchases to satisfy needs and wants

multibrand strategy Using two or more brand names in an existing product line or category

niches Small sub-segments of customers with distinct needs or requirements

objective and task budget method Method in which money is allocated according to the total cost of the tasks to be accomplished in achieving marketing plan objectives

objectives Shorter-term performance targets that lead to the achievement of organizational goals

opinion leader Person who is especially admired or possesses special skills and therefore exerts more influence over certain purchases made by others

opportunity External circumstance or factor that the organization aims to exploit for higher performance

organizational (corporate) strategy Strategy governing the organization's overall purpose, long-range direction and goals, the range of businesses in which it will compete and how it will create value for customers and other publics

penetrated market All the customers in the target market who currently buy or previously bought a specific type of product

percentage budget method Method in which senior managers set the overall marketing budget on the basis of a percentage of the previous year's annual turnover, next year's expected turnover, the product's price or an average industry percentage

personas Fictitious yet realistic profiles representing how specific customers in targeted segments would typically buy, behave and react in a marketing situation

podcasting Distributing audio or video files via the Internet

positioning Use of marketing to create a competitively distinctive place (position) for the product or brand in the mind of the target market

potential market All the customers who may be interested in a particular good or service

primary data Data from research studies undertaken to address a particular situation or question

product development strategy Growth strategy in which new products or product variations are offered to customers in existing markets

product life cycle Product's movement through the market as it passes from introduction to growth, maturity and decline

product line depth Number of variations of each product within one product line

product line length Number of individual products in each product line

product mix Assortment of product lines offered by an organization

productivity control Type of marketing control used to evaluate the marketing plan's performance in managing the efficiency of key marketing activities and processes

psychographic characteristics Complex set of lifestyle variables related to activities, interests and opinions that marketers study to understand the roots and drivers of consumer behaviour

public relations (PR) Promoting a dialogue to build understanding and foster positive attitudes between the organization and its publics

publics Groups such as stockholders, reporters, citizen action groups and neighbourhood residents that are interested in or can influence the organization's performance; also known as *stakeholders*

pull strategy Targeting customers with communications to stimulate demand and pull products through the channel

push strategy Targeting intermediaries with communications to push products through the channel

qualified available market All the customers within the available market who are qualified to buy based on product-specific criteria

quality Extent to which a good or service satisfies the needs of customers

reach The number or percentage of people in the target audience exposed to an advertisement in a particular media vehicle during a certain period

relationship marketing Marketing geared toward building ongoing relationships with customers rather than stimulating isolated purchase transactions

repositioning Changing the competitively distinctive positioning of a brand in the minds of targeted customers

retailers Intermediaries that buy from producers or wholesalers and resell to consumers

reverse channel Channel that allows for returning goods, parts or packaging

sales promotion Incentives to enhance a product's short-term value and stimulate the target audience to buy soon or to respond in another way

scenario planning Type of planning in which managers look beyond historical trends and short-term projections to envision broad, long-term changes in the marketing environment that could affect future performance, then prepare contingency plans to cope with the most likely scenarios

schedule Time-defined plan for coordinating and accomplishing tasks connected to a specific programme or activity

secondary data Information collected in the past for another purpose

segments Customer groupings within a market, based on distinct needs, wants, behaviours or other characteristics that affect product demand or usage and can be effectively addressed through marketing

selective distribution Channel arrangement in which a relatively small number of intermediaries distribute a product within an area

service recovery How the organization plans to recover from a service lapse and satisfy the customer

societal objectives Targets for achieving results in social responsibility areas

strategic control Type of marketing control used to evaluate the marketing plan's effectiveness in managing strategic areas such as the marketing function, key relationships and social responsibility/ethical performance

strength Internal capability or factor that can help the organization achieve its objectives, capitalize on opportunities or defend against threats

subculture Discrete group within an overall culture that shares a common ethnicity, religion or lifestyle

sustainable marketing Establishing, maintaining and enhancing customer relationships to meet the objectives of the parties without compromising the ability of future generations to achieve their own objectives

SWOT analysis Evaluation of an organization's primary strengths, weaknesses, opportunities and threats

target market All the customers within the qualified available market that an organization intends to serve

targeting Determination of the specific market segments to be served, order of entry into the segment and coverage within segments

threat External circumstance or factor that may hinder organizational performance if not addressed

undifferentiated marketing Targeting the entire market with one marketing mix, ignoring any segment differences

value From the customers' perspective, the difference between a product's perceived total benefits and its perceived total price

value chain (value delivery network) Sequence of interrelated, value-added actions undertaken by marketers with suppliers, channel members and other participants to create and deliver products that fulfil customer needs; also known as *supply chain*

variable costs Costs for supplies and other materials, which vary with production and sales

vlog A blog with mainly video content (*see* blog)

weakness Internal capability or factor that may prevent the organization from achieving its objectives or effectively addressing opportunities and threats

wholesalers Intermediaries that buy from producers and resell to other channel members or business customers

word of mouth People telling other people about a product, advertisement or some other aspect of an organization's marketing

Index

Note: Page references in **bold** refer to glossary entries